# Data as the Fourth Pillar

*Data as the Fourth Pillar* reasons that data should be considered the fourth pillar of every enterprise, alongside people, processes, and technology. Aimed at Boards, CEOs, and CxOs, this book provides a compelling case for why and how they should treat data as a strategic asset. It presents a comprehensive, success-by-design approach for enterprises, guiding them through a maturity framework to accelerate their data-centric journey.

This book addresses the "why," the "what," and the "how" of achieving this goal in measurable terms. It introduces key performance indicators (KPIs) such as total addressable value (TAV) and expected addressable value (EAV) through data to help measure the impact provided by the data pillar. This book also explores the symbiotic relationship between artificial intelligence (AI) and data, illustrating how both enable and benefit from each other. *A case study by Rüdiger Eck from Audi AG provides practical insights into the concepts and frameworks discussed.*

This book is an essential resource for business executives in both small to medium businesses (SMBs) and large enterprises, helping them navigate a highly complex and hypercompetitive business landscape while accelerating business value for their stakeholder communities.

"This book reveals how strategic data use fuels growth, unlocks value, and powers AI-driven innovation. It equips business leaders with practical frameworks and actionable insights to maximize data's potential, accelerate decision-making, and stay ahead in rapidly evolving markets."

**Liselotte Engstam,** *Professional Board Member and Strategic Advisor, Sweden*

"The future belongs to companies that see data not as an IT problem but as a strategic driver and the fourth pillar of the enterprise. Let this book be your guide to making that shift."

**Binny Gill,** *CEO of Kognitos, Inc., USA*

"This book underscores the critical role of data in scaling enterprise-grade AI systems. It provides foundational concepts, practical frameworks, and real-world examples. With actionable insights and a maturity journey for leveraging data to enhance business outcomes, this book is a compelling read for anyone wanting to stay ahead in the AI-driven world."

**Sandeep Kishore,** *Founder and CEO of Agivant Technologies, USA*

"The emphasis on the CEO and Board's critical role in driving this transformation is particularly insightful. This book is a must-read for any leader seeking to unlock the full potential of data and propel their organization towards a future of sustainable growth and competitive advantage."

**Mukundan Ramakrishnan,** *Managing Director of Tata Chemicals Limited, India*

"Data is the First Pillar, for me."

**Ramana Kumar,** *ex-CEO of Magnati, UAE*

"This book introduces the data intelligence layer as essential for optimizing business operations and fostering innovation. It also offers compelling insights and practical strategies for business leaders to boost efficiency and sustain a competitive edge by leveraging data as a strategic asset."

**Rüdiger Eck,** *Head of Data and Analytics Factory for Production & Logistics at Audi AG, Germany*

"This book distills the insights, frameworks, and strategies needed for every enterprise leader to take data seriously and unlock its full potential. Enterprises that capitalize on their data as a strategic asset and mature their data pillar will be able to create competitive advantages through initiatives like leveraging AI at scale."

**Sandeep Kalra,** *CEO, Member of the Board, Persistent Systems, USA*

# Data as the Fourth Pillar
## An Executive Guide for Scaling AI

Sujay Dutta and Siddharth Rajagopal

CRC Press
Taylor & Francis Group
Boca Raton  London  New York

CRC Press is an imprint of the
Taylor & Francis Group, an **informa** business

A CHAPMAN & HALL BOOK

Designed cover image: Sujay Dutta and Siddharth Rajagopal

First edition published 2026
by CRC Press
2385 NW Executive Center Drive, Suite 320, Boca Raton FL 33431

and by CRC Press
4 Park Square, Milton Park, Abingdon, Oxon, OX14 4RN

*CRC Press is an imprint of Taylor & Francis Group, LLC*

© 2026 Sujay Dutta and Siddharth Rajagopal

ISBN: 978-1-032-84460-2 (hbk)
ISBN: 978-1-032-83599-0 (pbk)
ISBN: 978-1-003-51277-6 (ebk)

DOI: 10.1201/9781003512776

Typeset in Minion
by Apex CoVantage, LLC

*To our families, friends, and supporters.*

# Contents

# Foreword

*By Rainer Deutschmann*

WE are living in an AI-first world – a world where access to cutting-edge technology is abundant, yet enterprises face a critical challenge: How to actually employ AI to create sustainable enterprise value and competitive advantage. The most successful companies not only leverage AI for top-line growth and operational efficiency but also establish a self-reinforcing flywheel effect whereby investments into AI capabilities generate greater cash flow, the fuel for further AI investments.

Over the past two decades, I have had the privilege of leading digital and AI-driven transformations across major telecommunications and technology enterprises worldwide. Whether in Europe and the Nordics, Asia, or in globally disruptive ventures, the common thread has always been unlocking value through data-driven innovation.

However, one lesson remains clear: Without a solid foundation and a structured approach, initiatives struggle to scale, business impact remains limited, and competitive advantage fades. While AI transforms industries, it is not the technology alone that drives success – it is how enterprises embed AI into their business models and organizational processes and build the necessary organizational capabilities to leverage AI at scale.

Traditionally, enterprises have structured their operating models around three pillars: People, processes, and technology. These pillars have served to drive productivity, efficiency, and innovation efforts across industries. However, this book – launched at a pivotal time – makes the compelling case that we are now at an inflection point at which enterprises must establish data as the fourth pillar – complementing people, processes, and technology – to successfully scale AI and unlock its full potential.

Four years ago, my team and I were faced with declining customer satisfaction and increasing cost to serve, due to broken processes and fragmented platforms in IT and customer operations. We radically simplified and digitized the end-to-end operations process, consolidated all ticketing systems, connected customer and IT operations, and harmonized data. As a result, system outages and call center volumes reduced significantly, and net promoter scores increased. However, this was only the beginning. On this digital and data foundation, we were able to establish a large language model (LLM)-based self-reinforcing flywheel. The data on *how* incidents were resolved was used to train an AI model, such that for further cases, the AI agent, rather than the human agent, could take over, thus continuously improving operations.

This case is a good example of how data complements people, processes, and technology to unlock the full potential of AI for better customer experience and lower cost. In this book, you will find similar real-world case studies that illustrate how enterprises can embed data-driven intelligence into business operations. The frameworks introduced offer structured guidance for execution.

Concretely, the authors introduce several key frameworks to help enterprises establish data as the fourth pillar and bridge the gap between AI aspiration and AI execution:

- To truly leverage AI, enterprises must ensure that the data is fit for purpose. The QCS framework (quality, compliance, and speed) helps leaders assess the data intensity required for AI-driven transformation – ensuring that the data is accurate, regulatory-compliant, and available at the speed of business needs. Without this, AI initiatives risk failure due to poor data quality, compliance risks, or slow decision-making.

- Furthermore, a successful AI-driven enterprise is not built on isolated data projects but on a structured and scalable foundation. The data operating model (DOM) serves as this blueprint, ensuring that people, processes, technology, and data are aligned to deliver trusted, governed, and accessible data across the enterprise. Without a well-architected DOM, enterprises risk data silos, operational inefficiencies, and AI initiatives that fail beyond experimentation.

- Achieving AI at scale is a journey, not a one-time project. The book's maturity model for the data pillar provides a structured roadmap to help enterprises evolve from basic data management to full AI automation. It defines three key stages – fundamental, scaled, and automated – each representing a critical milestone in AI readiness.

Many enterprises struggle because they try to implement advanced AI without first building a solid data foundation. By following this model, organizations can assess where they stand today, prioritize key enablers, and systematically progress toward AI-driven decision-making.

Besides the practical frameworks, what makes this book particularly valuable is the link to business value creation. It introduces the total addressable value (TAV) versus expected addressable value (EAV) model, guiding strategic investments in AI and data to maximize business impact.

I have seen data and AI initiatives succeed or fail depending on the clarity of leadership accountability. This book, therefore, rightfully details key roles, such as the chief operating officer (COO) and chief data officer (CDO), in the context of the organization's maturity. As enterprises progress on their data maturity journey, data is no longer a byproduct but a strategic asset, becoming deeply embedded across business functions. In such a mature state, every leader will have assumed data accountability, making data-driven decision-making a fundamental enterprise capability rather than a separate function.

This book is essential reading for business leaders, COOs, CDOs, CIOs, and executives responsible for driving digital transformation and AI adoption. As enterprises navigate an AI-first world, leaders must go beyond technology implementation and focus on establishing data as a strategic asset – one that fuels AI at scale, enhances operational efficiency, and drives competitive advantage. Whether you are a COO optimizing business processes, a CDO shaping data strategy, or a CEO looking to future-proof your enterprise, this book provides a practical roadmap to break down data silos, embed AI into core operations, and turn data into a sustained source of enterprise value.

This book is more than just an insightful read – it is a blueprint for action. The time to act is now. AI is no longer an experiment but an enterprise-wide imperative. Enterprises that fail to embed data as a core pillar will struggle to compete in the AI-first world.

I highly recommend this book to any leader looking to navigate the complexities of AI adoption, digital transformation, and data-driven value creation.

**Rainer Deutschmann**
*Senior Executive in Telecom and Technology Industries*
*Board Director, Advisor, and Investor*
February 2025, Malaysia

# Foreword

*By Sandeep Kalra*

W E stand at a pivotal moment in history – a time when the conflu-
ence of data and artificial intelligence (AI) is reshaping industries, redefining business models, and reimagining how enterprises create
value. In *Data as The Fourth Pillar – An Executive Guide for Scaling AI*, the
authors explore a fundamental shift: The recognition of data as the fourth
pillar of the enterprise operating model, alongside people, processes, and
technology.

For years, enterprises have focused on people, processes, and technologies as the core pillars of their operating models. However, my own
journey at Persistent Systems, as well as the experiences of our clients,
has demonstrated a significant evolution. The explosion of AI, fueled by
data, demands a fundamental shift. Data must be elevated to the same
level as people, processes, and technologies, a change that is now vital in
a hypercompetitive landscape. Data must not be treated as a "by-product"
of doing business; it is a key ingredient for innovation, powering AI and
enabling strategic decisions.

Data drives innovation, differentiation, and growth for enterprises. It is
the fuel that powers AI-driven business outcomes. At Persistent Systems,
our journey – from being a $500 million organization to a $1.4 billion
global leader in 5 years – proves that data, when elevated to a strategic
pillar, becomes the lifeblood of innovation, efficiency, and growth. Take
our AI-driven contract management system: It empowers sales teams with
real-time insights into pricing, deal terms, and risks. Similarly, our shift
from "systems of record" to "systems of insight" has democratized decision-making, enabling AI-powered forecasting, budgeting, and planning.

But scaling AI is not without challenges. Siloed data, fragmented governance, and cultural inertia hinder progress. This book offers a blueprint

to overcome these hurdles, emphasizing the need for data intensity – ensuring data is high-quality, accessible, and actionable.

Critically, this transformation requires leadership commitment: Boards and C-level executives (CxOs) must champion data as a strategic asset to enhance enterprise value. The Board must provide its sponsorship and commitment to establish and mature the data pillar. For Boards and CxOs, treating "data" as an operational topic to be handled by the IT is no longer an option. In my own experience, building a data-centric operating model has been transformative. At Persistent, our pivot to the SASVA AI platform, powered by a data-centric operating model, reflects this ethos – accelerating the entire application lifecycle.

This book distills the insights, frameworks, and strategies needed for every enterprise leader to take data seriously and unlock its full potential. Enterprises that capitalize on their data as a strategic asset and mature their data pillar will be able to create competitive advantages through initiatives like leveraging AI at scale.

To delay is to risk irrelevance. Enterprises that embrace data as a pillar will unlock AI at scale, drive competitive advantages, and shape the future. This book equips leaders with the frameworks to act decisively. The time to lead is now. Harness the power of data and thrive together.

**Sandeep Kalra**
*CEO, Member of the Board*
*Persistent Systems*
March 2025, USA

# Acknowledgments

## SUJAY DUTTA

Conveying thanks to my wife, Debashree, and my kids, Soham and Arna, would be an understatement. They have been my backbone throughout this journey. I want to thank my sister, parents, in-laws, friends, and well-wishers for their encouragement and blessings. I must also thank my co-author, Sidd, who came on board to join me in this journey – this book would not have been possible without his involvement.

## SIDDHARTH RAJAGOPAL

I want to thank my lovely wife, Deepti, and my son, Naman, first and foremost. They understood and patiently supported the marathon efforts of writing such a book. Their encouragement enabled me to be inspired and focused on writing this book. Special thanks to my father-in-law, V.R. Shyam Sundar, for reviewing parts of this book and providing practical insights from an outsider's perspective. Special thanks to my co-author Sujay – we spent long hours working together on late night calls, but the discussions are what has led to this book and its content.

***

We want to thank several individuals whose contributions helped this book immensely. To Rainer Deutschmann and Sandeep Kalra, thank you for writing thoughtful forewords for this book. Thanks to Rüdiger Eck and Audi AG for sharing their practical insights and examples in the case study. Thanks to Binny Gill and Ramana Kumar for their thoughtful quotes that enriched this book's content. Thanks to Gwellyn Daandels, Mike Ferguson, and Rainer Deutschmann (again) for reviewing this book extensively and providing such fantastic feedback to improve the content. Several people around the globe have given excellent advice as a sounding board: Amy McNee, Anand Krishnan, Julia Giona, Liselotte Hägertz

Engstam, Manuel Gomez, Mats Hanson, Mukundan Ramakrishnan, Nick Dobbins, Sandeep Kishore, Sauveek Ghosh, Steven Totman, and Thomas Hußlein. Your perspectives have been significantly helpful in shaping this book.

To the fantastic team at Taylor & Francis, thanks to Lucy McClune and her amazing team, Matthew Shobbrock and Danielle Zarfati. Your belief in this book and immersive support in bringing it to market are immensely appreciated.

Last but not least, several of our family, friends, colleagues, and the data community have provided immense support, learning, and mentorship. We would also like to thank those we have unintentionally left out or didn't want to be credited directly.

# About the Authors

**Sujay Dutta** is a seasoned technology and business leader with more than 25 years of global experience. He believes the future is being shaped at the intersection of AI, business outcomes, culture, and data ("ABCD"). He is passionate about helping organizations leverage data and AI at scale, to accelerate business impact. Throughout his career, Sujay has worked with top technology innovators such as Databricks, Informatica, and SAP, as well as leading IT services firms including Capgemini, Harman Connected Services, HCL Technologies, and Tata Consultancy Services. Having lived and worked across India, the United States, and Europe, Sujay brings a global perspective and expertise that spans data and AI strategy and execution, making him a trusted advisor to C-suite executives and business leaders worldwide.

**Siddharth Rajagopal** is a chief architect in the Field CTO Organization at Informatica. In his role, he engages with senior executives at the enterprise, providing thought leadership around data and data management by sharing his insights and learnings. Prior to this, he has worked as a consultant and architect in various large data management programs at Cognizant and Accenture. He lives in the Netherlands with his family.

# About the Case Study Author

**Rüdiger Eck** is an accomplished professional in the automotive industry with a distinguished career spanning over two decades. Working for two German premium OEMs, Rüdiger has over 20 years of technical track record in global automotive production, including winning two consecutive world champion titles with the Mercedes Formula 1 team. He has spearheaded various Audi teams from the early stages of digitalization in the production industry and now directs Audi's Data and Analytics Factory for Production and Logistics, as well as overseeing Volkswagen Group data activities. With a German master's degree ("Diplom-Ingenieur") in mechanical engineering, Rüdiger has a strong passion for managing technical and organizational change and bridging the gap between production and IT. His expertise and leadership continue to drive innovation and excellence in the automotive sector.

# Introduction

The world around us is changing at an unprecedented pace, and technology is fueling the transformation. With the Internet and the power of smartphones bringing unlimited information to our fingertips, we are now amid the most phenomenal transformation. With the democratization of GenAI, what will differentiate an enterprise from another will no longer be the technology itself but the data used by the people, processes, and technologies, not only for a competitive edge today but also to create a future-proof, long-term impact.

When we, the authors, started discussing this, drawing from cumulative five decades of professional experience, we concluded that most enterprises continue to struggle to harness the power of data strategically and sustainably. Most Boards and CEOs realize the power data possesses but struggle to comprehend the path to take to leverage it as a strategic asset. Their common perception is that data is a technical topic that should be handled within IT, analytics, or data offices. There is confusion about who is responsible and accountable for data. Some Boards and CEOs have taken "strategic" actions by appointing a chief data officer (CDO) or a data lead, considering it a "silver bullet" to leverage data as a strategic asset. Understandably, many CDOs and data offices struggle to deliver the expected impact. Data in most enterprises continues to be seen as a by-product of people, processes, or technologies. Technological advancements have happened in the data domain with innovative technologies; however, technologies alone do not create sufficient conditions for the needed change.

These observations led to the realization of this book's core purpose: To serve as a catalyst for structural change in enterprises – empowering

DOI: 10.1201/9781003512776-1

Boards and CxOs to drive a paradigm shift by elevating data as the "fourth pillar" of their operating model, along with its people, processes, and technology. We believe that this change would enable enterprises to develop a holistic and sustainable approach to reaping the benefits from data as a strategic asset.

Our core purpose for this book resonated with Rüdiger Eck, head of Data and Analytics Factory for Production and Logistics at Audi AG. They decided to come on board to provide their case study, which enriches the content with points of view and examples of an enterprise undergoing this journey. We share Rüdiger's introduction to the case study below.

Our book highlights the importance of data for Boards and CEOs and provides a roadmap for them and their CxOs to become mature in leveraging data and be prepared for future innovations that leverage data as a core foundation. Our book contains real-world examples, frameworks, maturity models, *Food for Thought* questions, and actionable insights that should give senior executives a practical guide to apply in their enterprises.

We have structured the content of this book in the following chapters:

- **Chapter 1:** This chapter addresses "Why data should be treated as the fourth pillar," highlighting the potential that data provides to enterprises looking to scale their artificial intelligence (AI) initiatives and the significant challenges they face to realize that potential. This chapter presents an assessment framework to assess and align the challenges and a framework to understand the varying data intensity of use cases.

- **Chapter 2:** This chapter delves into "data as the fourth pillar – what does it mean, and what does it include." Here, we share key principles for the data pillar and the data capabilities enterprises need to operationalize data as the fourth pillar. The CDO's role and key responsibilities are also provided in this chapter, along with an introduction to the agile data delivery framework, i.e., the data operating model (DOM), required to fulfill data needs.

- **Chapter 3:** This chapter covers "operationalizing data as the fourth pillar: the data operating model." This chapter dives deeper into the DOM, its layers, and how it can be operationalized with people, processes, and technologies.

- **Chapter 4**: This chapter presents a data maturity journey for enterprises leveraging a "maturity framework" we have developed. It enables enterprises to plan and execute their journey in a structured manner. The chapter highlights the importance of balancing data demand and data supply.

- **Chapter 5:** To conclude, the authors present a visionary view of "visualizing the future' with data and provide critical insights and takeaways for the key personas: Boards and the CxOs.

The case study provided by Audi furnishes a real-life example of a large global enterprise undergoing a journey to establish data as a new pillar in its operating model. We thoroughly enjoyed partnering with Rüdiger on the case study. We hope you will find the case study engaging and beneficial.

## 0.1  KEY PERSONAS AND PURPOSES FOR READING THIS BOOK

We have aimed to write this book in a manner that Boards and CxOs can read and benefit from.

- *Boards and CEOs* may struggle to realize the full potential of their data. This book enables them to understand how data can create a strategic differentiation and the actions that are required from them. This book also allows Boards and CEOs to measure and track their enterprises' data maturity journey.

- *CDOs* may find it challenging to deliver the impact expected from data to their enterprises. This book enables the CDOs to prioritize their data journey to build the data demand in their enterprises and fulfill these demands with an agile DOM enabled by defined people, processes, and technology capabilities.

- *Chief operating officers (COOs) and heads of business functions* may view data as a by-product of their business activities. This book enables them to identify and tap the data potential in their business operations and create new business models based on data. This book also calls out what is expected by these leaders and their teams to enable the data pillar.

- *Chief information/technology officers (CIOs/CTOs)* may view data within the boundaries of their applications and IT systems. This book enables them to decouple data from technologies, leveraging data to optimize their technology landscape strategically and operationally. With the knowledge of this book, these leaders also set up AI technologies with a robust and scalable data foundation.

- *Chief HR officers (CHROs)* can become the launchpads of data embedded into the enterprise. This book lets them view treating data as a strategic asset, as a cultural and enterprise mindset shift, and collaborate with the CDOs to accelerate data maturity.

- *Chief financial officers (CFOs)* may struggle to allocate funds and measure the enterprise value of using data. This book enables them to understand the return on investment (ROI) on data by understanding and measuring the relevant key performance indicators (KPIs) for data.

We hope this book inspires every business leader to act and succeed with data.

### 0.1.1 This Book's Website

Website for this book: *www.datathefourthpillar.com.* The website includes digital content like templates and videos that readers could leverage in their journey of operationalizing and maturing the data pillar in their enterprise.

Disclaimer: *The views expressed in this book are those of the authors and do not necessarily reflect those of their current or past employers.*

## 0.2 INTRODUCTION TO THE CASE STUDY BY RÜDIGER ECK

Long-standing business models throughout the industry have been undergoing profound transformational efforts in the past decade or so, many of them with data at the heart of this evolution. Integrating data into their operations, from fragmented sources to scaling insights for decision-making, is a significant challenge to many, often carefully balancing resources and aspirations. Recognizing these shared struggles, I was inspired to contribute to this book by detailing Audi Production's journey to provide on-the-ground implementation feedback on what works and what does not – a case study that offers practical lessons for others navigating similar terrain. My contribution is driven by the belief that real-world examples inspire action, hoping to empower others, thus helping to move our industries into a new phase of growth and productivity.

This book stands out because it introduces a viable model filled with actionable concepts that can be readily implemented. Beyond its practicality, this book addresses the critical need for cross-functional collaboration in leveraging data, a challenge many companies encounter. It helps clarify the purpose and deliverables of data lead roles (such as CDOs) and pinpoints operational strategies that can unlock internal efficiencies.

# CHAPTER 1

# Why Establish Data as the Fourth Pillar for Scaling AI?

## 1.1 SCALING THE USE OF AI FOR ENHANCING ENTERPRISE VALUE

"Can Machines Think?" was the question Alan Turing proposed to explore in his 1950 paper,[1] "Computing Machinery and Intelligence." That can be regarded as the initiation phase of AI. Decades later, the democratization[2] phase of AI is happening, like the democratization of the Internet that happened during the 1990s. In line with the popular adage of "Moore's law,"[3] according to which the number of transistors doubles roughly every 2 years, the growing capabilities of computing power, storage, and network capacity are accompanied by decreasing costs. This has also enabled advancements in AI algorithms, such as the development of generative AI (GenAI) models. GenAI models are increasingly becoming more intelligent and powerful. The availability of open-source AI models and abundant datasets to train and enhance AI models has provided further impetus to the proliferation of AI. These factors have lowered the entry barriers for enterprises to adopt AI by improving their ROI and reducing their payback period from AI investments. This is enabling the democratization of AI in enterprises. Today, AI is a topic in the boardroom of every enterprise.

DOI: 10.1201/9781003512776-2

*The rise of AI forces us to rethink everything. This isn't just another tool – it's a force multiplier, amplifying human decision-making and operational efficiency.*

*– Binny Gill, CEO of Kognitos, Inc.*

Enterprises can leverage AI in their products and services, increase the effectiveness and efficiency of their business processes, and improve the productivity of their people, thus enhancing their enterprise value (EV)[4] and contributing to the global economy. As per the projection[5] by PricewaterhouseCoopers (PwC), AI could contribute up to 14% or 15.7 trillion dollars to the global economy by 2030. However, with the significant potential value of AI also comes the responsibility to mitigate its potential risks. Such risks include biases, data privacy violations, cybersecurity threats, and deepfakes. To help mitigate the risks, globally, countries or regions have already introduced or are in the process of introducing AI regulations such as the European Union (EU) AI Act.[6] Enterprises need to develop internal standards and policies to mitigate the risks and to comply with the regulations. Additionally, AI's impact on the human workforce's role and relevance is a critical consideration. AI may replace humans in routine operational tasks, but at the same time, it will also enhance their skills and productivity. A skilled human workforce will still be essential to develop, deploy, and monitor complex AI capabilities. AI capabilities and the human workforce with the skills to build and leverage them will generate a "flywheel effect"[7] among themselves, benefiting each other in an upward spiral manner.

With such high stakes, the Boards and CxOs of enterprises cannot afford to ignore AI. AI's fast-paced innovation and democratization are pushing enterprises to execute AI at breakneck speed.

*AI does not offer any value on its own. It must be deployed in business processes to deliver business outcomes!*

Like the democratization phase of the Internet, enterprises that emerge as winners in the democratization phase of AI would be the ones that can significantly enhance their EV by leveraging AI at scale!

### 1.1.1 Meaning of Leveraging AI at Scale

Enterprises exist to continuously "give back more" (see Figure 1.1) to their stakeholder communities, outperform their competitors, and, as a result,

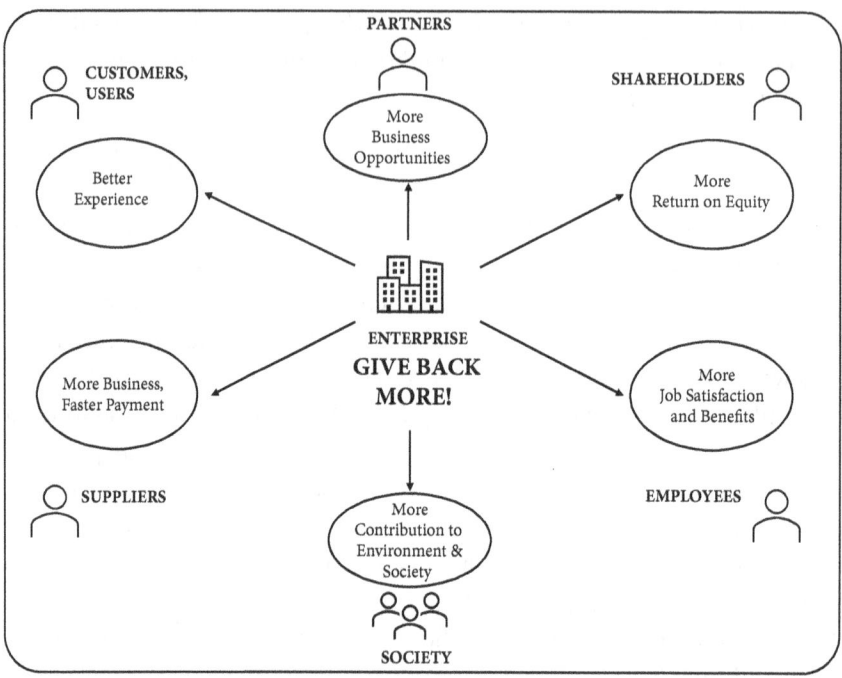

FIGURE 1.1 Enterprises Exist to Continuously "Give Back More" to Their Stakeholder Communities.

enhance their EV. However, they are constrained by limited resources. Enterprises must innovate continuously to deliver more with less. Those who can execute this will continue to flourish and exist.

Moore's law is more than a prediction of technological innovation: It is also closely linked to the dynamics of demand and supply. The exponential growth of transistors required growth in their applications. In alignment with this, enterprises need to continuously "give back more," anticipating growth in their stakeholders' demands.

Leveraging AI at scale (see Figure 1.2) means putting AI to work in business processes executed by the business functions, enabling them to innovate and continuously improve their outcomes and thus enhance their EV.

With scale, a "flywheel effect" (see Figure 1.3) is generated between AI and the people, processes, and technologies that enable business processes, resulting in a positive continuous improvement loop between them.

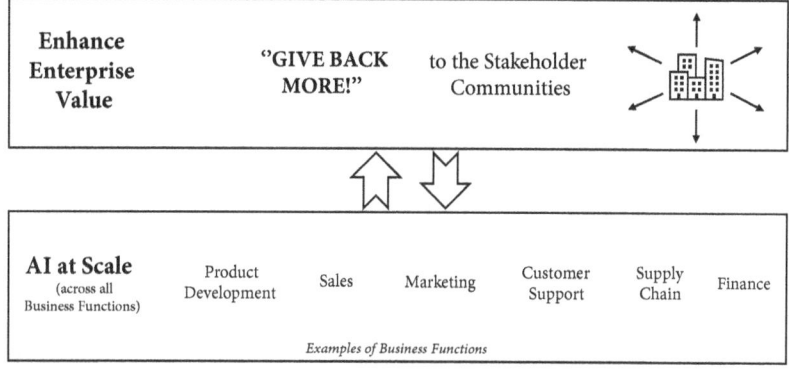

FIGURE 1.2    AI at Scale across Business Functions Enables Enhancing EV.

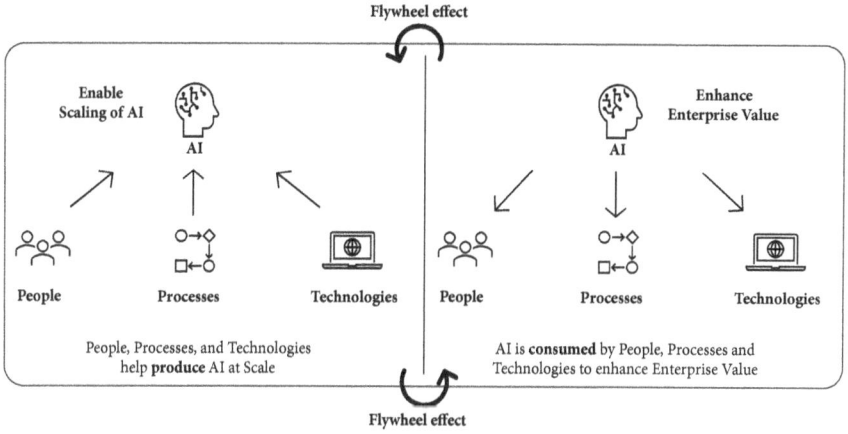

FIGURE 1.3    Flywheel Effect between AI and People, Processes, and Technologies.

On the one hand, as shown on the left side of Figure 1.3, AI solutions are produced and scaled by people, processes, and technologies. On the other hand, as shown on the right side of Figure 1.3, AI is consumed by people, processes, and technologies to enhance EV. The flywheel effect unlocks a continuously increasing EV from leveraging AI.

> *Food for Thought:* How can the flywheel effect benefit your enterprise rather than amplify incorrect or biased results?

People, processes, and technologies are necessary to scale the use of AI across the enterprise. However, are they sufficient? Is there another critical factor for successfully scaling the use of AI?

## 1.2 DATA IS CRITICAL FOR SCALING AI

Let us take the analogy of a restaurant wherein the "food" served with consistent high quality at scale by the restaurant is considered the "AI at scale," enabling the restaurant to succeed. To prepare and serve high-quality food, people involved in the restaurant, for instance, the manager, chef, host, waiter, and server, are critical. Processes such as how the kitchen is organized and how the dishes are prepared enable repeatability with high quality. The equipment used in the restaurant can be considered as the technologies that enable high-quality food to be prepared. All these components, i.e., the people, the processes, and the technologies, are necessary to deliver high-quality food at scale. However, they are not sufficient. High-quality ingredients such as fresh vegetables are also critical for high-quality food. Data is the ingredient required, together with people, processes, and technologies, for AI to scale. Stale or missing ingredients negatively affect the food quality; similarly, poor quality data negatively impacts the outcomes from AI, and then it does not scale.

> *Data, together with people, processes, and technologies, are required for AI to scale!*

Data is critical for the enterprises' use cases or initiatives,[8] like leveraging AI at scale, to improve their business outcomes.

> **Food for Thought:** *Are the data requirements of all use cases the same in your enterprise?*

### 1.2.1 Defining Data Intensity

To exemplify the variance in data requirements, a fraud detection use case in a financial institution requires reviewing all transaction data "as-is" and in real time. Conversely, for an email promotion campaign use case executed within the same financial institution, the accuracy of email addresses must be verified, customer consent must be confirmed, and the physical address and date of birth information must be removed before the data should be used. It can wait a couple of days to receive the data that is fit for use, as the content for the promotion is prepared in parallel.

The capabilities an enterprise requires to meet the data intensity (see Figure 1.4) requirements will vary. The Boards and CEOs cannot adopt

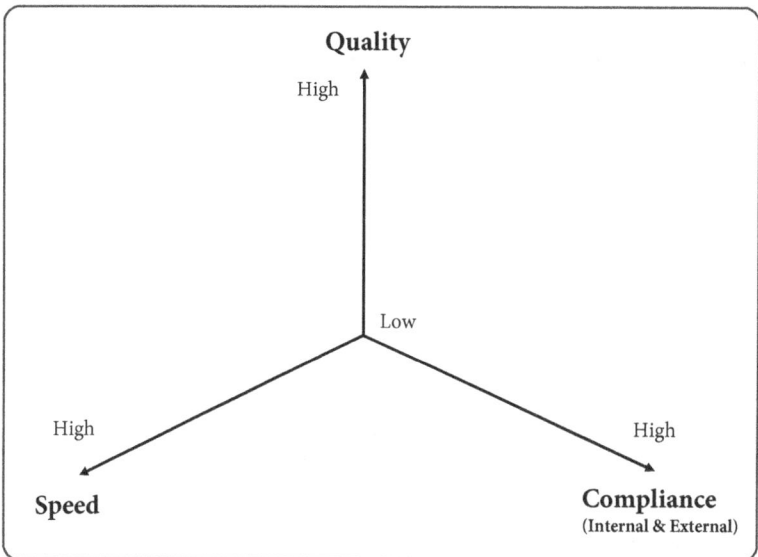

FIGURE 1.4   QCS Framework to Define Data Intensity.

a "one-size-fits-all" approach. They cannot configure themselves to only meet the most stringent data intensity requirement, such as the demand for accurate and compliant data in real time. Such use cases may be few. Otherwise, they would overinvest in capabilities, which would be wasted on many other use cases that would not have such stringent requirements. Conversely, they cannot configure themselves to meet the most relaxed data intensity requirement, such as the requirement for "as-is" data that could be provided in a few days. Once again, such use cases may be few. In this case, they would underinvest in capabilities and be unable to fulfill the needs of many other use cases that do not have such relaxed data intensity requirements.

Hence, understanding the data intensity requirement of each use case is critical to work toward fulfilling them.

To understand data intensity, we present a three-dimensional "QCS framework (see Figure 1.4)." "QCS" represents "quality, compliance, and speed," the three dimensions in the framework, which together determine the required data intensity of each use case.

As per the framework, the most stringent data intensity requirement would be "high quality + high compliance + high speed" data, and the most relaxed data intensity requirement would be "low quality + low compliance + low speed" data. A typical enterprise would have use cases that fill the spectrum from the most stringent to the most relaxed data intensity requirement.

> *The QCS framework enables stakeholders across the enterprise to align on the data intensity requirements of their use cases and collaborate to fulfill them.*

Let us now delve into each dimension of the QCS framework.

### 1.2.1.1 Quality ("Q") Dimension

"Garbage in, garbage out" – this popular adage could be applied to the relationship between data and business outcomes. "Garbage data" would lead to "garbage outcomes." Generating "garbage outcomes" at scale, such as while leveraging AI at scale, could severely impact enterprises and their stakeholder communities.

Data quality can be further expressed through multiple subdimensions such as accuracy, completeness, and freshness.

Accurate data is a well-understood requirement. For example, while diagnosing patients during COVID-19,[9] AI tools delivered little or no impact, as those tools were built using mislabeled data or data from unknown sources.[10]

The completeness of data is about having the required data attributes. For example, if the customer age segment information is missing, leveraging AI for segment-based marketing campaigns for the customer will not be possible.

The freshness of data is critical depending upon the expected purpose of the AI model. For example, suppose a fraud detection AI model is not trained with the latest fraudulent transactions displaying emerging fraud scenarios; as a result, it may miss potential fraudulent transactions due to not being trained on such data.

> *AI at scale with poor quality data will make incorrect decisions at scale!*

### 1.2.1.2 Compliance ("C") Dimension

With data being a key ingredient for AI, data privacy violations, biases, and manipulations caused by data become key concerns for AI users. Hence, regulators globally have developed or are developing frameworks for AI. For AI to comply with regulations such as the EU AI Act, data used to train and used by AI models when deployed in business processes must also be compliant. Global enterprises must also comply with multiple global regulations on data (such as General Data Protection Regulation (GDPR)[11] and CCPA).[12] These regulations also keep evolving, or new ones may come. The evolving compliance requirements require enterprises to set up internal policies and standards for data and build the capabilities required to adhere to those.

> *AI at scale without data compliance is like highways with fast cars that do not follow traffic rules and cause severe accidents!*

### 1.2.1.3 Speed ("S") Dimension

Scaling the use of AI would need the speed of data supply to match the speed of data required by the AI models and, thus, provide high-speed, real-time responses required by specific use cases. This requires high-speed processing and provisioning of data to AI and high-speed data transformation toward the form factor the AI model can consume, such as in a vector database. Based upon their purpose, AI models might require to be fed with more relevant and diverse information at high speed for training and inferences during usage. High speed becomes even more challenging to fulfill as the volume and variety of data increase. For example, when a customer interacts with a customer support AI agent[13] to seek support on an issue with an enterprise's product or service, the customer would expect real-time responses. The customer would expect that the AI agent has knowledge of the customer's historical interactions with the enterprise and provides context-sensitive responses. For this to happen, the AI agent must be fed with complete customer information in real time as it responds to customer queries in real time.

To clarify, the speed dimension and the freshness aspect of the quality dimension are interlinked. A data quality rule for the freshness aspect is leveraged to report the speed requirement of the use case.

> *Using AI without data provided at the required speed is like fueling a rocket with automotive gasoline!*

Each use case would have its specific data intensity requirement, which would be variances in the level of the quality, compliance, and speed dimensions. With the increasing usage of AI agents in business processes, enterprises will experience an increasing number of use cases that need them to execute at a "high" level on all three dimensions simultaneously and consistently!

> **Food for Thought:** *Can your enterprise execute at a "high" level on all three Q, C, and S dimensions simultaneously and consistently?*

Let us consider scenarios highlighting the impact of feeding data to AI, "high" on only two dimensions of the QCS framework:

- Leveraging AI agents to provide new offers to customers, with high data quality and compliance but at a low data speed, would make the AI agents slow to make offers and respond to customers' queries, thus negatively impacting the customers' decision to accept the new offers.

- Leveraging AI agents to provide new offers to customers with high data quality and speed but using their personal data without prior consent might result in heavy penalties from authorities and a tarnished brand. For example, as per GDPR,[14] penalties could be up to €20 million or 4% of annual global revenues.

- Leveraging AI agents to provide new offers to customers, with high data compliance and speed but with poor data quality, would lead to inaccurate offers and unsatisfactory responses to customers' queries by the AI agents, resulting in lost revenues or negative customer experiences.

  *Data is like "fire"! It could be harnessed into a source of energy (i.e., enhance EV), or it could burn down an enterprise (i.e., cease it to exist).*

Now that the data intensity has been defined through the QCS framework, let us delve into how the required data intensity differs based on enterprises' choice of AI journey.

## 1.2.2 Data Intensity Required on the Basis of Enterprises' AI Journey

Enterprises must judiciously plan their AI journey based on the investments required, expected ROI, payback period, etc. AI has various categories depending on the use case and application of AI in the use case.

Machine learning (ML) is a broad category in AI that enables a system to learn from data to make decisions and/or predictions. ML has subcategories such as "supervised learning," where the ML model is trained by a human expert, and "deep learning," a type of neural network with multiple nodes and layers to predict the outcome based on input features or attributes. GenAI is a further subset of deep learning that focuses on generating content. As we delve into the various categories and subcategories of AI, the role of data, the required data intensity, and the investment required vary substantially.

To illustrate this, let us first take an example of a simple AI model, an ML model to predict house prices.

In this example, as illustrated in Figure 1.5, a starting AI model is trained using sample training data to develop it into a trained model. Let us call this level as "Level 1." The training data enables the starting AI model to make accurate predictions over time and become a trained Level 1 AI model. For the AI model to understand and predict trends impacting house prices, it needs to be trained with past data on house prices. The training data must be accurate for the model to make accurate predictions. The training data must also include data on recent houses sold to reflect the prevailing market conditions. However, while doing so, to comply with privacy regulations, the personal information of the buyers and the sellers cannot be included in the training data. In addition to the training

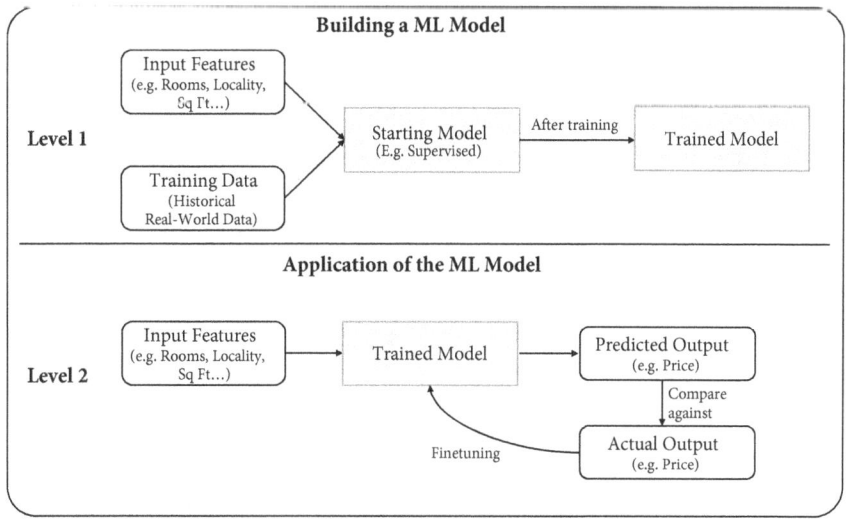

FIGURE 1.5   Abstracted View of a Simple ML Model to Predict House Prices.

data, selecting the right features decides the behavior of the AI model. For instance, if only input features, such as the size of the house and the number of rooms, are included for training the starting AI model and another critical parameter that affects house prices, like the locality of the house, is not included in the training data, the AI model will get trained to predict house prices that will not match real-life situations. It will then give the same price to houses across all localities, as it would not understand that house prices change across localities. In addition, caution must be exercised that biases such as data representation bias[15] are not introduced in the model through the training data. Thus, appropriate training data with the required data intensity, i.e., high on quality and high on compliance, in this case, is essential to get an adequately trained AI model.

Once the AI model is trained, it can be deployed to make predictions. The trained model can be fine-tuned continuously based on the data on the actual prices of the houses that get sold, compared with the price predicted by the AI model. Let us call this level "Level 2," referred to in Figure 1.5, wherein the AI model continuously learns and improves itself. If the use case demands the trained model to predict the house prices in real time, then real-time data, i.e., with high speed, would need to be fed to the AI model. Hence, this use case would require high data intensity, with high levels in the QCS dimensions.

To illustrate the importance of data in training AI models, in 2006, Fei-Fei Li[16] realized that AI models would not deliver the expected outcomes if the data used to train AI models were not real-world data. This realization led to the ImageNet[17] project, an ongoing research effort to provide researchers worldwide with image data for training large-scale object recognition models. ImageNet dataset enabled the models to deliver better results. ImageNet has catalyzed the "AI boom."

> *The paradigm shift of the ImageNet thinking is that while a lot of people are paying attention to models, let's pay attention to data. Data will redefine how we think about models.*
>
> – Fei-Fei Li[18]

Next, let us delve into the role of data in building and using GenAI models, as well as the required data intensity and investments. Figure 1.6 presents an abstract view of the way GenAI models are typically built[19] and the type of data that are needed at each level.

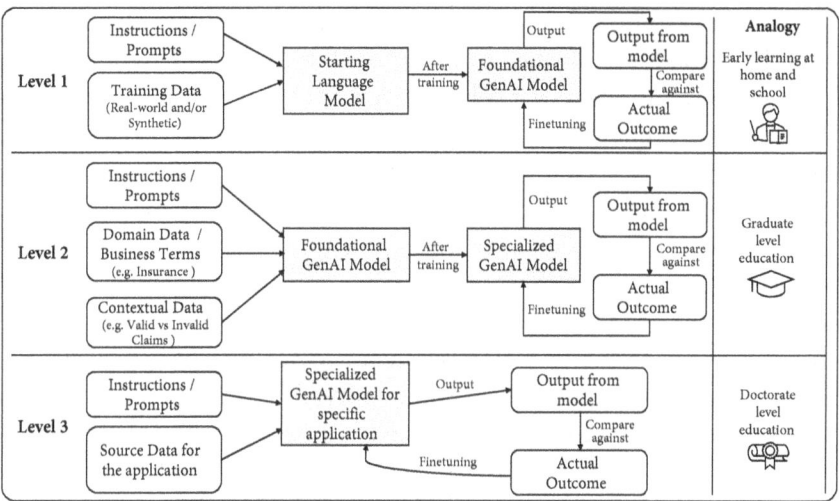

FIGURE 1.6 Abstract View of Building and Using a GenAI Model of Multiple Levels.

Let us call the first level of the flow "Level 1." To present a simple analogy, Level 1 is like taking a person through initial learnings, at home and school. The person is taught languages such as their family language and other local languages needed for communication and general subjects, such as science and mathematics, in their school to develop basic knowledge and survive in the world. Similarly, in an abstract view of how GenAI models are built in Level 1, a starting language model is trained with instructions or prompts and requisite data to understand the essential context of the type of output it needs to respond to. The training data used for training the model in Level 1 can be both actual and synthetic data[20] that mimic the actual data. Training GenAI models in Level 1 requires petabytes of diverse structured and unstructured data to enable the models to learn patterns, context, and relationships to generate adequate responses. In addition, highly skilled human resources are required to ensure that biases are not introduced in the model and that sensitive/inappropriate content is filtered out during the training process. Besides the knowledge of how the AI model functions and what data has been used to train it, they also need to develop the capability to explain the outcomes[21] from the GenAI model to comply with AI regulations. After the completion of the training in Level 1, the model becomes a foundational GenAI model.

After the training in Level 1, the foundational GenAI model moves on to the second level of the flow; let us call it "Level 2." Continuing the analogy, Level 2 is where the person graduates in chosen areas of knowledge such as computer science, mechanical engineering, or journalism. Similarly, in Level 2, specific knowledge training occurs for the foundational GenAI model to become a specialized GenAI model, with a specialty in performing tasks or roles in a specific domain. Such training includes instructions or prompts, domain data, and contextual data. Context is critical to generate relevant outcomes from the GenAI model. For instance, in the analogy, in the context of computer science specialization, a mouse is an input device, not an animal. At this level, enterprises can leverage their specialization and create differentiation by developing specialized GenAI models with their specific data, business terminologies, and contexts in their enterprise and industry domain. The goal would be to enable the specialized GenAI models to execute a variety of tasks and generate differentiated outcomes. For example, let us take a specialized GenAI model that is required to be specialized as an insurance AI agent for an insurance company. Customers might have various queries about their claims, policies, premiums, etc. However, only after being thoroughly trained in the specialized insurance domain, company-specific data, and contextual knowledge can the insurance AI agent understand customer queries and provide accurate answers. It can also create a new claim or provide the status of an existing claim.

After the specialized training in Level 2, as per the analogy, the next level, i.e., "Level 3," is where the person pursues further studies and acquires a doctorate level. Similarly, in Level 3, the specialized GenAI model is trained and deployed to perform highly skilled roles such as a fraud detection AI agent. This agent looks through claims in progress and identifies potential frauds. This agent cannot perform other tasks like responding to customer queries and opening a new claim.

The leverage of AI agents can be extended even further when an AI agent interacts with one or more other AI agents to perform additional tasks in the business process, with the required involvement of humans to execute critical tasks, validate the tasks performed by the AI agents, or improve the tasks performed by the AI agents. Continuing with the example of the insurance company, the insurance AI agent responsible for interactions with customers first interacts with a "New Claim Creation AI agent" to create a new claim and then with a "Claim Processing AI agent" to process the claim. When the claim is over a predefined threshold value or suspected of being fraudulent, a human expert could be notified to validate the claim.

In the future, an enterprise will have multiple such AI agents deployed across their business processes to improve their business outcomes.

Andrew Ng[22] stresses focusing on data to improve business outcomes from AI. He calls it "Data-centric AI" – "the discipline of systematically engineering the data used to build an AI system."

For adopting a data-centric approach to AI, each level of GenAI model development will require varying investment levels to meet the required data intensity, i.e., QCS requirements, based on the use case.

*The investment level required to meet data intensity for the different levels in the GenAI journey must be a key consideration for enterprises.*

With an understanding of the levels of AI and the required data intensity for each level, an enterprise must decide on a suitable level to start its AI journey. In the context of GenAI, enterprises can consider the three scenarios as explained in the next subsections. It is important to note that continued innovations in AI, like small language models (SLMs),[23] will continue to cause disruptions and offer new possibilities to enterprises.

### 1.2.2.1 Scenario 1: Start the AI Journey from Level 1

The most significant differentiation from leveraging GenAI is achieved when an enterprise starts its AI journey from Level 1 and then goes through Levels 2 and 3.

However, the cost and infrastructure needed to execute Level 1 are significantly high. For example, Meta's Llama 3[24] has been trained on over 15 trillion data tokens, consuming computing power equivalent to 350,000 Nvidia H100 chips and costing approximately US $10.5 billion.[25]

The investment level needed to meet the required data intensity is highest for Level 1, as compared to Levels 2 and 3 (see Figure 1.7). In this scenario, the enterprise must also bear the computing power and data intensity required for Levels 2 and 3 to make the GenAI model deployable in business processes. The enterprise would also need technically skilled resources to execute Levels 1, 2, and 3. Hence, the investments needed and the payback period would be the highest.

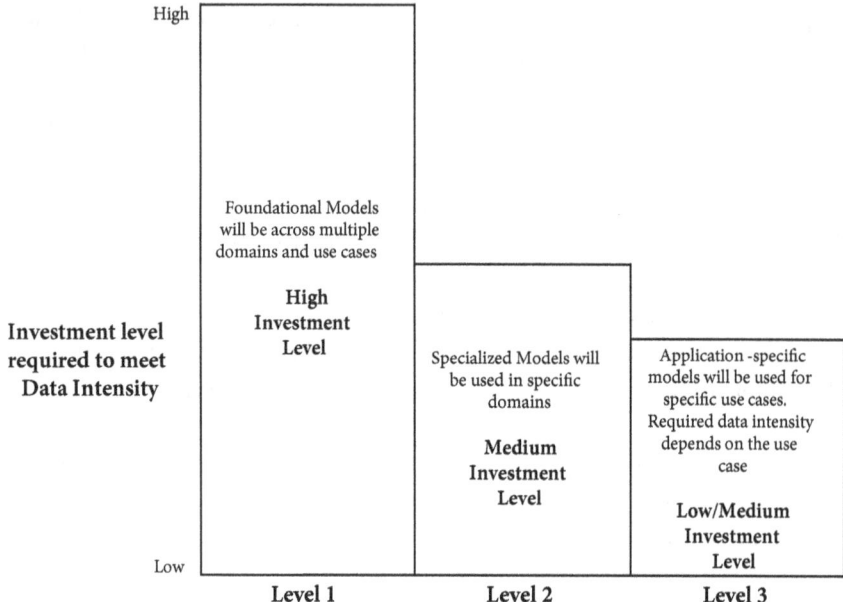

FIGURE 1.7   An example of Investment Level Required to Meet Data Intensity Based on AI Level and Use Case.

With the lure of this scenario creating the most significant differentiation, enterprises must evaluate the trade-offs before they adopt this scenario. This scenario would be most suited for large enterprises that can:

- Fund significant investment needed.

- Have use cases with significant expected business outcomes to achieve a positive return on their investment higher than their cost of capital.

- Sustain a long payback period.

- Have access to required technical resources.

- Can execute on the required data intensity for Levels 1, 2, and 3.

### 1.2.2.2 Scenario 2: Start the AI Journey from Level 2

In this scenario, an enterprise would leverage one or more existing foundational GenAI models available in the market. The enterprise would forego the differentiation that could be achieved in Level 1 while saving on the resources and time needed in Level 1. However, the enterprise would need to carefully evaluate the foundational GenAI models that suit their requirements, before proceeding with the Level 2 training. The enterprise would then need to focus on bringing differentiation through the specialized GenAI model it develops in Level 2. It would need to take care of the computing power and data intensity needed in Levels 2 and 3, which would be significantly lower than those in scenario 1.

However, before adopting this scenario, enterprises must thoroughly understand the investment needed and business outcomes targeted from the use cases, to achieve a positive return on their investment higher than their cost of capital, the expected payback period, required technical skills, and required data intensity for Levels 2 and 3. Differentiation in this scenario would be achieved through the instructions or prompts, domain data, and contextual data used to develop the specialized GenAI model. This scenario would suit enterprises that have the ability to allocate the required resources and the business case of making the required investment.

As an example of this scenario, Walmart[26] partnered with OpenAI and Microsoft to build a specific GenAI model with search capabilities to enable shoppers to search online based on prompts such as planning for a birthday party and shopping for relevant products.

### 1.2.2.3 Scenario 3: Play Only in Level 3

In this scenario, an enterprise would leverage the specialized GenAI models provided by enterprises adopting scenario 2. By doing so, the enterprise would forego the differentiation that could be achieved in Levels 1 and 2 while saving on the resources and time needed in those levels. As efforts would be spent only in Level 3, the investment level and payback period for this scenario would also be lower than those in the other two scenarios. The enterprise would, however, inherit any biasedness, performance issues, or limitation in capabilities, such as lack of cross-industry knowledge, that might exist in the selected specialized GenAI models.

Given the lowest investment needed and the fastest time-to-value for this scenario, this scenario is suitable for executing AI proof-of-value (POV) projects to develop a better understanding of the challenges involved in leveraging AI and their potential business value. When deploying AI in business processes, this scenario suits enterprises with specific use cases requiring a shorter payback period on the investments made. In this scenario, the key to achieving the expected business outcomes would be having access to data with the required intensity.

For example, several technology companies in scenario 1 or 2 have launched AI solutions integrated into their existing technology offerings, such as Microsoft Copilot,[27] IBM Watson,[28] Salesforce Einstein,[29] and OpenAI solutions such as text-to-video (Sora).[30] Enterprises that decide to play in Level 3 can leverage such offerings.

> **Food for Thought:** *Which AI journey scenario are you considering for your enterprise? Does it also vary across business functions and use cases?*

### 1.2.3 Data Intensity Required for Data Monetization

Data monetization[31] is another important use case for enterprises. There may be different types of enterprises leveraging data monetization, such as the following:

- Enterprises with their business entirely based on monetizing data by providing "data as a service" and insights based on data to their customers. For example, ZoomInfo[32] provides business-to-business (B2B) data and intelligence based on data monetization.

- Enterprises that monetize data by differentiating themselves based on the insights they provide to their customers to enhance the value proposition of their core products and/or services. For example, Magnati[33] helps its merchants increase their sales with its brand affinity tool based on the payment data.

- Enterprises that consider their business partners as "data partners" and monetize data by sharing it with them for joint go-to-market. For example, the Zalando Partner[34] team helps its partner brands to grow on the Zalando platform by sharing data insights.

One may consider the leverage of data by an enterprise to improve its business outcomes as data monetization.

While data is at the core of data monetization, each use case differs in the investment required toward data intensity. Let us consider a few examples:

1. For an enterprise providing "data as a service," its customers may ask for raw "as is" data in real time, such as payment transaction data for fraud detection. To meet the ask, the effort required by the enterprise

on the quality and compliance dimensions of the QCS framework would be "low." However, the enterprise would need to have or develop capabilities to provide the data in real time, so "medium to high" effort may be required for the speed dimension.

2. For a payment solution provider providing insights to merchants on its consumers, data would need to be curated, such as inaccuracies and inconsistencies removed, and sensitive data like the consumers' location need to be masked or removed. The effort required by the payment solution provider on the quality and compliance dimensions of the QCS framework would be "medium to high." Also, the merchants would need the data in real time to provide offers to the consumers as they visit their stores, so the effort required by the payment solution provider on the speed dimension could be "medium to high" as well.

With the understanding that each use case in enterprises has different data intensity requirements and enterprises cannot adopt a "one-size-fits-all" approach, enterprises may find the situation challenging. Also, the Board, the CEO, and the business leaders may not be aligned on the challenges and their severity. Let us next delve into the typical challenges enterprises face to meet the data intensity requirements.

## 1.2.4 Challenges to Meet the Data Intensity Requirements

To meet the data intensity requirements of its use cases, like scaling the use of AI, data monetization, and others, we recommend that each enterprise develop a holistic view of its challenges and achieve alignment among the business leaders. Once they have that view, they should work toward finding sustainable solutions for the challenges identified. We have categorized the expected challenges into nine categories to enable enterprises to develop a holistic view of their challenges. These challenge categories are collectively exhaustive but not mutually exclusive of each other; one challenge category might be dependent upon or exacerbate another one.

1. **Pressure of business execution:** Hyper-competition and the need to continuously give back more to their stakeholder communities pressure enterprises to focus on immediate business outcomes. This, unfortunately, creates a "chicken-and-egg" situation for some

enterprises that have not been able to focus on a long-term data strategy and build a strong data foundation. At the same time, they are hampered from meeting the required data intensity due to the lack of a data foundation. This situation gets aggravated for publicly listed enterprises that must continuously deliver the quarterly business results expected by the market. On the other hand, some enterprises may have established a data foundation and data operations to manage and deliver data. However, adoption by all business functions is still low on average. The low adoption could be because many business functions may not be aware of or believe that the data foundation and the data operations can deliver the data and data intensity required by their use cases. In such a scenario, data operations may not feel the pressure of business execution, and this challenge could be considered low.

2. **Complying with evolving regulatory requirements:** Data leveraged for AI, data monetization, and other use cases increase the risks of data privacy violations, biasedness, or manipulations based on data, etc. To mitigate such risks, regulatory requirements for AI and data are evolving at the local and regional levels. Understanding those implications and adhering to the evolving requirements make leveraging data more complex and incur additional costs. For example, the EU AI Act categorizes different risk levels for AI models. Classifying these risk levels will require enterprises to connect these AI models with a robust data governance process. The vital cost aspect of complying with evolving regulatory requirements increases the challenges for small to medium businesses (SMBs). For example, as per a Center for Data Innovation report,[35] a small business (with up to 50 employees/€10 million turnover) can expect total compliance costs of up to €400,000 for one high-risk AI product requiring a quality management system. Such challenges hinder enterprises from meeting the "compliance" dimension of the QCS framework for data intensity.

3. **Difficult to quantify the business value specifically generated by data:** Business functions generate value by leveraging people, processes, technologies (including AI), and data. It is not easy to separate and quantify the business value exclusively generated by data. This results in challenges to justify the investments needed to meet the data intensity requirements.

4. **Prioritization of resources:** Enterprises are constrained for resources. Prioritizing resources for areas where they can create the most value is critical. Measurement of business value generated by data is complex. Hence, prioritizing resources for managing data also becomes challenging, especially with other pressures such as driving revenue growth, improving profitability, or leveraging AI. In such a situation, technology applications that store/process data and their responsible stakeholders are given the added responsibility of managing data without allocating resources to focus on data. This leads to more efforts wasted by resources involved in the use cases, which must prepare the data to meet their required intensity before they can use it.

5. **Lack of role clarity for managing data:** As data exists in multiple business functions, business processes, technology applications, and with people across the enterprise with different data perspectives, who exactly should be responsible and accountable for meeting the data intensity requirements? That is a difficult question for most enterprises. Enterprises must clarify roles that are responsible and accountable for the data. Not having this clarity results in enterprises being unable to meet their data intensity requirements.

6. **Talent and cultural challenges:** The increasing need for data in enterprises results in the increasing demand for talent with experience in the data domain. Enterprises are facing challenges to meet this demand. For instance, a report[36] from the UK government shows that 46% of businesses in the UK have struggled to recruit the right data talent. We believe this issue is not just restricted to the UK but present globally. Enterprises must also have a data adoption mindset and culture. The talent and cultural challenges hinder enterprises from executing their plans to meet data intensity requirements.

7. **Complexity due to data growth:** As the volume, velocity, and variety ("3Vs") of data generation and consumption are increasing, it is becoming increasingly complex for enterprises to leverage data while complying with regulations (refer to point 2). In addition, with the increasing leverage of GenAI, the 3Vs of data will grow even further due to the higher demand for real-time and unstructured data, such as images, text, and videos, for GenAI. The complexities of data growth create challenges for enterprises to meet their data intensity requirements.

8. **Technological complexities:** Enterprises may have technological complexities such as proprietary technologies with proprietary data formats; legacy technologies with legacy data formats; and fragmentation in data storage, computing, and management technologies. These complexities hinder or slow enterprises from meeting their data intensity requirements.

9. **Growing data silos:** When data is considered a by-product of performing business activities, and together with prior challenges mentioned, it leads to growing data silos across the enterprise. When the data is scattered across various data silos, it makes it significantly difficult for enterprises to meet their data intensity requirements.

Due to the uniqueness of every enterprise, the level of challenges across the categories would vary for each enterprise. We recommend that each enterprise develop a scorecard of its challenges across each category. Figure 1.8 shows a sample scorecard. The numbers in the scorecard represent how the enterprise scores themselves in each challenge category. The higher the number, the higher the level of challenge in each category. The development of the scorecard need not be a scientific or quantitative exercise; it may be developed on the basis of the judgment of the business leaders, i.e.,

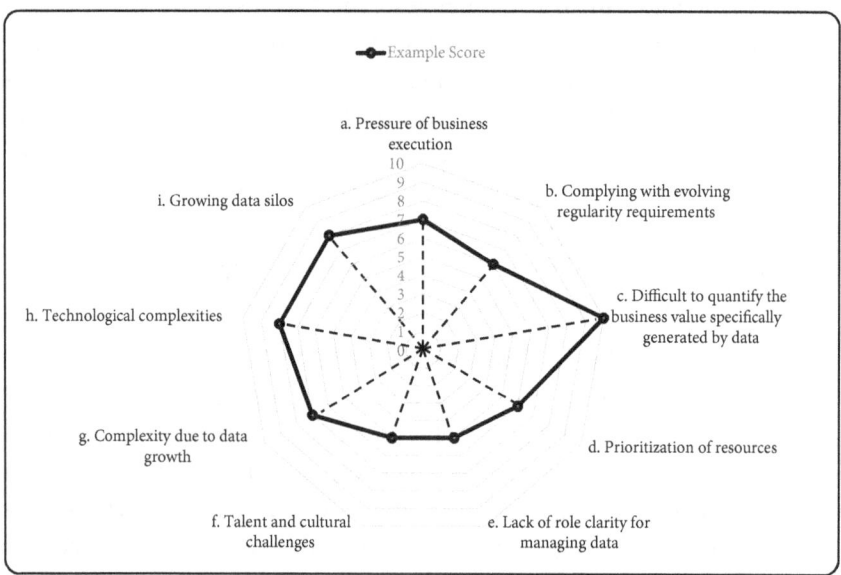

FIGURE 1.8  Sample Scorecard of Challenges an Enterprise Faces to Meet their Required Data Intensity.

the Board, the CEO, and the CxOs. The primary objective of the exercise is for the business leaders to be aligned on the severity of the challenges hindering the enterprise from meeting their data intensity requirements. Chapter 4 delves into how this scorecard becomes a vital input to devise the enterprise's maturity journey for the data pillar.

> *Food for Thought: Have you developed the above scorecard for your enterprise? Which challenges did you find to be rated differently from what you had earlier perceived? Why is that?*

### 1.2.5  For Enterprises to Alleviate Their Challenges – Treat Data Equally Important as People, Processes, and Technologies

People, processes, technologies, and data are necessary for use cases like leveraging AI at scale and data monetization to deliver their targeted business outcomes. From the data perspective, only providing the required data to the use cases is insufficient; their data intensity requirements must also be met.

However, enterprises face complex challenges while delivering data with the required data intensity. The attention and involvement of every stakeholder in the enterprise, from the Board, the CEO, and the leaders of the business functions to the stakeholders using data in their operational activities, are required to overcome these challenges. A structural change is required to secure that from the broad stakeholder base, including the Board and the senior management, and develop a holistic and sustainable approach to resolve the challenges.

That structural change would be enterprises making a paradigm shift and elevating "data" to become the "fourth pillar" of their operating model alongside their existing people, processes, and technology pillars (see Figure 1.9).

> *Paradigm Shift: Make "data" the fourth pillar in enterprises' operating model.*

When data is elevated as the fourth pillar of the operating model, data, together with people, processes, and technologies, enables use cases like leveraging AI at scale or data monetization to achieve their targeted business outcomes, which enhances EV.

Chapter 2 explores what "data as the fourth pillar" means for enterprises.

Let us now cover Audi's case study to understand why it has decided to make data a new pillar of its operating model.

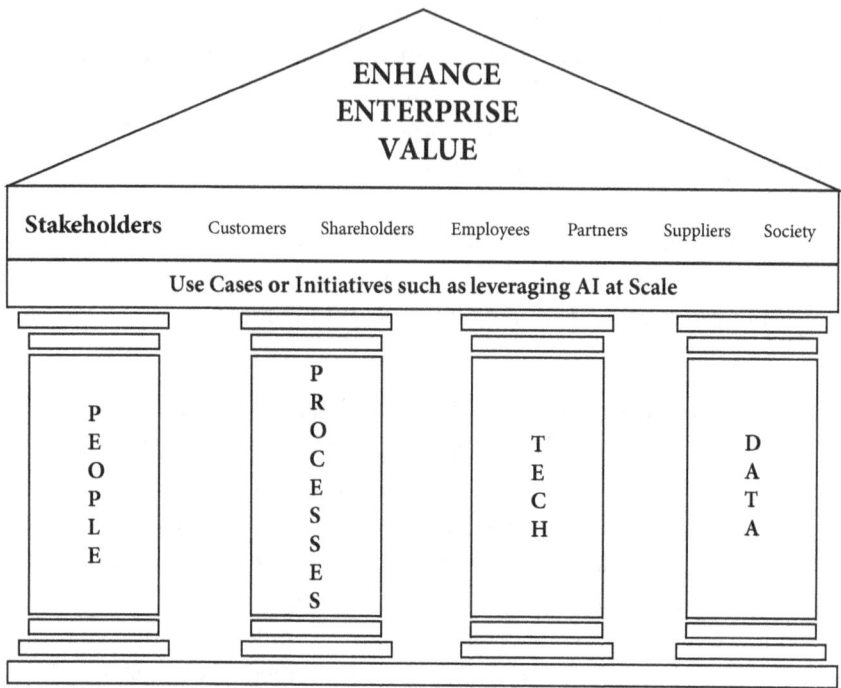

FIGURE 1.9    Data as the Fourth Pillar to Enhance EV.

## 1.3 CASE STUDY: WHY AUDI HAS DECIDED TO MAKE DATA A NEW PILLAR OF ITS OPERATING MODEL

As a subsidiary of the Volkswagen Group, the Audi Group[37] is a prominent manufacturer of premium and luxury automotive vehicles. In addition to producing vehicles with the Audi brand, it also makes vehicles with the Bentley, Lamborghini, and Ducati brands. In 2024, the Audi Group delivered approximately 1.7 million Audi brand vehicles, alongside other brands, employing over 88,700 people globally.

Audi's production and logistics operation is an advanced operation that spans 22 global locations. For this case study, "Audi Production" shall include production and logistics operations. Audi Production produces vehicles in four Audi-owned production facilities in Germany, Hungary, Mexico, and China and in several Volkswagen Group-owned sites worldwide.

Audi Production's strategy is centered around efficiency, innovation, and sustainability. It is pursuing the goal of achieving net carbon neutrality at all production sites worldwide by 2025. To execute its strategy, Audi Production relies on its global production and logistics network, its highly skilled workforce, and digital technologies in the manufacturing and logistics process.

It is often said that automotive OEMs[38] like Audi create some of the most complex industrial products. Audi Production is responsible for activities ranging from product and manufacturing engineering to operational manufacturing and supply chain processes. It is also responsible for the physical infrastructure and real estate management. The complexity involved in the entire value chain stems from a long chain of interlinked and interdependent processes. To describe it at a high level and in a simplified manner, the process starts with tooling and equipment preparation during the vehicle design stage. This involves setting up or adapting necessary machinery and tools for mass production, including stamping machines and paint booths. Once the tooling and equipment are prepared, the manufacturing process utilizes those, starting with shaping parts like doors and hoods from metal sheets. These parts are then welded together to form a vehicle's body. Next, the body undergoes painting, a meticulous process that adds protective and aesthetic layers to the vehicle. This is followed by the assembly stage, where various components such as the engine, transmission, and electronics are installed together with software commissioning steps to activate functions such as engine controllers or in-car connectivity and final calibration procedures of sensors and actuators. This is often done on a moving assembly line with the help of robotics and skilled workers. Finally, the vehicle undergoes quality control and testing to meet safety and performance standards before being distributed to dealerships. This structured process ensures that each vehicle is manufactured to high-quality standards while maximizing efficiency and resource utilization.

The viability of the business of automotive OEMs like Audi is perennially tested by significant technical challenges, high market and customer expectations, strong international competition, ever-tightening regulatory requirements, and a complex network of business processes accompanied by large workforce numbers, need for high investments, and relatively average profit margins.

To stay viable, Audi Production must continue to evolve itself. Through digitalization, it evolved from being an isolated operation to becoming unified across multiple manufacturing facilities. Audi Production created capability-focused technology applications leveraged across multiple manufacturing facilities during the digitalization phase. While it led to a standardization of business processes and a reduced number of applications, it also led to the creation of local data silos in each manufacturing facility. Data silos increasingly hinder the seamless flow of information across business functions, leading to inefficiencies and missed opportunities in leveraging data for strategic and operational initiatives. To understand this better, an almost classic example would be the different naming and hierarchical structural conventions of identical manufacturing assets between the equipment monitoring, plant maintenance, and manufacturing execution IT systems. Similar differences could be found in the data exchange protocol structures. Owing to the lack of an in-house concept for a single source of truth for asset data, the resulting machinery data either required elaborate data transformation or could not be used for further anomaly detection use cases. A data-centric approach has been adopted to progress further in the digital journey. It has helped to find ways in previously unsuccessful digitalization projects. To illustrate this, one must appreciate the automotive manufacturing process as a physical labor-intensive endeavor associated with great pride and craftsmanship. Hence, many quality initiatives rely on good local shop floor management, i.e., the robust handling and resolution of day-to-day occurrences such as supply and quality issues or technical problems. Historically, each manufacturing facility and subunit would have its own way of dealing with these. Hence, harmonizing these processes across multiple entities for digitalization was tedious. Digitalization was often frowned upon in the implementation phase because losing the physical connection to the real-world problem when collecting relevant information (such as root cause analysis or physical inspection) was too highly automated. With the advent of the data-centric approach, the focus could be shifted from tedious process harmonization to "simply" providing necessary data, thereby continuously supporting "self-empowered" harmonization over time and being better understood by the people working in the factories themselves.

This empowerment cycle through a data-centric approach has helped convince people at all levels that data-centric operations can vastly improve the speed and quality of day-to-day decision-making after digitalization. When carried out continuously, these efforts bring improvements across the organization, thus making data an unprecedented enabler and a new pillar of the operating model.

Figure 1.10 showcases Audi Production's digital journey and its present state. Audi Production expects the transformational efforts required for the data-centric phase to be the highest compared to that of the isolation and digitalization phases.

After digitalizing its operations and business processes and continuing its data-centric journey, the Audi Group considers AI a critical tool to differentiate and stay viable. The leverage of AI at Audi Production has gained pace recently. It is now evolving to play an ever more transformative role,

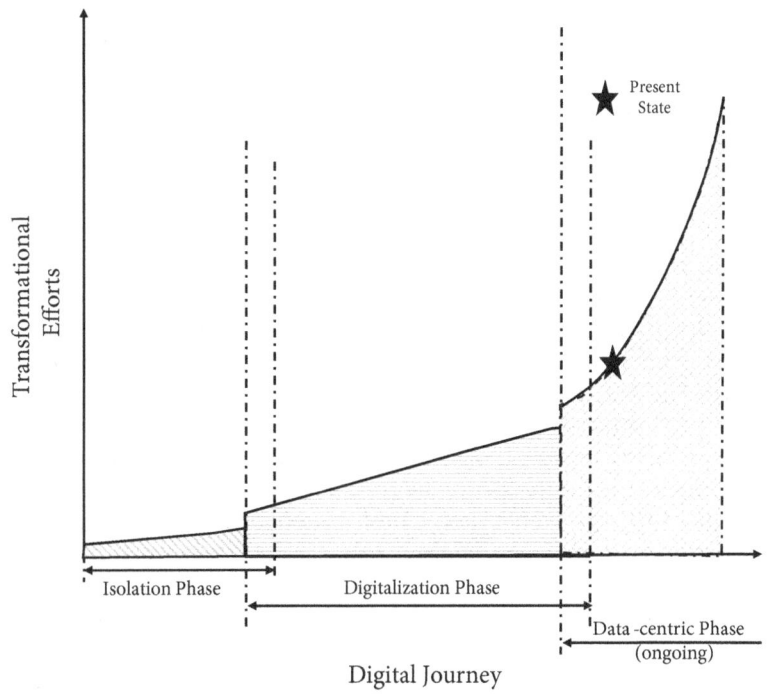

FIGURE 1.10   Audi Production's Digital Journey and Its Present State.

projected to provide fundamental new capabilities over the next 3–5 years to master the increasing business complexity.

The primary goal of leveraging AI is to enable the successful execution of Audi Production's overarching strategy, which focuses on four key areas:

- Enhancing profitability, measured by reducing factory costs (the sum of factory staff, overhead, and material provision costs)
- Promoting sustainability, assessed through environmental impact points
- Improving flexibility, evaluated mainly by the ability to adjust production volumes up or down promptly
- Boosting employer attractiveness, gauged through internal and external benchmarks for attracting and retaining talent

Currently, despite growing cross-business collaboration, AI initiatives and solutions within the Audi Group still largely remain fragmented, targeting specific functions such as localized predictive maintenance use cases or specific quality control tasks. However, these isolated AI applications are gradually evolving into more integrated solutions as the organization keeps on pushing the strategic importance of AI. This shift is reflected not only in strategic organizational adjustments but also in numerous data-driven proofs-of-concept (POCs), awareness campaigns, and educational programs designed to cultivate an AI-literate culture across the Audi Group.

A more strategic approach to AI becomes evident as Audi realizes tangible business value from its deployment. For instance, Audi Production's AI program is a cornerstone initiative to optimize manufacturing processes, minimize downtime, and improve product quality in response to growing, mainly externally driven business complexity that, among other implications, has led to new modular and flexible platforms for Audi products. Initially projected to deliver double-digit million euros in production efficiency gains, the program is also seen as a foundation for unlocking significantly larger business opportunities. This includes establishing a robust and efficient data- and AI-driven organizational structure.

The AI program is structured around ten strategic fields of action – such as digital shop floor management and data-driven logistics control – that combine immediate business case logic with long-term data management capabilities. Each field is supported by multiple use cases implemented through agile operating models. To ensure measurable ROIs, the program employs a "value tree methodology,"[39] linking AI initiatives directly to business outcomes and data management enablers.

Through this program, cross-functional AI solutions are emerging, breaking down silos and fostering more cohesive business processes. These solutions span core operations such as manufacturing execution and vehicle design, driving efficiency and innovation across the enterprise. A notable trend within this effort is developing a "large language model (LLM)" strategy, which enables the execution of increasingly complex tasks. However, scaling AI solutions also requires addressing internal ethical concerns and meeting external regulatory requirements.

One of the most significant challenges the AI program faces lies in providing and preparing trusted data for AI models. This underscores that technology (i.e., AI models) is no longer the primary bottleneck for scaling AI. Audi Production has recognized that data is the foundation for successful AI implementation. Scaling these efforts requires full adherence to data intensity in terms of data quality, compliance, and speed principles encapsulated in the "QCS framework" presented by the authors in Section 1.2. The ongoing data-centric phase of Audi Production's digital transformation (illustrated in Figure 1.10) will be pivotal for enabling success when scaling AI.

To illustrate this point, consider a recent use case involving an AI solution for anomaly detection in Audi Production's body shop monitoring spot welding quality. Previously, quality control relied on an additional offline ultrasonic sample-based process. The new AI solution aimed to predict anomalies directly from in-process data chains. While technically feasible during the POC phase, deploying (and scaling) this solution required permanent monitoring and compliance with welding parameter changes. This also had to be woven into customer quality approval procedures traditionally managed by the offline ultrasonic testing team.

This integration posed challenges due to differences in staff scheduling practices and a lack of (previously not required) established data management procedures within the maintenance team. Addressing these issues required implementing new processes and reevaluating the quality prediction algorithm. Ultimately, achieving success demanded transformational changes across people, processes, and technologies at multiple levels – requiring a strong collaboration across the organization.

Such organizational transformation efforts are particularly challenging, given the tasks' complexity. However, they underscore the critical role of cohesive teamwork and strategic alignment in realizing the full potential of AI within Audi Production's operations.

To summarize the challenges, the authors have presented a scorecard in Figure 1.8. Referring to it, the challenges Audi Production faces and its self-scoring in each challenge category are summarized in Figure 1.11.

The following is a detailed explanation of the self-assessment conducted for each challenge category represented in Figure 1.11:

1. **Pressure of business execution:** While there is significant pressure on business execution, this has not yet extended to data operations, as the potential business impact of data is not fully recognized. Consequently, the current pressure on data operations is low. However, many functional areas are nearing their performance limits without leveraging data, presenting an opportunity to enhance business impact through data utilization in the future. Based on that, Audi Production self-scores this challenge to be three out of ten.

2. **Complying with evolving regulatory requirements:** As a global automotive OEM, Audi must comply with a multitude of existing and emerging regulations across various regions, including GDPR, the EU AI Act, ESG regulations,[40] the EU Battery Passport,[41] and ZEV3[42] standards. The dynamic regulatory environment creates ongoing

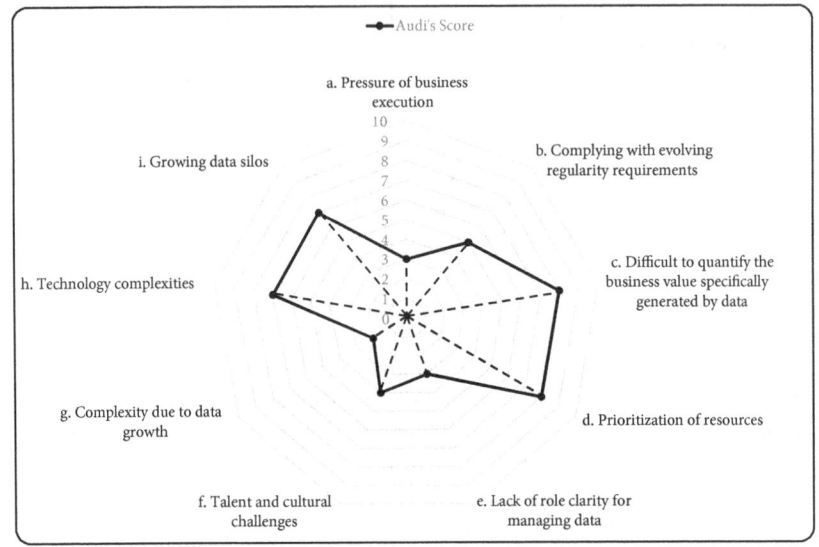

FIGURE 1.11   Challenges Audi Production Faces to Meet Their Data Intensity Requirements.

compliance challenges. Based on that, Audi Production self-scores this challenge to be five out of ten.

3. **Difficult to quantify the business value generated explicitly by data:** Audi Production is moving towards a fully structured product management approach to data. However, it remains challenging to accurately quantify the business value generated by specific data assets. This limitation impacts decision-making and resource allocation for data-driven projects. Based on this, Audi Production self-scores this challenge to be eight out of ten.

4. **Prioritization of resources:** Due to the difficulty in quantifying the business value of data (as noted in 3.), Audi Production works hard to prioritize resources for data initiatives. This challenge is further exacerbated by the high demands for data quality, compliance, and speed required to scale AI across operations. Based on this, Audi Production self-scores this challenge to be eight out of ten.

5. **Lack of role clarity for managing data:** Although Audi Production has a dedicated Data Factory organization in place and basic role clarity exists, further refinement is needed to adopt a product

management approach to data. A clearer delineation of responsibilities among the Data Factory, IT, and business units will be
crucial for effectively developing and maintaining data products.
Based on this, Audi Production self-scores this challenge to be
three out of ten.

6. **Talent and cultural challenges:** Audi recognizes that data management is a business rather than an IT issue. While talented resources
are available under current role understanding, additional expertise
and cultural alignment will be necessary to adopt a product management approach to data and meet the increasing demands for quality,
compliance, and speed across diverse production sites and organizational units. Based on this, Audi Production self-scores this challenge
to be four out of ten.

7. **Complexity due to data growth:** Audi Production primarily manages structured and machine-generated data and has historically
successfully handled its growth. The organization expects this trend
to continue without significant challenges in the foreseeable future.
Based on this, Audi Production self-scores this challenge to be two
out of ten.

8. **Technological complexities:** Audi focused on digitizing business
processes and reducing application redundancies during its digitalization phase but did not emphasize aspects like data sharing, reusability, or portability. Its existing technology landscape
is therefore considered complex due to these earlier oversights.
Based on this, Audi Production self-scores this challenge to be
seven out of ten.

9. **Growing data silos:** The diverse operational landscape across multiple countries has led to unintended data silos during the digitalization phase, fostering a "my data" versus "not my data" mindset within
teams. These silos hinder seamless information flow and collaboration across functions. Addressing this issue will be critical for scaling
AI initiatives effectively. Based on this, Audi Production self-scores
this challenge to be seven out of ten.

To summarize, the increasing demands for high-quality, compliant,
and fast-moving data necessitate significant transformational efforts across
people, processes, and technologies at Audi Production. Audi will adopt a
holistic approach to ensure success in leveraging data as a strategic asset:
A comprehensive integration of data into the operating model to meet the

evolving business needs (refer to the "QCS framework" from Section 1.2). Audi will also focus on enabling agility: Establishing an agile organization capable of delivering "data as a product" will empower teams across business functions and ensure alignment with strategic goals.

By addressing these challenges systematically, Audi Production can unlock greater value from its data assets while driving operational efficiency and innovation.

## KEY TAKEAWAYS FROM THIS CHAPTER

*"Companies that treat data as a core C-suite priority, on par with financial management and talent strategy, will thrive. Those that don't will struggle to compete."*

*– Binny Gill, CEO of Kognitos, Inc.*

- Democratization of AI is a reality. The onus is on the Boards and CEOs of enterprises to leverage AI as a differentiator in their business to increase their revenues and the efficiency and efficacy of their operations, thereby enhancing their EV. To achieve significant benefits, the Boards and CEOs must scale the use of AI. While the Boards and CEOs must push for leveraging AI at scale, they need to safeguard and mitigate potential significant adverse impacts from AI.
- Boards and CEOs must strategically leverage their people, processes, technologies, and "data" to generate expected business outcomes from leveraging AI at scale or data monetization.
- While data is an essential ingredient, each use case has unique and varying data and data intensity requirements. The data intensity defined through the QCS framework must be understood for each use case. The Boards and CEOs should not adopt a "one-size-fits-all" approach to meet the data intensity requirements of all use cases in their enterprises.
- Multiple challenges exist across an enterprise that hinder it from meeting the data intensity requirements. To align on the severity of the challenges among the business leaders, the Boards and CEOs must develop a scorecard of the challenges in their enterprise.
- To overcome the challenges, Boards and CEOs must adopt a holistic and sustainable approach: A structural change and a paradigm

shift that elevates data as the "fourth pillar" of their operating model alongside people, processes, and technologies.

- Audi's case study provides insights into their reasoning to make data a new pillar of their operating model, their data-centric journey to date, and the challenges they face to meet their data intensity requirements.

## NOTES

1 Turing, A. M. (1950). *Computing Machinery and Intelligence*.
2 Democratization of AI or the Internet refers to the general population having access to and benefiting from such capabilities.
3 Moore's law. (2025, January 27). In *Wikipedia*.
4 EV is an economic measure reflecting the market value of a business.
5 PWC. (n.d.). *PWC AI Study*. Global Artificial Intelligence Study.
6 European Commission. (n.d.). *EU AI Act*. EC Digital Strategy.
7 Collins, J. (n.d.). *The Flywheel Effect*.
8 Going forward, in this book, use cases would refer to both use cases and initiatives.
9 COVID-19 was a global pandemic that emerged in late 2019.
10 Heaven, W. D. (2021, July 30). Hundreds of AI Tools Have Been Built to Catch Covid: None of Them Helped. *MIT Technology Review*.
11 General Data Protection Regulation (GDPR) is a EU regulation on information privacy in the European Union and the European Economic Area.
12 California Consumer Privacy Act (CCPA) is a state statute intended to enhance privacy rights and consumer protection for residents of the state of California in the United States.
13 An AI agent is a program that can perform tasks independently to achieve specific goals.
14 GDPR Fines and Notices. (2024, November 22). In *Wikipedia*.
15 Bias might occur when the training data predominantly contains houses from certain localities/price ranges and/or misses houses from certain localities/price ranges.
16 Fei-Fei Li. (n.d.). *Stanford People*.
17 Gershgorn, D. (2017, July 26). The Data That Transformed AI Research – And Possibly the World. *Quartz*.
18 Fei-Fei Li. (2021, August 27). *ImageNet: A Pioneering Vision for Computers*. History of Data Science.
19 Advancements are being made in building GenAI models. The abstract view presented here may not be valid in the future.
20 Synthetic Data. (2025, February 23). In *Wikipedia*.
21 Explainable AI. (2025, February 19). In *Wikipedia*.
22 Ng, A. (n.d.). *Andrew Ng Homepage*.

23 CIO Dive. (2025, February 18). *Why Enterprises Are Turning to Small AI Models.*

24 Llama. (n.d.). *Meta Llama.*

25 Kan, M. (2024, January 18). Zuckerberg's Meta Is Spending Billions to Buy 350,000 Nvidia H100 GPUs. *PC Mag.*

26 Bransten, S. (2024, January 9). *Walmart Unveils New Generative AI-Powered Capabilities for Shoppers and Associates.* Microsoft Blogs.

27 Microsoft Copilot. (n.d.). *Copilot Homepage.*

28 IBM Watsonx. (n.d.). *Watsonx Code Assistant.*

29 Salesforce. (n.d.). *Salesforce Einstein.*

30 Open AI Sora. (n.d.). *Sora.*

31 Data Monetization. (2023, November 11). In *Wikipedia.*

32 Zoominfo. (n.d.). *Zoominfo About Us.*

33 Magnati. (n.d.). *Magnati Super Surprises.*

34 Zalando. (n.d.). *Zalando Partner Insights.*

35 Mueller, B. (2021, July). *How Much Will AI Act Cost Europe?* Center for Data Innovation.

36 Gov.UK. (2021, May 18). *Quantifying the UK Data Skills Gap – Full Report.* UK Gov.

37 Audi AG. (n.d.). *Company.*

38 OEM stands for original equipment manufacturer. An OEM is a company that produces parts and equipment that may be marketed by another manufacturer.

39 The value tree methodology recognizes that analytics projects are often fiendishly hard to scale while early progress can often be misleading. Hence, this approach aims to ensure that a consistent lineage from strategic business opportunities down to the data product level is derived, ensuring that all projects contribute to a long-term data enablement roadmap.

40 ESG. (2025, February 25). In *Wikipedia.*

41 Battery Pass. (n.d.). *Advancing the Implementation of the Battery Passport in Europe and Beyond.*

42 ZEV. (2025, February 4). In *Wikipedia.*

## REFERENCE LIST

Audi AG. (n.d.). *Company.* https://www.audi.com/en/company/

Battery Pass. (n.d.). *Advancing the Implementation of the Battery Passport in Europe and Beyond.* https://thebatterypass.eu/

Bransten, S. (2024, January 9). *Walmart Unveils New Generative AI-Powered Capabilities for Shoppers and Associates.* Microsoft Blogs. https://blogs. microsoft.com/blog/2024/01/09/walmart-unveils-new-generative-ai-powered-capabilities-for-shoppers-and-associates/

CIO Dive. (2025, February 18). *Why Enterprises Are Turning to Small AI Models.* https://www.ciodive.com/news/small-language-models-AI-LLMs/740281/

Collins, J. (n.d.). *The Flywheel Effect.* https://www.jimcollins.com/concepts/the-flywheel.html

Data Monetization. (2023, November 11). In *Wikipedia*. https://en.wikipedia.org/wiki/Data_monetization

ESG. (2025, February 25). In *Wikipedia*. https://en.wikipedia.org/wiki/Environmental,_social,_and_governance

European Commission. (n.d.). *EU AI Act*. EC Digital Strategy. https://digital-strategy.ec.europa.eu/en/policies/regulatory-framework-ai

Explainable AI. (2025, February 19). In *Wikipedia*. https://en.wikipedia.org/wiki/Explainable_artificial_intelligence

Fei-Fei Li. (2021, August 27). *ImageNet: A Pioneering Vision for Computers*. History of Data Science. https://www.historyofdatascience.com/imagenet-a-pioneering-vision-for-computers/

Fei-Fei Li. (n.d.). *Stanford People*. http://vision.stanford.edu/people.html

GDPR Fines and Notices. (2024, November 22). In *Wikipedia*. https://en.wikipedia.org/wiki/GDPR_fines_and_notices

Gershgorn, D. (2017, July 26). The Data That Transformed AI Research – And Possibly the World. *Quartz*. https://qz.com/1034972/the-data-that-changed-the-direction-of-ai-research-and-possibly-the-world

Gov.UK. (2021, May 18). *Quantifying the UK Data Skills Gap – Full Report*. UK Gov. https://www.gov.uk/government/publications/quantifying-the-uk-data-skills-gap/quantifying-the-uk-data-skills-gap-full-report

Heaven, W. D. (2021, July 30). Hundreds of AI Tools Have Been Built to Catch Covid: None of Them Helped. *MIT Technology Review*. https://www.technologyreview.com/2021/07/30/1030329/machine-learning-ai-failed-covid-hospital-diagnosis-pandemic/

IBM Watsonx. (n.d.). *Watsonx Code Assistant*. https://www.ibm.com/products/watsonx-code-assistant

Kan, M. (2024, January 18). Zuckerberg's Meta Is Spending Billions to Buy 350,000 Nvidia H100 GPUs. *PC Mag*. https://www.pcmag.com/news/zuckerbergs-meta-is-spending-billions-to-buy-350000-nvidia-h100-gpus

Llama. (n.d.). *Meta Llama*. https://www.llama.com/

Magnati. (n.d.). *Magnati Super Surprises*. https://www.magnati.com/en/super-surprises/

Microsoft Copilot. (n.d.). *Copilot Homepage*. https://www.microsoft.com/en-us/microsoft-copilot

Moore's Law. (2025, January 27). In *Wikipedia*. https://en.wikipedia.org/wiki/Moore%27s_law

Mueller, B. (2021, July). *How Much Will AI Act Cost Europe?* Center for Data Innovation. https://www2.datainnovation.org/2021-aia-costs.pdf

Ng, A. (n.d.). *Andrew Ng Homepage*. https://www.andrewng.org/

Open AI Sora. (n.d.). *Sora*. https://openai.com/index/sora/

PWC. (n.d.). *PWC AI Study*. Global Artificial Intelligence Study. https://www.pwc.com/gx/en/issues/data-and-analytics/publications/artificial-intelligence-study.html

Salesforce. (n.d.). *Salesforce Einstein*. https://www.salesforce.com/eu/artificial-intelligence/

Synthetic Data. (2025, February 23). In *Wikipedia*. https://en.wikipedia.org/wiki/Synthetic_data

Turing, A. M. (1950). *Computing Machinery and Intelligence*. https://redirect.cs.umbc.edu/courses/471/papers/turing.pdf

Zalando. (n.d.). *Zalando Partner Insights*. https://partner.zalando.com/services/marketing/insights

ZEV. (2025, February 4). In *Wikipedia*. https://en.wikipedia.org/wiki/Zero-emissions_vehicle

Zoominfo. (n.d.). *Zoominfo About Us*. https://www.zoominfo.com/about

# Data as the Fourth Pillar

## *What Does It Mean, and What Does It Include?*

With data as the fourth pillar of the operating model, enterprises leverage their people, processes, technologies, and data to continuously give back more to their stakeholder communities, thus enhancing enterprise value (see Figure 2.1).

The data pillar enables people, processes, and technologies (including AI) to make accurate and timely decisions or inferences in the use cases in which they are involved. In return, these people, processes, and technologies enable the data pillar to provide data at the required data intensity. This creates a flywheel effect between the data and other pillars (see Figure 2.2). As the flywheel effect gathers momentum, it leads to continuous higher business impact by each pillar, thus, conceptually, creating a multiplier effect on the enterprise value.

> *The flywheel effect creates value for each pillar of the operating model and, thus, a multiplier effect on the enterprise value.*

To enable the establishment of the data pillar and the flywheel effect, the Board and the CEO must establish principles for the data pillar that guide every stakeholder in the enterprise that produces or consumes data. Let us next delve into the principles for the data pillar.

DOI: 10.1201/9781003512776-3

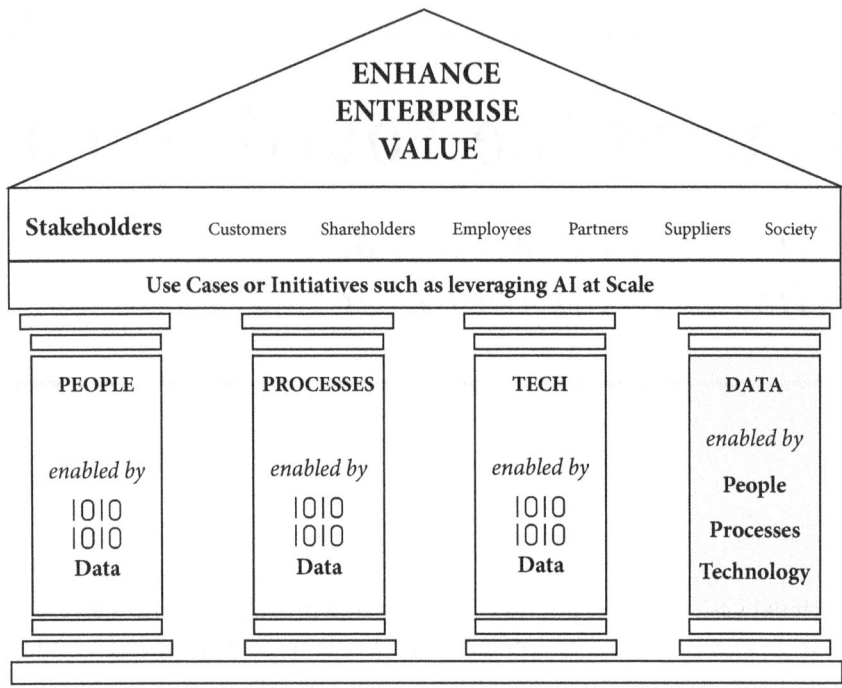

FIGURE 2.1    People, Processes, Technology, and Data Pillars Enable Each Other and Enhance Enterprise Value.

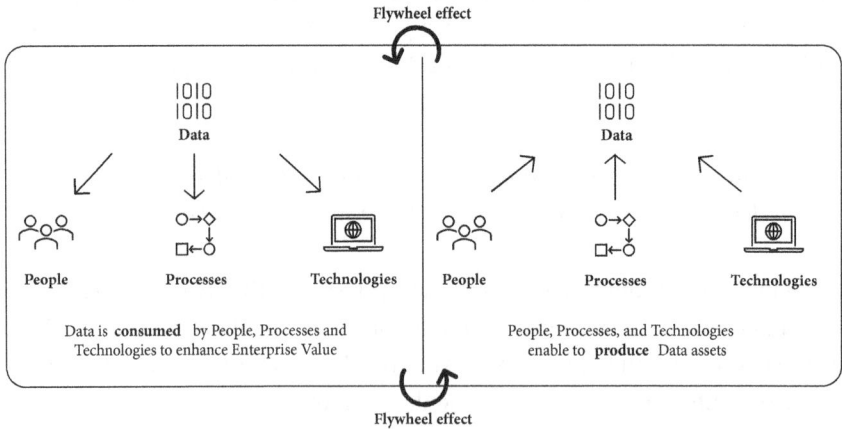

FIGURE 2.2    Flywheel Effect between the Data Pillar and the People, Processes, and Technology Pillars.

## 2.1 PRINCIPLES FOR THE DATA PILLAR

*First, data needs to move out of IT's shadow and into the board-room as a strategic priority. Second, companies must shift their culture – rewarding data-sharing instead of hoarding, and evaluating managers based on data fluidity, not control.*

*– Binny Gill, CEO of Kognitos, Inc.*

Learning from the existing people, processes, and technology pillars, we propose the following five principles for the data pillar (see Figure 2.3). These principles are not mutually exclusive.

1. **Provide Board-Level Sponsorship:** The Board provides its sponsorship to the people, process, and technology pillars. The sponsorship by the Board provides a stamp of strategic importance to each pillar and is critical for their success. Sponsorship by the Board also means that it allocates necessary resources to each pillar, including its bandwidth to collaborate closely with the leader of each pillar to help achieve their goals and resolve any hurdle they face. With data as the fourth pillar, the Board acknowledges the strategic importance of data for the enterprise's success and sponsors the data pillar.

2. **Define Data Strategy:** Enterprises have defined people, processes, and technology strategies aligned with their enterprise business strategy. They enable enterprises to take a long-term view of their

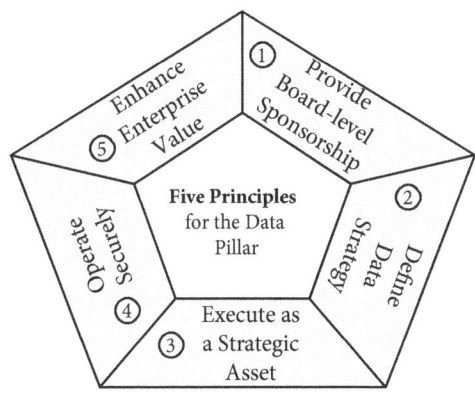

FIGURE 2.3   Five Principles for the Data Pillar.

people, processes, and technologies and leverage them strategically to achieve their business objectives. For instance, the people strategy determines the critical skills and competencies required to serve the enterprise immediately and in the future. The process strategy determines the necessary business processes and the approach to operate them effectively and efficiently and improve them continuously. The technology strategy lays out how technological capabilities (like AI) will enable the enterprise, now and in the future. When data is the fourth pillar, the stakeholder(s) responsible for the data pillar must define a data strategy and align it with the enterprise business strategy and the strategies for the people, processes, and technology pillars. The data strategy outlines how the data pillar would deliver data with the required data intensity to the use cases, now and in the future.

3. **Execute as a Strategic Asset:** The data pillar must execute the defined data strategy to enable the use of data as a strategic asset. Data assets must be shared and utilized by all stakeholders across the enterprise, creating a multiplier effect on enterprise value. This necessitates making data assets findable, accessible, interoperable, and reusable.[1]

4. **Operate Securely:** While strategic assets are to be shared and leveraged across the enterprise, the enterprise must ensure their secure usage to enable the execution of business operations securely and in compliance with the required regulations. To do so, enterprises must have defined standards and policies for their people, processes, and technologies. For example, which individuals have permission to do what, how do processes align with regulatory compliance, and how do technology selections undergo a clear privacy and security evaluation such as role-based access controls?[2] Likewise, data assets must be shared and utilized securely and in a compliant manner. That does not mean that people, processes, and technologies should keep their data locked – that violates the third principle. At the same time, sensitive data must not be accessed by unauthorized people, processes, and technologies. The data pillar must prevent unauthorized or incompliant data usage. It must also prevent inadvertent or intentional data breaches.

5. **Enhance Enterprise Value:** Every pillar of the operating model must enhance enterprise value. As the fourth pillar, the data pillar must

enhance enterprise value by delivering data at the required data intensity to the use cases. The Board, the CEO, the leaders of the business functions, and the leaders of the other pillars must also leverage the data pillar to enhance enterprise value.

*The Board and the CEO must communicate the principles for the data pillar to every stakeholder in the enterprise, which will guide them as they produce or consume data in their strategic and/or operational activities.*

In alignment with the principles for the data pillar, the Board, with its sponsorship, must develop a mandate for the data pillar. The mandate must include creating the leader role for the data pillar, i.e., the CDO. It must also include requirements for the leaders of the other pillars to collaborate with the CDO to establish the data pillar and consider data a strategic asset in their respective pillars. The following section focuses on the CDO role – its goal and responsibilities, the impact it creates in the organization structure, and the key attributes of the CDO persona.

## 2.2 THE CHIEF DATA OFFICER

*The North Star goal of a CDO would be to enable all stakeholders to enhance their business outcomes by leveraging data as a strategic asset.*

With data as the fourth pillar, the North Star goal of a CDO would be to enable all stakeholders in the business functions to enhance their business outcomes by leveraging data as a strategic asset. Figure 2.4 summarizes the seven key responsibilities of the CDO to achieve this goal. The CDO must set up the "Data office" to deliver its responsibilities.

Let us now delve into each responsibility, including potential pitfalls and suggestions for mitigation.

1. **Capture and create demand for data across the enterprise:** Fulfilling the demand for data is the reason for the existence of the data pillar. First, the CDO must engage with business stakeholders to capture the existing demand for data. That would entail understanding their use cases, the role of data in enhancing business outcomes,

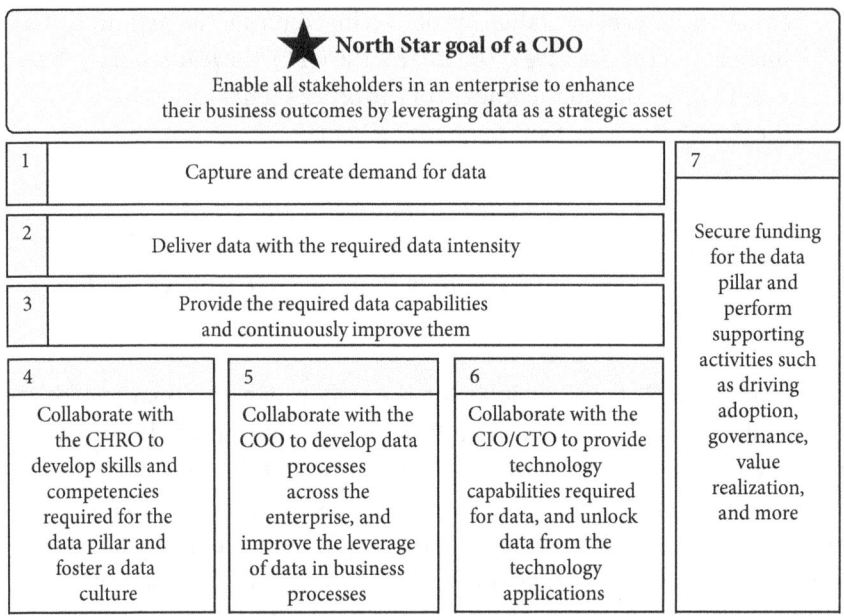

FIGURE 2.4   Seven Key Responsibilities of the CDO.

and the data intensity requirements. Next, as the CDO takes steps to fulfill the existing demand, they must also create demand for data by engaging with business stakeholders who may not yet have considered leveraging data as a strategic asset to enhance their business outcomes. To enable the CDO to measure and communicate the demand for data, we have coined two KPIs:

i   **Total addressable value (TAV) through data**: i.e., potential business value that can be unlocked by leveraging data. In line with the concept of an enterprise's total addressable market (TAM), this KPI would measure the aggregate business value goal for all use cases in an enterprise that can use data assets.

ii   **Expected addressable calue (EAV) through data**: i.e., expected business value data from leveraging data. This would be the aggregate business value expected from all use cases that leverage the data assets provided by the data pillar. EAV increases due to two factors: a) An increase in the number of use cases that leverage the data assets provided by the data pillar or b) an increase in the business value generated by the in-scope use cases. The maximum value of EAV would be equal to TAV when all use cases that can use data assets leverage the data assets provided by the data pillar.

Under this responsibility, the goal of the CDO would be to continue increasing the TAV and EAV.

- *To increase the TAV*, the CDO, as a visionary, influences the Board and the CEO to consider new strategic initiatives, such as data monetization, which would be powered by data and enhance the enterprise value. For example, in a retail consumer brand enterprise, the CDO influences the Board and the CEO to consider wholesalers as "data partners." By exchanging data with them in a compliant manner, the enterprise can improve product mix, optimize inventory levels with the wholesalers, and improve the customer experience of the end users. These actions result in enhancing the enterprise value and, thus, the TAV.

- *To increase the EAV*, the CDO engages with the business leaders and stakeholders of use cases and highlights how data leveraged strategically could enhance their business outcomes. For example, in a retail consumer brand enterprise pivoting its go-to-market (GTM) model toward a direct-to-consumer (D2C) focused model, the CDO engages with the stakeholders in the supply chain management function and showcases that by leveraging the data assets provided by the data pillar for making predictions about inventory levels in each store, they would achieve "10% inventory cost savings," equal to 15 million dollar savings. The 15 million dollars become the EAV from this use case. At the enterprise level, the EAV would be the aggregate EAV from all use cases leveraging data assets provided by the data pillar.

Chapter 4 delves further into the measurement of TAV and EAV. Table 2.1 provides the potential pitfalls and mitigation suggestions for this responsibility of the CDO.

2. **Deliver data with the required intensity:** Use cases generate business outcomes when they get data with the required data intensity. Therefore, this is another key responsibility of the CDO. The CDO and the data office must collaborate with stakeholders to understand their use cases, data needs, and intensity requirements. They must also comprehend the enterprise's challenges to fulfill these

TABLE 2.1 Pitfalls and Mitigation Suggestions for the CDO's First Responsibility.

| Potential Pitfall | Mitigation Suggestion |
|---|---|
| • The CDO only focuses on "friendly" business stakeholders to capture and create demand<br>• The CDO and the business stakeholders take an accounting approach to measure TAV and EAV and either spend too much time agreeing on the values or do not align | • While initial success must be attained by engaging with the "friendly" business stakeholders, the CDO must broaden the impact of the data pillar by engaging with the "skeptics" and "nay-sayers." The CDO needs to turn them around by highlighting the business benefits from the success stories<br>• The CDO and the business stakeholders must take a pragmatic approach. The TAV and EAV provide them with information on the direction of travel – to mature the data pillar and enhance enterprise value |

TABLE 2.2 Pitfalls and Mitigation Suggestions for the CDO's Second Responsibility.

| Potential Pitfall | Mitigation Suggestion |
|---|---|
| • The Board and the CEO assign additional delivery responsibilities to the CDO, such as business intelligence[3] reporting or AI technology development. This might dilute the CDO's focus on delivering data<br>• The responsibility of the CDO for delivering data gets misinterpreted as being accountable for data | • Data delivery must be a core focus of the CDO. It is a challenging and critical responsibility. The CDO must leverage the five principles for the data pillar to get support from the Board and the CEO, avoiding additional responsibilities that might dilute their focus<br>• The Board and the CEO must mandate the business functions that the accountability for data remains with them, like the accountability for the execution of business processes. The business domains must treat the data office as an enabler to get the required data, fulfilling their data intensity requirements |

requirements (see Figure 1.8). Given the dynamic nature of the business environment, the CDO must establish an agile framework for data delivery (refer to the DOM in Section 2.14) that can be incrementally set up and refined throughout the maturity journey of the data pillar (see Chapter 4). Table 2.2 provides the potential pitfalls and mitigation suggestions for this responsibility of the CDO.

3. **Develop the required data capabilities and continuously improve them:** To execute their data delivery responsibility and enable the stakeholders for the use cases to leverage data, the CDO must develop the required data capabilities and continuously improve them based on feedback received. Such capabilities include data strategy, architecture, semantic data management, governance, and engineering. Section 2.3

TABLE 2.3    Pitfalls and Mitigation Suggestions for the CDO's Third Responsibility

| Potential Pitfalls | Mitigation Suggestions |
|---|---|
| • The CDO rushes to deliver data without understanding and developing the required capabilities<br>• The CDO and the data office develop data capabilities without involving the stakeholders, leading to a lack of buy-in<br>• Data capabilities are not consistently updated to meet the evolving business needs | • The CDO must continuously align with the stakeholders to understand their needs and the required data capabilities<br>• The CDO must involve the stakeholders while developing the data capabilities<br>• To cater to the needs of the evolving business, the CDO must continuously improve the data capabilities in alignment with the stakeholders involved |

details the data capabilities. Table 2.3 provides the potential pitfalls and mitigation suggestions for this responsibility of the CDO.

4. **Collaborate with the CHRO to develop skills and competencies required for the data pillar and foster a data culture:** Even though businesses are undergoing perpetual change, people, in general, are hesitant to change. The outlook of people across the enterprise needs to change so that they consider data as a strategic asset and not a by-product of performing business activities. And, corollary to that, strategic assets must be handled responsibly and securely. In addition, the stakeholders in the business functions must realize and accept accountability for data. They must be trained to be capable of doing that. To make these changes happen, the CDO must collaborate with the CHRO to design and execute a structured change management program. It should include data literacy training for the people in the business functions to enhance their data skills and competencies, thereby creating positives for them by leveraging data. Data privacy and security training are also essential to train people on the potential privacy and security risks that could be created through data and on how to mitigate those. People must also experience data as fun and easy to work with, and it must help them deliver a higher business impact, leading to their personal career growth. Data and HR offices can introduce gamification initiatives like competitions and recognition programs to increase engagement. The CDO and the data office must also promote success stories from diverse stakeholders, leveraging data to enhance business outcomes in varied use cases and motivate more people. When the enterprise fosters a culture of leveraging data as a strategic asset, it becomes easier for the CDO to

TABLE 2.4    Pitfalls and Mitigation Suggestions for the CDO's Fourth Responsibility

| Potential Pitfall | Mitigation Suggestion |
|---|---|
| • The CDO and the CHRO only take a top-down approach of asking or mandating people to treat data as a strategic asset<br>• Having slower than the necessary pace of skill and competency build-up in the data office negatively impacts the development of the data capabilities | • The CDO and CHRO should find pockets of interest within the enterprise, which could be early adopters of the change, and share their success stories. The leaders of the business functions must lead by creating and sharing examples of leveraging data as a strategic asset in their decision-making<br>• Adopt a multipronged approach: Motivate internal people in the business functions and information technology (IT) to join the data office and hire experienced external people |

fulfill their other responsibilities successfully. In addition, the capabilities of people in the data office should be continuously enhanced as the data pillar matures. Chapter 3 delves into the people capabilities required for the data pillar. Table 2.4 provides the potential pitfalls and mitigation suggestions for this responsibility of the CDO.

5. **Collaborate with the COO to improve the use of data in business processes and develop processes required for the data pillar:** The CDO must collaborate with the COO to improve the use of data in business processes and improve their outcomes. For example, the lead time of the quote-to-cash (Q2C) process can be enhanced by leveraging data effectively in multiple steps of the Q2C process, such as for accurate and quick quote generation based on the accurate information of the customer, their past purchases, the segment of the customer, and applying discounts as per pricing rules. Some process steps might need to be modified to improve data usage. In addition, data processes are required in the data pillar to deliver data at the required data intensity to the use cases. Chapter 3 delves into such data processes. New data processes could result in new ways of working and change existing ways. The CDO and the COO must collaborate to overcome change management challenges through a structured change management program. Table 2.5 provides the potential pitfalls and mitigation suggestions for this responsibility of the CDO.

6. **Collaborate with the CIO/CTO to provide the technology capabilities required for data and unlock data from the technology applications:** Technology capabilities are critical for the data pillar

TABLE 2.5  Pitfalls and Mitigation Suggestions for the CDO's Fifth Responsibility

| Potential Pitfall | Mitigation Suggestion |
|---|---|
| • The CDO and the COO take a big-bang approach to implementing new processes and changing existing ways of working<br>• Misalignment between the COO and CDO on who is accountable for data | • Develop a prioritization of the new processes and take an incremental approach involving data domains (like customer or product domains), business functions (like supply chain or manufacturing), or operating units<br>• Referring to the mandate from the Board and CEO in Table 2.2, the CDO and COO must ensure that the accountability for data remains with the business functions, which are also accountable for the business processes |

TABLE 2.6  Pitfalls and Mitigation Suggestions for the CDO's Sixth Responsibility

| Potential Pitfall | Mitigation Suggestion |
|---|---|
| • The CDO overlaps with the CIO/CTO by getting involved in technology management and focusing on reducing the cost of technology for data operations, such as reducing the cost of technology used for data quality | • The CDO must maintain the focus on leveraging technology to achieve the goals of the data pillar, not dilute its focus by getting involved in technology management. The CDO must partner with the CIO/CTO to fulfill the required technology capabilities and overcome the challenges |

to deliver data with the required data intensity to the use cases. The stakeholders involved in the use cases also require technology capabilities to consume data and provide feedback. The key challenges for the CDO to fulfill their data delivery responsibility would be the existing data silos across the enterprise and tight coupling of data with the existing technology applications for operations and transactions. The CDO must partner with the CIO/CTO to provide the required technology capabilities and overcome the challenges. Chapter 3 delves into the technology capabilities required for the data pillar. Table 2.6 provides the potential pitfalls and mitigation suggestions for this responsibility of the CDO.

7. **Secure funding for the data pillar and perform the supporting activities:** The data pillar would require adequate funding for it to operate. The CDO develops the data strategy, gets it approved by the Board and the CEO, and leverages it to secure funding. To measure and track the data pillar's performance vis-à-vis the funding

TABLE 2.7    Pitfalls and Mitigation Suggestions for the CDO's Seventh Responsibility

| Potential Pitfall | Mitigation Suggestion |
| --- | --- |
| • Due to budget constraints in the enterprise, the Board and the CEO do not allocate the funding the CDO asks<br>• The CDO defines complex KPIs that are difficult to measure. Also, the KPIs are not outcome-focused, and the respective stakeholders do not validate the KPIs.<br>• The supporting activities consume most of the bandwidth of the CDO and the data office, and as a result, the other responsibilities do not get the required attention | • The CDO must base the funding request on the data strategy approved by the Board and the CEO. If the requested funding is not approved or the approved funding is not released, the CDO must scale down the data pillar's scope according to the available funds and reset the expectations with the Board, the CEO, and the business functions<br>• The CDO must first align the KPIs with the Board, the CEO, and the leaders of business functions before measuring and reporting them. The CDO must also opt for an incremental approach to measure and report KPIs aligned with the maturity journey of the data pillar<br>• The CDO must also opt for an incremental approach in supporting activities, such as developing the artifacts, based on their need. In addition, the CDO must develop strong execution leaders within the data office, enabling them to delegate effectively |

received, the CDO must measure and report the KPIs related to the demand and supply of data to the Board and the CEO. This is one of the key supporting activities performed by the data office. Business outcomes would be enhanced when business functions adopt the data assets delivered by the data pillar. Data must also be used in a governed and secure manner. Hence, driving data adoption and data governance would also be key supporting activities. Another supporting activity would be developing reusable artifacts,[4] such as data engineering templates, data quality rules, and data access policies, which enable standardization and improve time-to-value while producing or consuming the data assets. Chapter 3 provides further details on the supporting activities and examples of relevant KPIs. Table 2.7 provides the potential pitfalls and mitigation suggestions for this responsibility of the CDO.

*Food for Thought: As a CDO, what would be your most challenging responsibility? How do you plan to be successful with that?*

It is important to note that the CDO's responsibilities will evolve as the data pillar matures. The CDO should be agile in prioritizing their responsibilities throughout the maturity journey, which Chapter 4 delves into.

### 2.2.1 Business Impact Delivered by the CDO

The business impact delivered by the CDO and the data office can be measured through the realized value (RV) – the business value already realized by the use cases that are leveraging data assets provided by the data pillar. The RV can be compared with the EAV and TAV.

The size of the circles in Figure 2.5 represents the dollar or equivalent currency values of RV, EAV, and TAV.

> *All actions by the CDO and the data office culminate into this one goal: "Keep expanding the RV, EAV, and TAV circles!"*

### 2.2.2 Positioning of the CDO in the Organization Structure

This is a crucial decision by the Board and the CEO. The position of the CDO in the organization structure would be key to enabling the CDO to overcome the change management challenges they would face, execute their responsibilities successfully, and make the data pillar successful.

The Board and the CEO must consider the following factors to make that decision:

- Size of the enterprise

- Complexity of business operations

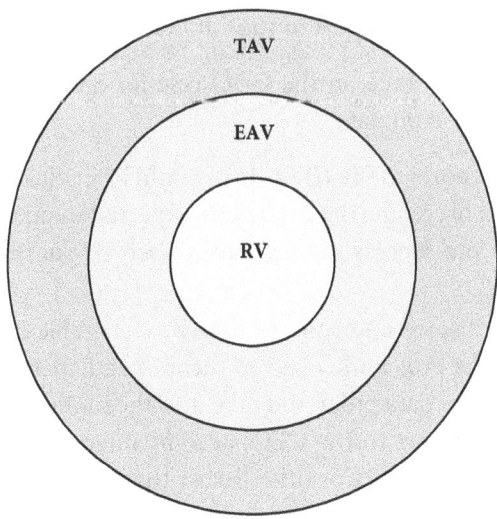

FIGURE 2.5   Business Impact by the CDO: RV vs EAV vs TAV.

- The existing organization structure
- Level of data intensity required
- Data maturity of the organization

Based on the above factors, enterprises may consider the following options:

1. Large enterprises may have a Group CDO (Hub), and different business functions have their CDO (Spokes). The Group CDO reports to the Group CEO, and the business function CDO reports to the head of the business function.

2. Enterprises that expect notable change management challenges in establishing new processes for the data pillar may have the CDO report to the COO, who in turn reports to the CEO. The COO works closely with the CDO to establish new processes for the data pillar and help resolve the change management challenges.

3. Enterprises driving significant transformation initiatives may have a chief transformation officer or a chief digital officer for digital transformations. Data is key to the success of transformations; such enterprises may have the CDO report to the chief transformation officer or chief digital officer.

4. Enterprises that consider data to be tightly coupled with technologies may have the CDO report to the CIO/CTO.

5. The CEO might take on the CDO role for SMBs whose business is primarily based on data.

6. The CDO reports to the CEO. This would be critical for empowering the CDO to overcome the challenges expected in operationalizing the data pillar and successfully executing their responsibilities.

Each option has its pros and cons, as presented in Table 2.8.

Considering the pros and cons, we recommend that when enterprises need to establish the data pillar and take it to the highest level of maturity, the CDO should report to the CEO, accompanied by a strong mandate and clear communication from the Board that making the data pillar a success is a priority for the enterprise. For large enterprises with CDOs in their business functions, the business function CDO should report to the

TABLE 2.8    Pros and Cons of the Different Positions of the CDO in the Organization Structure

| Option | Biggest Pro | Biggest Con |
|---|---|---|
| 1. Overall, Group CDO and different business functions have their CDO | The hub (Group CDO) and spoke (business function CDOs) model ensures group-wide alignment with a business function focus. The hub could also leverage the higher level of maturity of one spoke to improve the maturity of other spoke(s) | Each spoke could be at a varying level of maturity, leading to a broad spectrum of data maturity. This situation may become complex and challenging for the hub to manage and improve upon |
| 2. CDO reporting to COO | Drives business process improvements leveraging data. Implements data processes to leverage data | The data pillar is considered a subset of the process pillar. With COOs focused internally, data could become purely an operational tool for business process optimization rather than a strategic asset that could also enable new business models and revenue streams |
| 3. CDO reporting to the chief transformation officer or chief digital officer | Data is leveraged as a core ingredient in every transformation initiative | The leverage of data is focused on the transformation initiatives in scope. Hinders the democratization of data |
| 4. CDO reporting to the CIO/CTO | Reduces change management issues within the technology pillar | The data pillar is considered a subset of the technology pillar. Data continues to be locked in within technology applications, which hinders it from being shared and leveraged across the enterprise as a strategic asset |
| 5. CEO playing the role of a CDO | Data is leveraged right from the top as a strategic asset. This enables the entire organization to be aligned on its importance | The CEO focuses on fulfilling the demand for data only for strategic initiatives. The CEO may be unable to focus on developing the DOM, which, as the enterprise grows, would negatively impact data delivery at the required intensity |
| 6. The CDO reports to the CEO | The CDO receives attention and importance from the CEO and the Board, which enable them to resolve the challenges faced and mature the data pillar to fulfill the data requirements now and in the future. This is critical for establishing and maturing the data pillar | Without a strong mandate and clear communication from the Board, the CDO can create overlap or confusion with existing CxOs. Also, the CDO, as another executive team reporting to the CEO, adds to the CEO's responsibilities |

TABLE 2.9  Key Attributes of the CDO Persona

| **Key Attributes of the CDO Persona** |
| --- |
| 1.  Be a pioneer, visionary leader with delivery expertise |
| 2.  Have/can develop a good understanding of the business |
| 3.  Prioritize generating business outcomes through the data pillar |
| 4.  Build partnerships with stakeholders in the business functions, HR, and IT offices |
| 5.  Have high emotional quotient (EQ) and intelligence quotient (IQ) |

head of the business function, and the Group CDO should report to the CEO. For SMB enterprises, the CEO may play the role of CDO until they can focus on continuing to mature the data pillar. During the maturity journey, the reporting structure should be reevaluated. Chapter 4 delves into the maturity journey.

> *CDO reporting to the CEO or head of business function is critical for enterprises to establish the data pillar and accelerate its maturity!*

### 2.2.3  Selecting the Right Person for the CDO Role

The Board and the CEO make a key decision of onboarding a suitable CDO. To make that decision, they must be aligned on the attributes of the CDO persona. Table 2.9 provides the key attributes of the CDO persona.

> *When data is the fourth pillar, a successful CDO would be the leading indicator of a successful enterprise!*

To adhere to the five principles for the data pillar and execute their responsibilities, the CDO must identify and prioritize the required capabilities, i.e., "data capabilities." Prioritizing them will guide the CDO in developing the required people, process, and technology capabilities for the data pillar (see Chapter 3). Let us next delve into the data capabilities needed for the data pillar.

### 2.3  DATA CAPABILITIES

Enterprises develop a business capability map[5] to have a comprehensive view of the capabilities they currently possess and the capabilities needed in the future to support their strategic and operational goals. A multitier structure is typically adopted for business capabilities,[6] which enables focus and prioritization and improves manageability. Level 1 capabilities in the business capability map are the ones that are strategically important for the enterprise, now and in the future.

Aligning with the principles for the data pillar, the Board and the CEO must include "data management" as a Level 1 capability in the enterprise's business capability map. As a Level 1 capability, the data management capability includes all data capabilities the CDO decides to develop.

The data capabilities enable the data pillar to fulfill the demand for data by delivering data with the required data intensity to the use cases. Data capabilities also enable all pillars to operate efficiently, effectively, and securely. During the initial phase of developing the data management capability, the Board and the CEO must focus on helping the CDO resolve the challenges identified in the scorecard (see Figure 1.8) in collaboration with the CHRO, the COO, and the CIO/CTO.

### 2.3.1 Hypothetical Example – A Retail Enterprise Undergoing a D2C Business Transformation

Let us revisit the example of a retail consumer brand enterprise executing a strategic initiative to transform its GTM model from being a traditionally wholesale-focused model to a D2C focused model.

Multiple business capabilities, like customer experience management and supply chain management, will enable the success of the strategic initiative. To enable the initiative through strategic leverage of data, the Board and the CEO of the enterprise include "data management" as a Level 1 capability in the enterprise's business capability map, as depicted in Figure 2.6.

The business capabilities are enabled by the people, process, technology, and data capabilities (see Figure 2.7). The data capabilities are developed under the Level 1 data management capability.

The CDO identifies and prioritizes the required data capabilities in collaboration with stakeholders of the other business capabilities to increase their impact and make the strategic initiative successful. The data capabilities would enable the data pillar to deliver the required data to develop the transformation execution plan, develop predictions to highlight potential pitfalls, and recommend alternate approaches based on insights from the data. The data pillar would also enable insights during the execution of the plan, which empower the Board, the CEO, and the business functions to adapt and make changes during execution. An example would be insights on the speed of pivoting the GTM model. Such insights could highlight

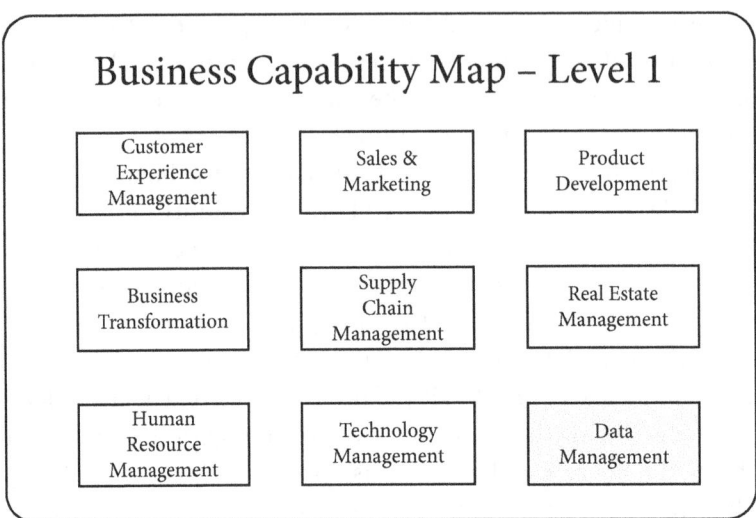

FIGURE 2.6   Data Management Added as a Level 1 Capability in the Business Capability Map.

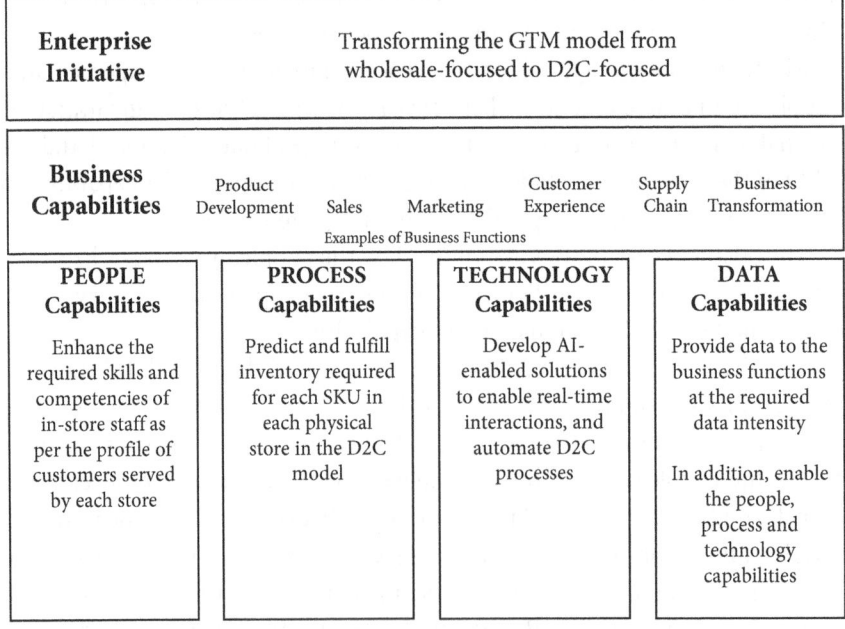

FIGURE 2.7   Example: Business Capabilities Are Enabled by People, Processes, Technology, and Data Capabilities.

supply chain complexities to prevent potential out-of-stock situations in physical stores with a global manufacturing set-up. As the pivot from the wholesale-focused model to the D2C-focused model would take time to implement, the data pillar would also recommend approaching wholesalers as data partners and motivating them to share more granular data on orders and customer preferences to improve KPIs for the wholesaler and the brand company. Also, the "real estate management" Level 1 capability leverages the data capabilities to identify the locations of physical stores based on data on customer demographics, real estate prices, and competition stores.

In addition, the data capabilities enable the capabilities provided by the people, processes, and technology pillars required for the success of the strategic initiative.

The people pillar, led by the CHRO, provides the people capabilities, such as skilled in-store staff, to execute the GTM transformation and the business processes in the D2C model. The people pillar leverages data to enhance people's skills and competencies required for the initiative. For example, based on data, the store operations team aligns the skills of the in-store staff with the profile of customers served by a particular store.

The processes pillar, led by the COO, provides the D2C process capabilities in collaboration with the leaders of the business functions. These include establishing physical stores globally, managing the complex supply chain from global production facilities to geographically diverse physical stores and fulfillment centers for online stores, inventory management across the complex supply chain, and delivering cohesive in-store and online customer experiences. These processes would leverage data to enhance their outcomes. For example, the store fulfillment process leverages data to predict the inventory required in each store. The accuracy of the predictions relies on the accuracy of the data used.

The technology pillar, led by the CIO/CTO, provides the technology (including AI) capabilities to execute real-time customer interactions, predict customer behavior, and enable the D2C processes mentioned earlier. The technology pillar leverages structured, semi-structured, and unstructured data to deliver such capabilities. For example, a personal shopping AI agent in a mobile app for online customers uses data on products, customers' past purchases, and social media activity to recommend products.

*Data management as a Level 1 business capability drives alignment across the depth and breadth of the enterprise, focusing on the strategic importance of data in enhancing enterprise value.*

The sub-capabilities within the Level 1 data management capability are referred to as Level 2 data capabilities. As an enterprise progresses on the maturity journey of its data pillar (see Chapter 4), a particular Level 2 capability may need to be broken down further into its sub-capabilities, referred to as Level 3 data capabilities, to identify areas for sharper focus or reflect changes in the data strategy. The multilevel structure provides a composable view of the data capabilities that an enterprise can leverage to prioritize and configure the data capabilities as per its unique situation.

Let us next delve into the Level 2 and 3 data capabilities.

### 2.3.2 Level 2 and 3 Data Capabilities

Enterprises' Level 2 and 3 data capabilities vary based on multiple factors, such as their enterprise business strategy, size, industry, geographic locations for doing business, requirements of their stakeholder communities, and the maturity level of their data pillar. Chapter 4 delves into the maturity journey.

A good starting point for identifying data capabilities is the data management framework DMBoK (Data Management Body of Knowledge),[7] provided by the Data Management Association (DAMA).[8] The framework includes data management knowledge areas that could be good candidates for Level 2 data capabilities. A CDO should identify Level 2 data capabilities that are relevant to their enterprise based on the aforementioned factors.

Figure 2.8 presents an example of Level 2 data capabilities.

*The success of the data pillar relies on the data capabilities and leveraging them to enhance business outcomes through data.*

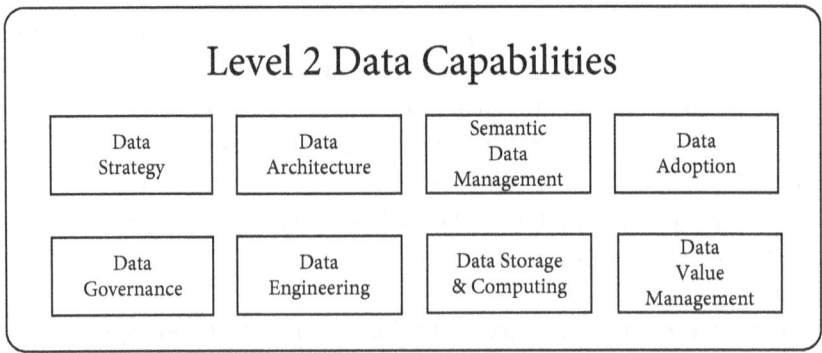

FIGURE 2.8   Data Management – Level 2 Capabilities.

The CDO and the data office are responsible for developing and providing these Level 2 data capabilities. Let us explore them.

## 2.4 DATA STRATEGY

This is one of the five principles for the data pillar. It specifies what the enterprise needs to do with data to enhance business outcomes. Data strategy takes inputs from the enterprise business strategy along with the strategies of the other pillars, keeping in mind the requirements of other Level 1 business capabilities. To execute the data strategy, additional requirements may be created on the other Level 1 business and Level 2 data capabilities (see Figure 2.9).

To illustrate this, let us continue with the retail consumer brand enterprise example. The enterprise has devised a business strategy to transform its wholesale-focused GTM model to a D2C-focused one. As depicted in Figure 2.6, the enterprise has created its Level 1 business capability map. The "customer experience management" capability in the map would need real-time, accurate, and compliant data (i.e., QCS requirements) about customers' activities at its online and physical stores to deliver cohesive and positive customer experiences. This requirement would be a use case for the data strategy. Similar use cases could come from other Level 1 business capabilities, like the supply chain or product development capability mentioned in the capability map. The data strategy capability considers such use cases as inputs, prioritizes them, and establishes the data strategy to fulfill the data needs of the prioritized use cases. In turn, to execute the data strategy, new requirements are created on multiple Level 1 business capabilities like the

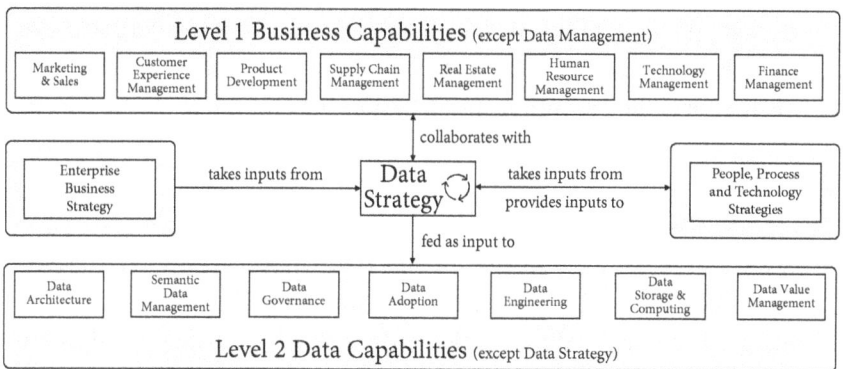

FIGURE 2.9 Data Strategy Synergizes with Level 1 Business Capabilities and Provides Input to Level 2 Data Capabilities.

human resource management capability, which needs to recruit or develop talent for the data office, and the marketing and sales capability, which needs to capture additional data about customers' preferences and buying behavior. The interdependency between data strategy capability and other business capabilities requires the CDO to collaborate with the stakeholders of the business capabilities for the successful execution of the data strategy, resulting in the achievement of overall business goals.

When the CDO and the data office develop the data strategy, it also becomes a reference for other Level 2 data capabilities to be aligned with.

Data strategy must also be revised on the basis of updated inputs. This iterative process helps engage the stakeholders and consider their feedback, making them feel part of the data strategy development. The CDO must get every version of the data strategy approved by the Board and the CEO. The CDO can then leverage the approved data strategy to secure funding for the data pillar and support from the business functions and other operating pillars and overcome the challenges mentioned in Figure 1.8.

The Level 3 capabilities under the data strategy capability could be as follows:

- **Data Strategy Development and Update:** This capability develops the data strategy with inputs from the enterprise business strategy, the strategies of other operating pillars, and the requirements of Level 1 business capabilities. It also updates the data strategy based on changes to the inputs and feedback received during its execution.

- **Data Strategy Execution:** This capability follows the execution of the data strategy, engages with the stakeholders involved, collects feedback on the updates needed for the next iteration of the data strategy, and shares those with the data strategy development capability. It also reports the execution status to the CDO.

## 2.5 DATA ARCHITECTURE

The data architecture capability connects the "what" captured in the data strategy to the "how," i.e., the realization of the data capabilities. Data architecture is a blueprint for implementing the data strategy and developing Level 2 data capabilities over time. The data office updates the data architecture based on the revisions to the data strategy. The data architecture is realized through the DOM, covered in Section 2.14.

The data architecture capability also looks beyond the immediate business needs to the potential needs of the enterprise in the future. For example, as covered in Chapter 1, unstructured data is critical for AI initiatives. Even though an enterprise may not consider leveraging AI at scale immediately, the data architecture capability should include the need for unstructured data for AI initiatives in the future.

> **Food for Thought:** *How do you ensure your enterprise adopts and aligns data architecture with information and technology architecture?*

The data architecture capability must align with the information architecture capability, an already established Level 2 or 3 capability under Level 1 business capabilities for an enterprise. The information architecture capability develops a presentation of the information used in business and the interlink between critical business information and processes. Each aspect of the information architecture would have linkages with the data elements captured in the data architecture.

The data architecture capability must also align with the technology architecture capability, which may be a Level 2 or 3 capability for an enterprise under technology management Level 1 capability. The technology architecture provides a blueprint of the technology landscape, which may include data catalog, data lake, warehouse, or lakehouse technologies. The data architecture can drive new requirements for the technology architecture, and the technology architecture might create limitations when such requirements are not fulfilled. Take the example of the retail consumer brand enterprise, which needs to predict the next-best action toward its consumers. The data architecture would include unstructured data required for the predictions, like social media posts, images, and audio/video. Different storage and computing technologies are required to process unstructured data and to combine unstructured data with structured data, such as consumers' social media activity and transaction history. The technology architecture must include the required storage and computing technologies for unstructured data.

Level 3 capabilities under data architecture capability could be as follows:

- **Data Architecture Development:** Capability to develop the data architecture aligned to the data strategy.

- **Data Architecture Review:** Capability to review and update the data architecture based on the updated enterprise business strategy.

## 2.6 SEMANTIC DATA MANAGEMENT

Semantic data management is a critical capability that provides the business and technical context of data through the metadata in the enterprise. The context enables accurate, compliant, and timely decision-making by all stakeholders (refer to the QCS framework in Figure 1.4). It also enables the data pillar to adhere to the findability, interoperability, and reusability sub-principles for making data a strategic asset (refer to the five principles for the data pillar in Figure 2.3). These are key for the stakeholders to use the data. The context also provides benefits like effective data governance and data engineering. Thus, the semantic data management capability enables other data capabilities such as data adoption, governance, and engineering.

Figure 2.10 presents the Level 3 capabilities under the semantic data management capability. The semantic data management capability would leverage a data catalog as a technology capability to enable these Level 3 capabilities.

### 2.6.1 Knowledge Graph Management

This capability involves building and maintaining the "enterprise knowledge graph (EKG)." The EKG enables every stakeholder to understand the context of the data through the lens of their needs, with ease and speed. This graph, depicted at a high level in Figure 2.11, provides information on the relationships between the business/data domains, business terms, processes, policies, people, and technical metadata.

Other data capabilities would provide subsets of information presented in the EKG. For example, the metadata management capability provides information on business and technical metadata, and the data governance capability provides information on the policies. The information on the data delivered through the DOM further enhances the EKG. The EKG becomes the map for finding data and understanding its context to fulfill business needs. We will delve into the DOM in Section 2.14.

For example, in the retail consumer brand enterprise, the marketing function would leverage the EKG to develop in-store customer promotion

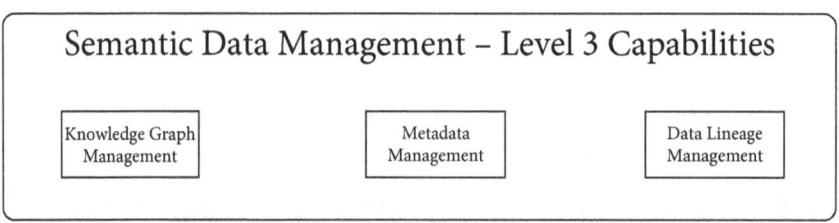

FIGURE 2.10   Semantic Data Management – Level 3 Capabilities.

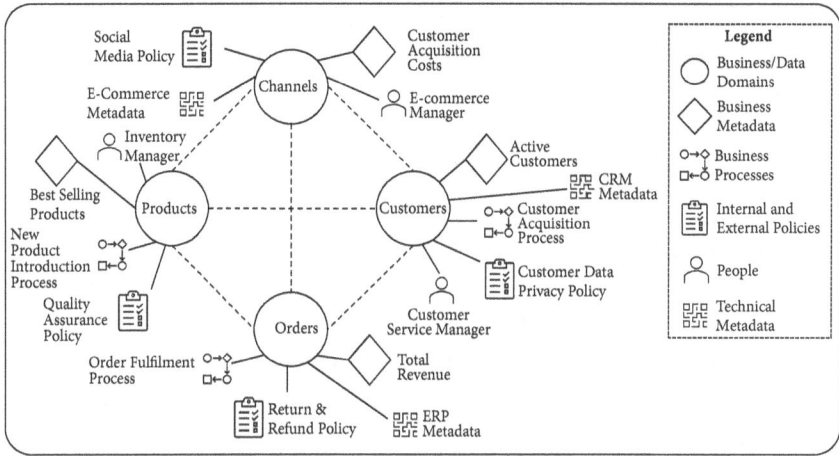

FIGURE 2.11    Example of a High-Level EKG for a Retail Consumer Brand.

campaigns. The EKG enables the marketing function's stakeholders to find data that provides a 360-degree view of its customers and understand the context of that data by learning about related policies such as customer data privacy policy, processes such as a customer campaign process, glossaries such as the definition of an existing customer versus a new customer, and technical metadata in the customer relationship management (CRM) application. By leveraging the EKG, the marketing function could develop the campaign faster and more effectively.

## 2.6.2  Metadata Management

This capability manages the enterprise's business and technical metadata lifecycle and creates a single source of truth for the metadata across the enterprise. The metadata includes business metadata, such as a business glossary describing standard business terms; metadata for stakeholders (people), processes, policies; usage metadata; and technical metadata linked to physical data stored in data stores or technology applications. The metadata management capability enriches the EKG with business and technical metadata information. Such information enables the enterprise's stakeholders to understand the business and technical perspectives of its structured, semi-structured, and unstructured data. This is like understanding the components of a physical or digital product or service produced by an enterprise but applied to data.

For example, for the retail consumer brand enterprise, the metadata in the "customer" business/data domain includes business metadata like "active customers," which means customers who have purchased in the past 90 days; the people involved, such as the "customer service manager"; the process involved, such as the "customer acquisition process"; and the technical metadata of the CRM application.

### 2.6.3 Data Lineage Management

This capability focuses on tracing the data flow from the origin of specific data to its point of consumption, including changes made to the data and data quality information along the value chain. The data engineering capability provides information about the changes to data. The data quality and observability sub-capability under the data governance capability enrich the data lineage by overlaying the data quality and observability information over the lineage. The data lineage provides data flow from a business and a technical perspective. The business perspective is helpful for business users to understand the origin of data, the processing done on the data before it has reached the point of consumption, and to develop trust in the data through the data quality and observability information through the data flow. The technical perspective is helpful for technical users to perform operational impact analysis and execute the required remediation actions. The business and technical data lineage also enables their users to understand and appreciate each other's perspectives and thus collaborate effectively and efficiently.

For example, in the retail consumer brand enterprise, if a final dataset contains customer segmentation data for a particular physical store, the data lineage capability enables to show how different datasets, such as regional demographics, social media data, and purchase history, have been combined to build the final dataset. Suppose a stakeholder in the marketing function, i.e., a business user, identifies data quality issues in the final dataset. It can collaborate with the data quality engineer, i.e., a technical user, to fix the problem. The technical lineage would enable the data quality engineer to perform a quick root cause analysis of the data quality issue in the final dataset and execute the appropriate remediation measure in collaboration with the business user, i.e., fix the identified quality issues at the right step in the data flow.

*Key Considerations for Semantic Data Management Capability*

Semantic data management is a critical capability that enterprises require to mature their data pillar. As this capability interfaces with the business and technical users to harvest the relevant metadata and interplays with other data capabilities, it may also be the most challenging capability for enterprises to develop. We recommend that the CDO and the data office consider the key points provided in Table 2.10 for developing this capability.

TABLE 2.10 Key Considerations for Developing the Semantic Data Management Capability

---

1. **Approach to follow for harvesting the business and technical metadata.** Options available are as follows:
   a) **Domain-centric, i.e., going by individual business/data domain:** This approach would be focused on selected business/data domains, helping to get attention from the stakeholders in each business/data domain to onboard their business metadata. The technical metadata is onboarded for the in-scope business metadata, which may be in limited applications covering the scope of the specific business/data domain. However, this approach may not deliver significant business value derived from end-to-end business processes that cut across multiple business/data domains.
   b) **Use case-driven, i.e., based on the use cases prioritized in the data strategy:** This approach would enable focused actions to support the in-scope use cases, thus delivering business value linked to them. However, it may be a complex approach to execute for complex use cases that cut across multiple business/data domains and technology applications, involving multiple stakeholders to collaborate with.
   c) **Bottom-up, i.e., going by technology applications.** This approach would provide speed in harvesting the technical metadata. After that, each business/data domain could schedule onboarding their respective business metadata based on their priorities and bandwidth availability. However, in this approach, business users cannot fully leverage the capability unless both business and technical metadata have been onboarded, hence a longer path to providing business value. This approach thus faces a significant risk of being a technology initiative without the involvement of the business stakeholders.
   The approach enterprises take would depend on their data pillar's maturity level. We recommend that enterprises with low maturity levels start with the domain-centric approach and pivot to the use case-driven approach when the maturity level increases.

2. **Understanding and clarifying perceived overlap with other business capabilities:** The information and process models, developed as part of information architecture in Level 1 business capabilities, may be perceived to overlap with the EKG. To clarify, information models contain logical information leveraged across all Level 1 business capabilities, their meaning, and the relationships between them. In contrast, the EKG provides information on the relationships between the business domains, business metadata, processes, policies, people, and technical metadata, thus providing the context for data in the enterprise. Information models can help develop the EKG.
   Process models could benefit from the EKG. For instance, the order fulfillment process model could learn from the EKG about the critical data elements (CDEs) relevant to the process. That knowledge will enable quick identification of the root cause of unfulfilled orders.

3. **Scale of required change management in large enterprises:** Developing this capability necessitates collaborating with multiple stakeholders in large enterprises' business functions and IT office(s), each with its own priorities and bandwidth challenges. In addition, business metadata would be scattered across each business capability, and technical metadata would be scattered across the diverse technology landscape in a large enterprise. To overcome the challenges, the CDO and the data office must develop and execute a structured change management program in collaboration with the business leaders.

---

## 2.7 DATA ADOPTION

The primary goal of the data adoption capability is to drive the usage of the data assets (see Section 2.14) by the data consumers, which include the Board, the CEO, the business functions, the processes, and the technology applications. The data pillar will be successful only when the adoption happens. Hence, the CDO must prioritize this critical capability.

To fulfill its objective, this capability focuses on two aspects:

- Capturing the demand for data assets, along with the data intensity requirements, from the data consumers.

- Driving up the consumption of the data assets by the data consumers.

For example, when the marketing function of the retail consumer brand enterprise wants to offer real-time in-store promotions to customers, this capability captures the demand and recommends the customer data asset to the marketing function. This capability also develops the success story based on the marketing function's successful data asset usage. It also promotes the customer data asset and the success story with the marketing function to other stakeholders who might benefit from it.

This capability aligns closely with the data value management capability to capture the business value the data consumers have generated by leveraging the data assets. The CDO and the data office use such information to share success stories, motivate more data consumers to leverage the data pillar, and grow the consumption of data assets.

The Level 3 capabilities under the data adoption capability could be as follows:

- **Data Demand Capture:** This capability is responsible for capturing the demand for data from various data consumers across the enterprise.

- **Data Consumption Growth:** This capability is responsible for continuously growing the consumption of the data assets provided through the DOM. It works with the data governance capability to understand the present usage of the data assets and the improvements needed. It would then execute the improvement measures to grow consumption, such as promoting and recommending data assets, sharing data stories, and enabling the data consumers.

## 2.8 DATA GOVERNANCE

The data governance capability governs the fulfillment of data consumers' needs – to get data with the required data intensity. It also enables enterprises to comply with the regulations and mitigate the risks from data usage, such as data privacy violations, unauthorized usage, data breaches, and biases created on the basis of data.

The data governance capability also influences other related business capabilities. For instance, AI governance[9] extends from data governance to regulating AI models so they operate safely and competently. This may also drive new requirements toward the technology management capability for audits and compliance checks on AI models adopted by the business functions for various business use cases. Another example would be when the marketing capability of the retail consumer brand wants to offer real-time in-store promotions to customers and needs to capture images of customers entering a store; the data governance capability enforces the marketing capability to take customers' consent to opt-in.

> **Food for Thought:** *How can data governance be perceived as an enabler of business value in your enterprise?*

To fulfill its objectives, the data governance capability develops ways of working for people, governance processes, and required technology capabilities. The new ways of working may give rise to change management issues, which this capability also works to resolve.

Figure 2.12 presents the Level 3 capabilities under the data governance capability.

### 2.8.1 Data Quality and Observability

The data quality and observability capability focus on mitigating incorrect decision-making due to inferior data quality. This capability is critical for

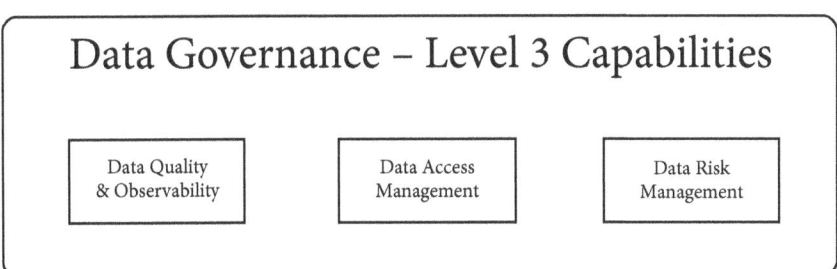

FIGURE 2.12 Data Governance – Level 3 Capabilities.

measuring, monitoring, and resolving quality issues in all data assets consumed by all data consumers; thus, it fulfills the quality dimension of the data intensity requirement.

This capability also helps fulfill the speed dimension of the data intensity requirement. Determining and resolving the potential choke points early in the data delivery process positively impacts the data delivery speed. Data observability extends the data quality capability by proactively identifying the potential choke points for data delivery and determining the people, processes, technologies, and data it could impact.

This capability works with semantic data management capability and acts as a radar to link detected data quality issues across the data flow. Early detection and improvement of data quality help reduce the "cost of quality."

In the retail consumer brand enterprise example, the data quality capability might detect that the distribution dataset is missing some customers' zip codes in the address. The data observability capability proactively notifies the data quality issue to the stakeholders of the in-scope applications – the mobile apps and fulfillment application; processes – the order fulfillment process; and datasets – the weekly order fulfillment dataset. The data quality capability can resolve the identified data quality issue.

It is important to note that the leverage of data quality and observability capability must go beyond internal and structured data and extend to external and unstructured data. For instance, data shared with suppliers might include weather data, traffic data, and GPS routes. The data quality and observability capability would provide notifications such as incorrect latitude and longitude coordinates detected in a delivery location provided to a supplier.

AI capabilities will enhance data flow monitoring, specifically for real-time streaming data, providing real-time insights and recommending quality improvements. The technology management Level 1 capability needs to support the data quality and observability capability for such AI requirements.

### 2.8.2 Data Access Management

Data must be accessible by the people, processes, and technologies across the enterprise that need it and when they need it. The data access management capability enables the data pillar to fulfill the last mile of data delivery and consumption in a governed manner. This capability also allows governed data access to business partners outside the enterprise. The data access management capability thus enables the data pillar to adhere to the accessibility principle of the data pillar.

The data access management capability works together with the data risk management capability to enable the data consumers to access trusted data at the required speed in a governed manner. By making the data accessible to different people, processes, and technologies with the required speed, this capability prevents the creation of multiple copies of data, thereby reducing data quality issues, data risks, and costs of data operations. This capability also reduces data risks by making specific data accessible only to the people, processes, and technologies allowed to use such data, as per the standards and policies. This also includes data protection capabilities such as masking, anonymization, or erasing the required data. Thus, the broader objective of this capability also includes delivering on the compliance dimensions of the data intensity requirements and reducing the cost of data operations.

The data access management capability enables various Level 1 business capabilities to meet their data access requirements. Take the retail consumer brand enterprise example. The supply chain management Level 1 capability needs access to additional regional data as the enterprise pivots its GTM strategy. This requires the data access management capability to ensure that the regional supply chains get up-to-date data restricted to their regions at their required time.

Data access management will increasingly be applied to unstructured data to enable AI models to access such data while securing sensitive information. For instance, sensitive information in a PDF document containing customer shipment information or an audio file containing customer name and address information must be masked or removed before an AI model uses such data for training purposes. In addition, AI agents could analyze data and, based on the analysis, recommend data policies to be applied to datasets. The technology management Level 1 capability needs to support the data access management capability for such requirements.

The hidden gem among the benefits of the data access management capability is data usage monitoring and insights. This capability monitors and provides insights into who is accessing a particular data asset, when, and for which purposes. The usage insights enable the data value management capability to capture the value generated by the data pillar by measuring and tracking the KPIs presented in Chapter 3. They also enable the data adoption capability to learn about the data consumers' adoption of the data assets and work toward making the required improvements. The usage insights also enable an effective governance of access to data assets.

### 2.8.3 Data Risk Management

As another sub-capability of data governance capability, the primary objective of the data risk management capability is to identify and mitigate data risks, together with the data quality and observability and the data access management sub-capabilities.

Examples of data risks created internally would be when people, processes, and technologies

- do not comply with the internal standards and policies and access data they are not authorized to, such as accessing customer confidential data;

- do not comply with external regulated policies such as GDPR and/or CCPA; and

- create inadvertent data breaches.

The data risks could also be created externally, such as rouge attacks from external agents causing data breaches or asking for ransoms by threatening to cause data breaches.

This capability performs data risk assessment for different situations. For example, as the retail consumer brand enterprise pivots its GTM model toward D2C, it gathers and uses more privacy-sensitive data, such as customers' personal information, videos, and social media activities. A customer data breach could jeopardize their entire GTM transformation initiative, significantly impact customers' confidence in the brand, and even risk the enterprise's existence.

The data risk management capability works with other data capabilities, such as the semantic data management capability to perform the data risk assessment, data quality and observability, and data access management capabilities to mitigate data risks. The data risk management capability also creates requirements for other business capabilities, such as the technology management Level 1 capability, to develop AI capabilities to safeguard structured and unstructured data and results from an AI model.

Data risk management is a critical data capability for enterprises that control and/or process personal data of individuals or country-specific sensitive data. At enterprises in sensitive industries such as public services, defense, energy and utilities, financial services, healthcare services, and telecommunication services, the CEO and the CDO may promote the data risk management capability as a Level 1 capability.

In some enterprises, enterprise risk management capability may include managing data risks. For instance, enterprise risk management is core to a financial institution's business. In such a case, enterprise risk management is a Level 1 business capability, and the data risk management capability is mapped into it.

The data risk management capability could include additional data capabilities, depending upon the use cases, risk exposure, and risk averseness of specific enterprises:

- **Data Privacy Management**: manages the data privacy of individual customers.

- **Data Loss Prevention Management**: prevents inadvertent data breaches.

- **Data Retention Management**: manages data retention as required by specific business processes or legal hold requirements. Longer data retention exposes enterprises to higher risks and costs.

- **Data Sharing Risk Management**: manages risks from data sharing with business partners and/or customers.

## 2.9 DATA ENGINEERING

The data engineering capability enables the collection or ingestion of diverse structured, semi-structured, and unstructured data from various internal and external sources in different latencies, such as real-time, near-real-time, and batch, along with their transformation and processing.

The data engineering capability is critical in producing the various data assets delivered through the DOM (see Section 2.14). This capability must be agile and flexible to support various use cases' diverse and changing requirements. This capability would also need to scale with the growth in use cases.

The data engineering capability will increasingly leverage AI capabilities to auto-ingest data, auto-generate data engineering pipelines, process unstructured data, and more. The technology management Level 1 capability needs to enable the data engineering capability with the AI technology capabilities.

The Level 3 capabilities under the data engineering capability could be as follows:

- **Data Ingestion Management:** The capability to ingest structured, semi-structured, and unstructured data by moving or replicating them in real-time and batch mode from the data sources to targets.

- **Structured and Semi-structured Data Transformation Management:** The capability to transform structured and semi-structured data in real-time and batch mode.

- **Unstructured Data Transformation Management:** The capability to transform unstructured data, including operational data, is critical for AI initiatives.

## 2.10 DATA STORAGE AND COMPUTING

The data storage and computing capability enables the efficient and effective storage and computing of data. The storage capability enables enterprises to store an increasing volume of structured, semi-structured, and unstructured data for transactional, operational, or analytical purposes. The computing capability enables enterprises to improve their performance by processing their increasing volume, velocity, and variety of data. This impacts the "speed" dimension of the data intensity (refer to the QCS framework in Figure 1.4). If the data pillar cannot meet the speed requirements of the use cases, then the adoption of the data would be negatively impacted, thus influencing the success of the data pillar. This capability thus enables other data capabilities, such as data engineering, governance, and adoption. Hence, this capability is a foundational capability for the data pillar.

The Level 3 capability under the data storage and computing capability could be as follows:

- **Requirement Management:** This is the capability of developing the data storage and computing requirements for the data assets delivered by the data pillar and developing the technology specifications of the required technology capabilities like the data lake, data warehouse, and data lakehouse. The technology specifications include the scalability and performance requirements from the technology capabilities based on the requirements of the different use cases in scope. It also coordinates with the data operations management capability for managing the operations of these technology capabilities.

## 2.11 DATA VALUE MANAGEMENT

Use cases generate value by leveraging the four pillars of the operating model: People, processes, technologies (including AI capabilities), and data. The data value management capability periodically measures and tracks the RV, EAV and TAV.

The RV, EAV, and TAV are the three essential KPIs the CDO must report to the Board and the CEO. The trendline of these KPIs would indicate the impact delivered by the data pillar. Based on the performance of these KPIs, the CDO will be able to secure additional funding for the data pillar. The data value management capability works with the financial management Level 1 business capability to get the required funding for the data pillar.

*The RV, EAV, and TAV are the essential KPIs for the CDO – to showcase the business impact of the data pillar, track the execution of the data strategy, and get funding for the data pillar.*

The data value management capability defines, measures, and reports additional KPIs relevant to the DOM. Chapter 3 delves into such KPIs.

The Level 3 capabilities under the data value management capability could be as follows:

- **KPI Identification and Definitions Management:** This capability identifies and defines the KPIs that will be measured and reported as value delivered by the data pillar. It also works with data adoption and governance capabilities to identify new KPIs as the data pillar matures.

- **KPI Measurement and Reporting:** This capability measures and reports the identified KPIs. It also enables the CDO to provide an executive summary of the KPIs, which the CDO leverages to report to the Board and the CEO.

- **Data Value Feedback and Improvement Management:** This capability provides feedback to the data strategy, architecture, adoption, and governance capabilities based on the reported KPIs. If a KPI value is lower than forecasted, the data strategy and architecture might require adjustments; the data adoption capability could modify the adoption initiatives to drive up the KPI; or the data governance capability could relook into the governance controls and explore if changing any control could help improve the KPI.

## 2.12 OTHER DATA CAPABILITIES

Enterprises must also investigate their existing business capabilities and identify the data capabilities under such capabilities. Such a situation might have happened when data management was not considered a Level 1 capability. When data management is classified as a Level 1 capability, most data capabilities should become a sub-capability of data management. However, there may be a few exceptions. Such exceptions would vary for enterprises based on their organizational structure and expected benefits from economies of scale and scope.

An example would be the data operations management capability. This capability manages the data infrastructure, network security, network latency, and related change management to enable the Level 1 data management capability. This capability could be under the Level 1 technology management capability or brought under the Level 1 data management capability.

Another example would be the recruitment, onboarding, training, and people enablement required for the data management capability. This capability could be under the Level 1 human resource management capability or brought under the Level 1 data management capability.

## 2.13 ROADMAP FOR DATA CAPABILITIES

An enterprise cannot develop all the data capabilities in one go – a staggered approach must be adopted. We recommend CDOs build a roadmap for the data capabilities, develop each capability iteratively, and expand them as their business requirements grow/change and their data pillar matures. Leveraging the capabilities to deliver data as the CDO and the data office develop them provides essential feedback to improve or adjust the capabilities.

Figure 2.13 presents an example roadmap of the Level 2 data capabilities in the retail consumer brand enterprise transforming its wholesale-focused GTM model to a D2C-focused model.

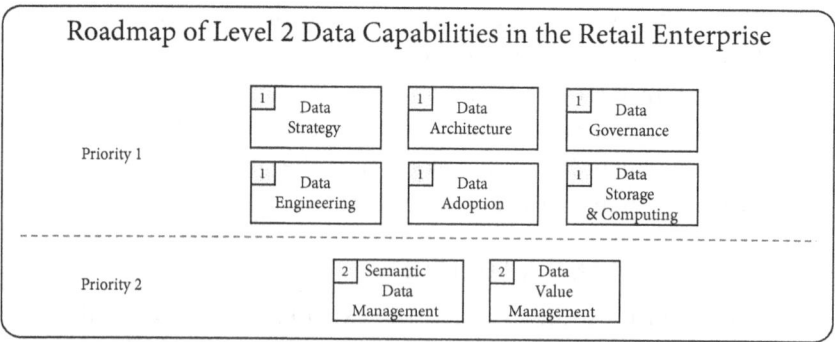

FIGURE 2.13 Roadmap of the Data Capabilities in a Retail Enterprise Transforming Its GTM Model.

As per the example, the CDO of this enterprise plans to build its data capabilities with "Priority 1" on the data strategy, architecture, engineering, governance, and adoption capabilities to enable the various use cases involved in the GTM transformation initiative with data at their required data intensity. The CDO and the data office develop "Priority 2" capabilities, semantic data management, and data value management after "Priority 1s" are operationalized and the enterprise has matured enough to benefit from Priority 2s.

*Food for Thought: What are your prioritized data capabilities? What hindrances do you expect in realizing them?*

An agile and robust data delivery framework is needed to deliver data with the required data intensity in a governed manner. The framework is operationalized by leveraging the developed data capabilities. The following section delves into the data delivery framework.

## 2.14 WHAT IS A DATA OPERATING MODEL?

A DOM is an agile data delivery framework that enables the data pillar to provide data assets to data consumers, i.e., the Board, the CEO, the business functions, and the other operating pillars, with the required data intensity for the dynamic needs of their use cases.

The stakeholders in the use cases, i.e., the data consumers, need data that is ready to use and fulfills their required data intensity. However, the data created from the transactions, business processes, or operations are raw data. Raw data can be structured, semi-structured, or unstructured data. The raw data is not in a form or shape that the data consumer can understand, does not meet the required data intensity, and thus is not readily consumable. For every data consumer to perform the required processing of raw data, making it consumable would lead to significant delays in time-to-value and a waste of efforts and, thus, funds. In addition, such data processing would be complex for most data consumers to perform independently and would need time and bandwidth allocation from the IT office.

To resolve such challenges and enable data consumption, the raw data sourced from diverse data stores should be processed and packaged for the data consumers to find and use readily. Such packaged data are referred to as "data products." A data product would enable data consumers to focus and spend time on their use cases and not waste their bandwidth on operational activities to make the data ready to use. Also, to promote the reusability of data, which would lead to further savings in time, efforts, and funds, a new data product could be produced from other existing data product(s), thereby potentially creating a "network effect"[10] from data products.

To help understand how data products differ from raw data, let us consider a simple analogy. End consumers create demand for stainless steel bottles and staplers to meet their specific needs. A manufacturer producing stainless steel bottles and staplers would require minerals like iron ore, nickel, and chromium as raw materials to make such products. In this analogy, the bottle and the stapler are "data products" consumed by the end consumers for their specific needs. And the minerals that come from different sources and are used to produce the bottles and the staplers are the "raw data." The end consumers readily use the bottles and stapler as and when needed without needing to know or spending time/money to process the raw materials.

Similarly, in our example of the retail consumer brand enterprise, the "regional customer segmentation" data product contains data on various customer segments based on age, location, buying behavior, etc., at a regional level. This data product has been created from raw data from multiple business applications like order management and CRM applications. In the data product, data quality issues like duplicate or missing data have been resolved, sensitive customer information has been removed, and the data product is refreshed daily to include new customers and update the buying behavior of the existing customers. This data product is used by multiple data consumers who have the roles of brand managers, advertising managers, and supply chain managers. These data consumers use the data product for their use cases, such as improving the effectiveness of promotional programs, advertising campaigns, and supply chain planning. By leveraging the data product, the data consumers enhance the business value by creating additional revenue impact from the promotional programs, increasing brand value, and reducing inventory carrying costs. It would have been inefficient, wasteful, and challenging due to the lack of required skills if each data consumer, i.e., the brand manager, advertising manager, and supply chain manager, had to find the raw data, get access to it, understand it, and perform the required processing of the raw data to fulfill the required data intensity, before being able to use the data.

Let us delve into the key characteristics of raw data and data products to clarify how they differ. These have been provided in Table 2.11.

The DOM enables the stakeholders involved in the use cases, i.e., the data consumers, to readily get the required data products. It also enables the efficient creation and provisioning of data products and the efficient collection, processing, and provisioning of raw data (see Figure 2.14).

TABLE 2.11    Key Characteristics of Raw Data and Data Products

| Characteristic | Raw Data | Data Product |
|---|---|---|
| Example | Point-of-sale data | Regional customer segmentation |
| Reason for existence | A by-product of business activities | To meet the data and data intensity requirements of specific use cases |
| Business value from the data | Does not have an EAV goal. The value provided is not quantifiable | A data product carries an EAV goal |
| Creation of the data | Created as a by-product of transactions, business process execution, and/or operations | Created by stakeholders in the business functions based on the demand for data |
| Sharing of the data | Complex, complicated, and/or risky to share | Readily shared across the enterprise, shareable with external parties as well |
| Use cases can readily consume the data | Cannot consume "as-is" | Finished product to be consumed "as-is" |
| Self-service consumption by nontechnical users | It is not possible, as it lacks the business metadata | Yes, it is packaged for self-service consumption by nontechnical users |
| Volume | Significant high volume, depending upon the scale and scope of business activities | Comparatively low number. The number of data products increases over time with the increasing maturity of the data pillar |
| Time and effort needed for creation | Low to negligible, generated as a by-product of business activities | High, to perform the packaging activities |
| Lifecycle management | Not managed for most. Managed for some due to data sensitivity/legal requirements | Actively managed for all |

Key considerations before embarking upon producing data products are presented in Table 2.12.

Considering the high likelihood of producing data products by processing raw data till the "network effect" from data products kicks in and the challenges involved in producing data products from raw data, we present an enhanced approach. For that, let us revisit the earlier presented analogy.

The manufacturer of the bottles and staplers, i.e., the data products, does not process the minerals, i.e., the raw data, every time to produce another bottle or stapler. They produce or buy an intermediate stainless

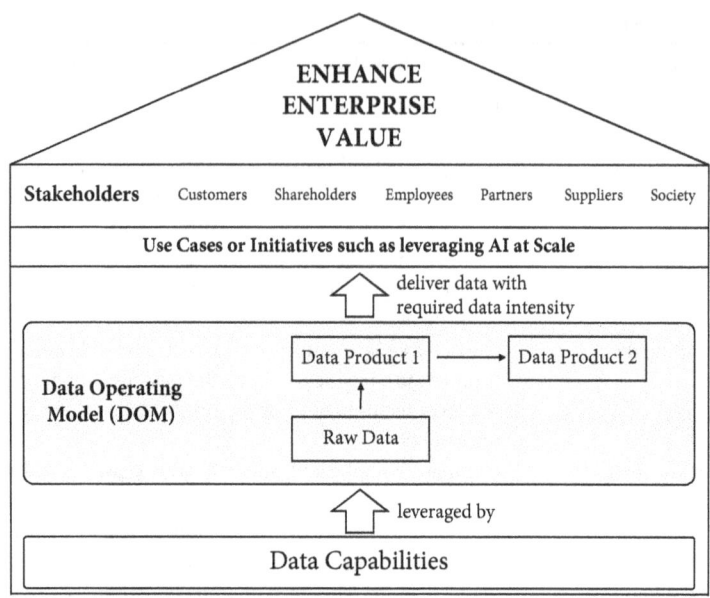

FIGURE 2.14   DOM Delivers Data to the Stakeholders of Use Cases.

TABLE 2.12   Key Considerations before Embarking upon Creating Data Products

1. *Achieve clarity and alignment regarding what the data products are and which ones to produce.* For example, is a business intelligence report a data product, or is a dataset focusing on a specific data domain a data product? Which use cases require each data product?

2. *Establish the process for producing data products. Also, expectations should be aligned with the lead time required to produce specific data products.* The production process for data products should be standardized. Develop an understanding of the lead time to execute the process and align with the data consumers. Chapter 3 delves into the process

3. *"Network effect" from data products may take long to materialize.* When few data products exist or the existing products are not suitable for reuse, new data products are seldom created from existing ones. Until then, producers will have to utilize raw data to produce data products

4. *Data engineers could become a bottleneck due to their limited bandwidth.* When new data products are not created from existing data products, raw data processing is required to produce new data products. Data engineers will need to do this until the producers of data products are skilled enough to do it themselves

steel product and use it to produce bottles and staplers. Stainless steel helps speed up and scale the production of bottles and staplers, as the manufacturer does not need to wait to process the minerals first. The economies of scale and focus on skills to process stainless steel allow the manufacturer to reduce the unit cost of bottles and staplers. Also, suppose the manufacturer decides to produce another type of product to fulfill new market demand, such as a spoon, i.e., another data product. In that case, it cannot produce spoons from bottles and staplers, the existing data products, but can produce them from stainless steel, the intermediate product. Thus, stainless steel also promotes interoperability and enables the manufacturer to achieve faster time-to-value when producing new types of end products.

Referencing the analogy, we introduce the concept of "data foundation block (DFB)" as the intermediate product, like stainless steel (see Figure 2.15).

A DFB is an intermediate product produced by processing raw data. It helps improve the speed and self-serviceability of data producers and, thus, enables scalability in producing data products. It provides the foundation to produce multiple data products that data consumers can readily use. Depending on the requirements of the use cases, a DFB may need further processing before the data consumers can use it.

For example (see Figure 2.16), in the customer data domain of the retail consumer brand enterprise, the "customer foundation block" will contain holistic information about customers across multiple operating units and geographies. Similarly, in the product data domain, the "product foundation block" will contain holistic information about products across multiple business units and geographies. In collaboration with the relevant business functions, the data office produces these foundation blocks by

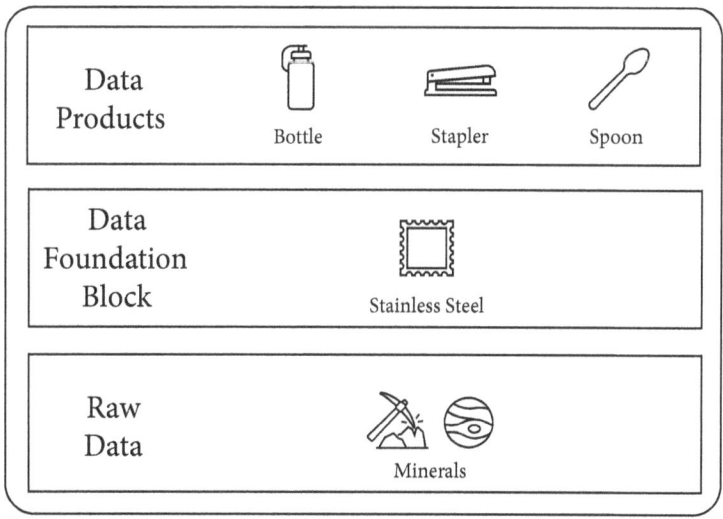

FIGURE 2.15   Analogy of Data Products, Data Foundation Block, and Raw Data.

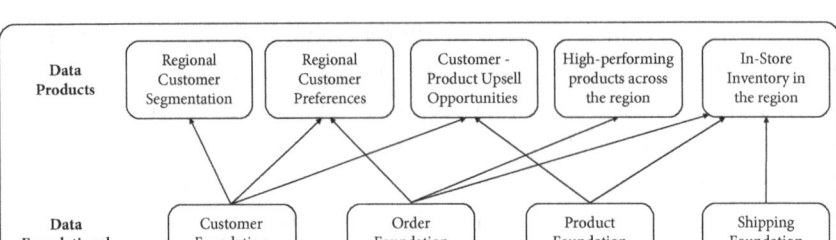

FIGURE 2.16   Examples of Data Foundation Blocks and Data Products.

processing the raw customer and product data collected from various sources like transactional, operational, and analytical applications. The customer foundation block includes individual customers' demographics, location, preferences, and consent details. Data products built by reusing the customer foundation block may not need all the data.

Business stakeholders reuse these foundation blocks for their use cases or for producing specific data products. The marketing function reuses the customer foundation block to self-produce the "regional customer preferences" data product. It also combines the customer and product foundation blocks to self-produce the "customer-product upsell opportunities" data product. To produce these data products, they would need to do additional processing, such as aggregating customers' preferences and removing individual customers' personal information. Benefitting from the availability of the DFBs, the marketing team will not have to spend time or possess the skills required to access and process the raw customer and product data or wait on the IT office to do it for them.

Let us delve into the key characteristics of raw data, DFBs, and data products to clarify how they differ. These have been provided in Table 2.13.

Given the role and benefits of DFBs, we recommend enterprises adopt them as a data asset provided through the DOM.

The DOM enables the stakeholders involved in the use cases, i.e., the data consumers, to readily get the required data products and foundation blocks. It also enables the efficient creation and provisioning of data products and foundation blocks and the collection, processing, and provisioning of raw data (see Figure 2.17).

*The producers of data products need the DFBs, the intermediate products, to speed up and scale the production of data products.*

TABLE 2.13  Key Characteristics of Raw Data, DFB, and Data Product

| Characteristic | Raw Data | DFB | Data Product |
|---|---|---|---|
| Example | Point-of-sale data | Customer foundation block in the customer data domain | Regional customer segmentation |
| Reason for existence | A by-product of business activities | Provides speed to data producers and consumers. Promotes reusability | To meet the data and data intensity requirements of specific use cases |
| Business value from the data | Does not have an EAV goal. The value provided is not quantifiable | Does not have an EAV goal. Has reusability goals | A data product carries an EAV goal |
| Creation of the data | Created as a by-product of transactions, business process execution, and/or operations | Created by the data office in collaboration with the stakeholders responsible for defined data domains centrally or in different business functions/operating units | Created by stakeholders in the business functions based on the demand for data |
| Sharing of the data | Complex, complicated, and/or risky to share | Readily shared across the enterprise with governed access | Readily shared across the enterprise; shareable with external parties as well |
| Use cases can readily consume the data | Cannot consume "as-is" | Semi-finished product that can be used by the data producers "as-is." Consumers may need additional processing before consuming | Finished product to be consumed "as-is" |
| Self-service consumption by nontechnical users | It is not possible, as it lacks the business metadata | Yes, it is packaged for self-service consumption by nontechnical users | Yes, it is packaged for self-service consumption by nontechnical users |
| Volume | Significant high volume, depending upon the scale and scope of business activities | The number is dependent on the number of identified data domains. The number does not increase significantly over time | The number is dependent on the number of use cases in scope. The number increases over time with the increasing maturity of the data pillar |

*(Continued)*

TABLE 2.13 (Continued)

| Characteristic | Raw Data | DFB | Data Product |
|---|---|---|---|
| Time and effort needed for creation | Low to negligible, generated as a by-product of business activities | Medium, to perform basic packaging for producers | High, to perform the packaging activities |
| Lifecycle management | Not managed for most. Managed for some due to data sensitivity/legal requirements | Actively managed for all | Actively managed for all |

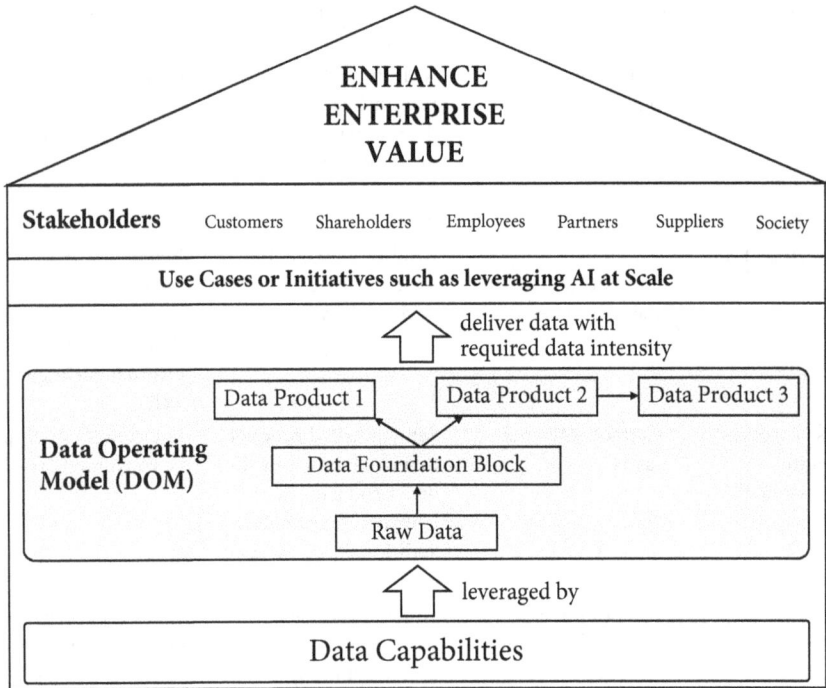

FIGURE 2.17 DOM Delivers Data to the Stakeholders of the Use Case.

Key considerations for introducing DFBs are presented in Table 2.14.

Figure 2.18 depicts the referencing of the data products, foundation blocks, and raw data in the EKG.

The next section delves into the layers of the DOM.

TABLE 2.14 Key Considerations for Introducing DFBs

1. *DFBs are intermediate products that enable data consumers to leverage them when finished products are unavailable.* Data consumers would save time and effort by not processing raw data multiple times. That results in faster time-to-value

2. *Take a long-term view of the benefits of DFBs.* The benefits of using the foundation blocks in the long term would outweigh the additional effort spent creating them in the short term

3. *Enterprises with DFBs create new data products from these blocks and/or existing data products without processing raw data.* This reduces the time, effort, and funds spent producing new data products

4. *Developing people capabilities to produce DFBs by processing raw data and reuse them to produce data products.* The CDO must collaborate with the CHRO to develop the required skills and competencies among people in the data office and data producers to produce and reuse DFBs, respectively.

5. *Creating DFBs requires collaboration between the data office and the stakeholders responsible for the data domains.* Collaboration is required to appropriately define and design the DFBs for reuse.

6. *Large enterprises with a federated model, wherein business functions have individual data offices, would immediately benefit from adopting DFBs.* By creating DFBs, the data office of one business function can enable sharing its data with others. Refer to the Audi case study as an example

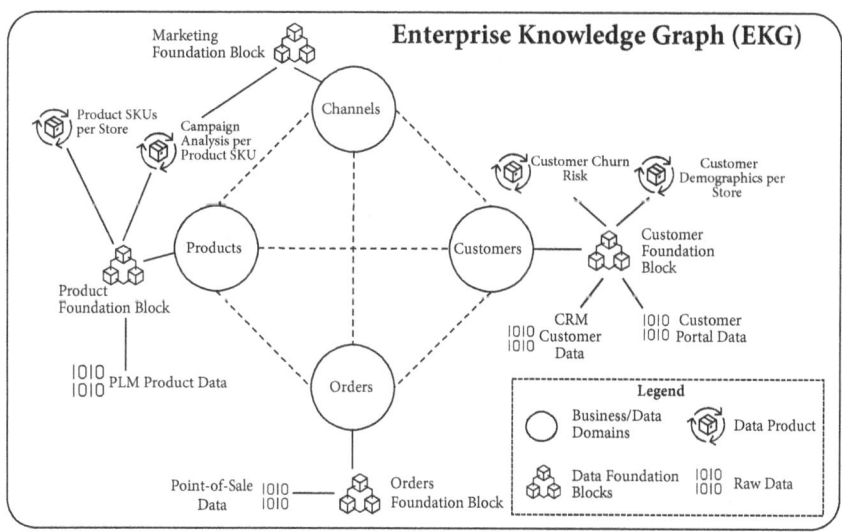

FIGURE 2.18 All Data Assets Referenced in the EKG.

## 2.14.1 Layers of the DOM

To establish and operationalize the DOM, we have structured it into four layers (see Figure 2.19): The data products layer, the data intelligence layer, the raw data layer, and the supporting layer.

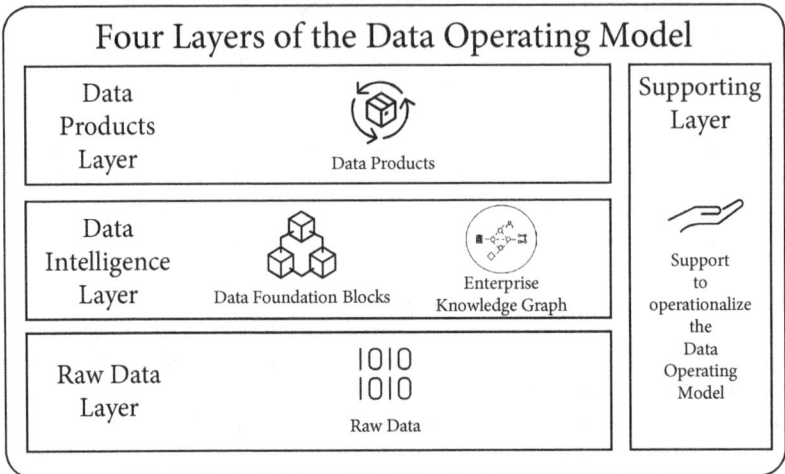

FIGURE 2.19   Four Layers of the DOM.

The *data products layer* enables enterprise-wide production and consumption of data products by the data consumers.

The *data intelligence layer* enables the creation and provisioning of the DFBs and the EKG.

The *raw data layer* collects structured, semi-structured, and unstructured raw data from operational, transactional, and analytical sources within and outside the enterprise.

The *supporting layer* supports establishing and operationalizing the DOM. In this layer, the CDO and the data office drive the adoption, governance, and realization of business value through the data pillar. This layer also provides reusable artifacts like templates, frameworks, rules, and guidelines and, together with the IT office, brings the required technology capabilities across the DOM.

> *A successful AI-driven enterprise is not built on isolated data projects but on a structured and scalable foundation. The DOM serves as this blueprint, ensuring that people, processes, technology, and data are aligned to deliver trusted, governed, and accessible data across the enterprise.*
>
> Rainer Deutschmann, Senior Executive in Telecom and
> Technology Industries.
> Board Director, Advisor, and Investor

The next chapter, Chapter 3, delves into establishing and operationalizing each layer of the DOM.

However, before moving to the next chapter, let us go through the case study on Audi: What does data as a new pillar mean for Audi?

### 2.15 CASE STUDY: WHAT DOES DATA AS A NEW PILLAR MEAN FOR AUDI?

Recognizing the immense strategic value of data, the Audi Group undertook a significant shift in its approach to providing and utilizing data within its business framework. Traditionally a hardware-focused manufacturing company, Audi acknowledged the challenges of "harvesting" data and elevated it as a core pillar of its operating model. This shift underscored the critical role of data in driving innovation and operational efficiency, managing complexity, and maintaining a competitive edge. The new strategy aimed to embed a data-centric approach across all business dimensions, from product development to customer service, while ensuring robust data quality, security, privacy, and compliance systems.

Transitioning to this data-centric approach required fundamental changes across multiple organizational dimensions. The initial focus was on defining top-down strategic goals while simultaneously establishing bottom-up structures and processes to support these objectives across business functions and IT. Beyond setting value-based ambition levels aligned with business targets, the expectation was also that this approach would empower the organization, inspiring it to decentralized, continuous improvement initiatives that had previously been difficult to implement efficiently. A key enabler for this transformation was improving data provisioning and quality to make working with data intuitive and effective for solving localized problems.

Audi Production, having undergone iterations of less efficient setups in its digital journey, was among the first within the Audi Group to recognize the importance of a designated "data lead" role (similar to what the authors call the CDO). This became foundational for driving governance and delivering consumable data products to the business. The data lead's mandate extended beyond governance to fostering new ways of working with data – such as promoting data sharing and establishing ethical guidelines – to create a robust organizational environment. Sponsorship of the Board was deemed essential to achieve success.

While some aspects of this transformation could be driven top-down, significant challenges emerged in reprioritizing resources, accessing localized knowledge, and achieving horizontal integration across process silos.

Cultural and skill gaps, particularly in areas of information architecture and enterprise architecture management, also surfaced. These challenges were compounded by uncertainties around methods and implementation strategies, leading to setbacks that occasionally eroded trust in the agreed roadmap.

To address the challenges of managing and leveraging data effectively, Audi Production established a dedicated "data factory" delivery unit (similar to what the authors call the "data office") under the new data lead role. The data factory was designed to oversee all aspects of data from both business and IT perspectives, with the primary goal of delivering measurable business outcomes. It operates as a "shared services" provider for Audi Production, combining data delivery and governance functions within joint teams to ensure alignment and efficiency.

As is common in evolving data organizations, integrating the data lead into the business structure has undergone significant changes. Currently, the role reports hierarchically to the central digitalization function while being technically embedded within a "hub-and-spoke" data organization. This structure is still maturing in terms of scale and scope. The "hub" is temporarily housed within the IT organization to address the immediate need to reduce technical complexity – a prerequisite for enabling value generation. Meanwhile, the "spokes" represent key business functions such as development, production, and sales. These spokes are divided into 13 distinct data domains (e.g., product design, business partner management, and asset management), ensuring comprehensive coverage across the organization.

It is critical for the data lead role to acknowledge that this internal business model will continue to evolve. Transformation efforts must remain adaptable to new insights and foster collaboration with other business functions, including IT. This flexibility is essential for overcoming challenges such as aligning priorities across business functions, accessing localized knowledge, and integrating processes horizontally across organizational silos.

The success of this model also depends on addressing cultural and skill gaps within the organization. For instance, expertise in information architecture and enterprise architecture management remains limited in some areas. Additionally, uncertainties around implementation strategies have occasionally led to setbacks, eroding trust in the agreed roadmap. However, Audi Production is committed to create a robust foundation for leveraging data as a strategic asset by fostering continuous adaptation and building strong alliances across teams.

In the early stage of the data lead role, one of the most significant challenges was identifying and engaging "data producers" within the business and helping them understand that data is primarily a business concern, with IT playing a supporting role. This effort was further complicated by a common misconception that AI could diminish the importance of data quality and availability, whereas, in reality, these factors become even more critical for success with AI.

Key initiatives during the data-centric phase included securing long-term financing stability, setting up data warehousing solutions, and continuously connecting data sources. A major hurdle was satisfying the business-case-driven financing logic, which had partially contributed to the creation of data silos during the digitalization phase. However, while this initially slowed progress, it also helped gathering the organization behind a sustainable data strategy that now increasingly links data products as an enabler to tangible business benefits. This foundational work required extensive cooperation across all levels of the business, especially as timing expectations of early projects could often not be met.

Today, Audi Production has developed a robust methodology that aligns with financial rationales while ensuring a sustainable data architecture. This methodology has enabled the organization to transition from having fragmented approaches to a cohesive strategy that supports long-term goals.

Since the beginning of Audi Production's data-centric phase (referenced in Figure 1.10), its strategic roadmap has focused on building consolidated and innovative data capabilities. Establishing the data factory under the leadership of a designated data lead role was a pivotal step in this journey. Recognizing that not all capabilities can be developed simultaneously, Audi adopted a staged approach to prioritize initiatives based on current needs, resource availability, and business objectives.

The following are the top-priority data capabilities for Audi Production, each playing a principal role in advancing its data-centric transformation.

### Data Governance

During Audi Production's digital transformation, key aspects of data governance – such as data access, data quality, and data risk management – were prioritized to establish a robust and efficient data management framework. The data factory plays a central role in continuously adapting guidelines to meet internal needs while providing staff training, even as the number of available data products remains relatively low.

Historically, data access was managed in isolation within individual units, leading to fragmented approval processes and inconsistent practices. To address this, Audi adopted a paradigm where data was generally shared and only withheld in exceptional cases. This shift enabled streamlined and standardized access procedures supported by technological capabilities. While significant progress has been made, building this capability remains an ongoing effort to ensure seamless and secure data access across the organization.

As Audi Production moves toward industrializing its data products, maintaining high-quality data has become essential. Data quality management is closely tied to real business use cases that demand reliable and trustworthy information. A forward-looking approach involves developing data observability capabilities to proactively identify failure patterns, safeguard process robustness, and foster trust in data-driven decision-making. This capability is expected to become a top priority as Audi's data-centric journey progresses.

Data risk management has been well-established at Audi Production, initially driven by concerns over external threats and sensitive company data. It includes organizational structures supported by procedures, training programs, and KPIs for monitoring progress. However, updates are now required to align with new priorities such as internal data sharing, AI applications, and ethical considerations in AI usage. These updates will be essential for evolving data risk management alongside broader organizational goals.

## DATA VALUE MANAGEMENT

Often misunderstood but critical for long-term success, data value management goes beyond simply calculating the financial contribution of new business cases. While initial POCs can be implemented relatively quickly, scaling solutions require sustainable building blocks that link data products to strategic business opportunities.

At Audi Production, value generation is evaluated using five "degrees of hardness," ranging from broad estimates to adjusted financial budgets. This approach accounts for the unpredictable nature of certain data products while ensuring their contribution is measurable against distributed costs and medium-to-long-term operational requirements. Effective data value management requires close collaboration among the data lead role, business units, IT, and finance teams. The data factory facilitates this by encouraging structured articulation of business needs linked to internal process hierarchies, avoiding duplication of demands, and fostering stability in data product management.

## DATA ADOPTION

Data adoption ensures that existing data products are utilized effectively while driving the demand for new ones. Developed alongside data value and data access management capabilities, significant effort has been invested in making data products easily consumable with high service levels and a strong focus on internal customer needs.

Audi has directly linked its strategic data-driven portfolio to the demand for data products, ensuring consistency and alignment with business objectives. This approach has made it more acceptable for business units to take on roles and responsibilities for impactful data products. This continuous "deployment process" also supports sustainable change management by fostering the acceptance of rules and policies. Over time, this effort is expected to drive a cultural tipping point toward an even more data-centric mindset across the organization.

### DATA ENGINEERING MANAGEMENT

Data engineering management was central to the initial setup of Audi Production's data organization. It focused on de-clustering the existing data provisioning pipelines, including central connectivity services and standards for data warehousing, as well as machinery and industrial Internet-of-things (IIoT)[11] communication standards.

Historically viewed as "operational technology (OT)"[12] rather than as IT, machinery connectivity straddles both automation and IT departments. Setting and implementing standards required significant effort due to the distribution of legacy equipment across production plants. Whether dealing with machine or IT systems data, the data factory focuses on supporting the "big data loop," enabling business functions to generate new data that can provide value across other functions.

### DATA ARCHITECTURE

Audi's application-centric approach during its digitalization phase resulted in significant data silos that now need to be addressed through modernized data architecture. Overcoming this legacy landscape is essential for enabling progress in the current data-centric phase.

Defining and implementing the data architecture capability early alongside associated business and IT roles are crucial for success. As expectations from business functions grow throughout the journey, visible results ("proof on the ground") are necessary to maintain momentum and avoid setbacks that could jeopardize the transformation effort.

Beyond the top-priority data capabilities, Audi Production has identified the following as the next-level priorities essential for sustaining its data-centric transformation.

### DATA STRATEGY

Developing a comprehensive data strategy is critical but requires a certain level of organizational maturity and structure to ensure its effectiveness. At Audi Production, a detailed data strategy was formalized 2 years into the data-centric phase of its digital journey. This strategy comprises eight chapters – covering motivation, organization, data products, fields of action, data management, architecture, qualification, and culture – presented in a narrative format to align the entire business around a unified vision.

The strategy serves as a "living document," revised annually to reflect evolving priorities and foster internal discussions. It aims to clarify seemingly unrelated tasks and challenges while securing formal management approval for addressing pain points and implementing mediating actions that expedite ongoing developments.

## SEMANTIC DATA MANAGEMENT

Semantic data management, as termed by the authors in Section 2.6, has been a cornerstone of Audi Production's roadmap from the outset but remains one of the most challenging capabilities to develop. It relies heavily on business functions to document and share internal knowledge while grappling with unclear best practices, KPIs, and engagement levels.

This capability is driven by the dual need to build more data-centric IT applications and make data products broadly consumable. Currently, efforts are focused on defining a target information model supported by graph technology to enhance the metadata for the existing data products. This initiative will remain a key focus area in the foreseeable future as Audi works toward creating a more structured and accessible data ecosystem.

These capabilities are integrated into a sustainable DOM, which Audi Production is actively developing. The model addresses not only analytical data – traditionally used by management for decision-making – but also transactional or raw data, which forms the foundation of long-term data quality and usability.

In large enterprises like Audi, raw data generated by IT systems often results from complex, undocumented data lineages. These lineages can branch off unpredictably due to time-sensitive requirements from various business domains, leading to inconsistencies and inefficiencies. To address this issue, Audi is devising a clear information architecture strategy that incorporates semantic metadata. This involves creating "sources of truth" fine-tuned to specific business purposes while reconciling informational knowledge across the organization.

Implementing this architecture is conceptually and practically challenging but essential for ensuring long-term success. Once established, governance and quality control based on this architecture will be significantly easier to manage than attempting to operate without it.

As informational knowledge expands across the organization, data becomes increasingly contextualized, enabling deeper insights into the root causes of problems and uncovering previously hidden connections. When qualified contributors of informational context are distributed throughout the organization, the potential for insights and business opportunities grows exponentially. Fostering this dynamic is a key responsibility of the data lead role and a cornerstone of Audi Production's data strategy. Progress in this area is measured using KPIs such as data catalog completeness and informational model development.

Once the path for raw data creation is addressed, data domain groups must define an initial configuration of datasets, referred to as "data foundation blocks (DFBs)" in Section 2.14. Ideally, these blocks are derived from the existing use cases and include clear, documented lineage back to the raw data and its owners. These foundation blocks must be continuously validated to ensure that they meet the business requirements for QCS as outlined in Chapter 1's QCS framework. Well-managed DFBs that fulfill QCS criteria are highly valuable, as they provide powerful insights and demonstrate the value of data within the organization.

However, there is a risk that DFBs may proliferate uncontrollably over time, diluting their impact. To mitigate this, Audi Production emphasizes extending the existing blocks where possible rather than creating new ones unnecessarily. Governance structures are essential to enforce consistency in structuring and naming conventions across all DFBs.

With well-managed DFBs in place, data products can be developed efficiently by leveraging the foundation blocks as building blocks to deliver quick, actionable insights and value for specific business use cases. These products must be thoroughly documented and made accessible through a data marketplace supported by automated processes. Transparency regarding the costs and benefits of each data product is vital to ensure alignment with business objectives.

Like physical or digital products in any business, data products require ongoing management to maintain their operational performance (e.g., availability, quality, and cost) and strategic relevance (e.g., vision and technology alignment). Effective product management ensures their long-term viability and scalability.

The flowchart presented in Figure 2.20[13] illustrates two key data products used in daily factory shopfloor management at Audi Production and their foundation blocks:

- **Direct Run Rate:** This KPI measures the percentage of cars with zero defects at specific checkpoints on the final assembly line. Both physical location and time stamps define this.

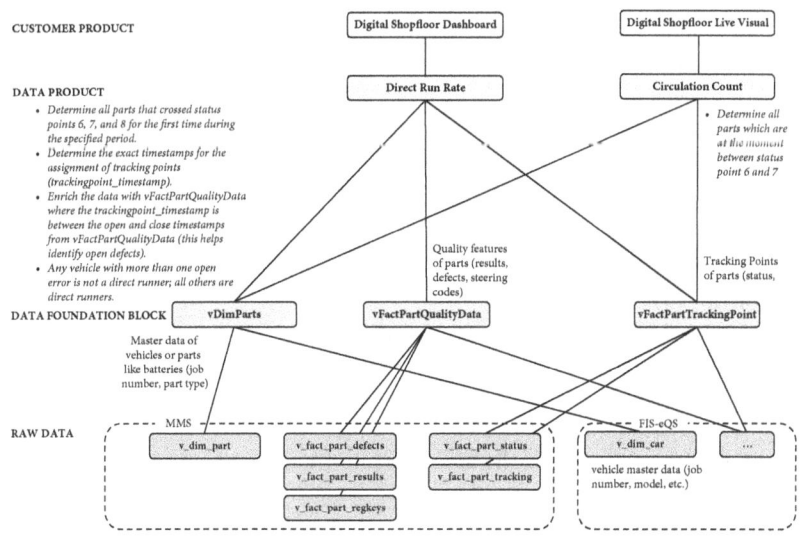

FIGURE 2.20  Example of Data Products, Data Foundation Blocks, and Raw Data at Audi Production.

- **Circulation Count:** This KPI tracks the number of cars between specific status points to estimate the total rework effort required at any given time.

Both data products share several identical foundation blocks and can be applied to vehicle assembly and parts manufacturing lines. These shared components highlight the efficiency of well-structured foundation blocks in supporting multiple use cases. The foundation blocks are created by transforming raw data and provide data persistence while avoiding potential performance issues.

## KEY TAKEAWAYS FROM THIS CHAPTER

*"Data is the First Pillar, for me."*

*— Ramana Kumar, ex-CEO of Magnati*

### For the Board and the CEO

- **Recognize and sponsor data as a core enterprise asset:** An enterprise with data as a core pillar of its operating model creates a multiplier effect on the growth of enterprise value and competitive advantage.
- **Champion adherence to the principles:** The principles for the data pillar guide the enterprise in leveraging data in their strategic and operational use cases and enhancing business outcomes.
- **Appoint and empower a CDO:** To maximize the impact of the data pillar and fast-track its maturation, the CDO should directly report to the CEO. Provide a clear mandate for the CDO to establish and mature the data pillar and the other CxOs to enable the CDO.
- **Fund and track performance:** Prioritize investments in data capabilities. Track performance from data investments using key metrics: RV, EAV, and TAV.

### For the CDO

- **Achieve the North Star goal:** Enable all the stakeholders to enhance their business outcomes by leveraging data as a strategic asset. Execute its responsibilities to achieve the goal. Operationalize the DOM.
- **Be aware of pitfalls and mitigate them:** Common pitfalls: Slow data adoption, restricted by lock-in with technology applications, focusing on efficiency improvement and compliance. Mitigate by developing a structured change management plan with success stories and incentives, involving the Board and the CEO, and balancing compliance with revenue and market share impact.

**For the CxOs**

- **COO:** Leverage data insights to improve outcomes from processes. Partner with the CDO to establish agile data processes and execute a structured change management program that promotes the maturation of the DOM.
- **CHRO:** Partner with the CDO to foster a data culture, improve data literacy, and ensure data ethics and compliance. Enable the CDO with people capabilities for the data office.
- **CIO/CTO:** Unlock data from technology applications, provide technologies for the DOM, and ensure secure and scalable technology infrastructure.

## NOTES

1 FAIR principles. (2025, February 4). In *Wikipedia*.
2 Role-based access control. (2025, January 16). In *Wikipedia*.
3 Coursera. (2024, April 3). *Business Intelligence Reporting.*
4 An artifact is a reusable template, framework, library, or piece of code that can be reused and extended for multiple data assets.
5 Business capability model. (2025, February 9). In *Wikipedia*.
6 Capability management in business. (2024, December 14). In *Wikipedia*.
7 DAMA. (n.d.a). *Data Management Body of Knowledge.*
8 DAMA. (n.d.b). *DAMA.*
9 Process to ensure that AI models are safe, compliant, and ethical.
10 Network effect. (2025, January 22). In *Wikipedia*.
11 Industrial Internet of things. (2024, December 30). In *Wikipedia*.
12 Operational technology refers to specialized industrial equipment and software to integrate large amounts of physical sensors and actuators into a low latency, often safety-critical machinery environment; this robust and proven technology is now gradually converging toward IT architectures, thus enabling additional sensor and field device data-driven capabilities.
13 Referring to Figure 2.20, "crossed status points" are the following: Status point 6: Assembly complete; status point 7: Setup and testing complete; and status point 8: Final inspection and ready for shipment to customer.

## REFERENCE LIST

Business Capability Model. (2025, February 9). In *Wikipedia*. https://en.wikipedia.org/wiki/Business_capability_model

Capability Management in Business. (2024, December 14). In *Wikipedia*. https://en.wikipedia.org/wiki/Capability_management_in_business

Coursera. (2024, April 3). *Business Intelligence Reporting.* https://www.coursera.org/articles/business-intelligence-reporting

DAMA. (n.d.a). *Data Management Body of Knowledge.* https://www.dama.org/cpages/body-of-knowledge

DAMA. (n.d.b). *DAMA.* https://www.dama.org/cpages/home

FAIR Principles. (2025, February 4). In *Wikipedia.* https://en.wikipedia.org/wiki/FAIR_data

Industrial Internet of Things. (2024, December 30). In *Wikipedia.* https://en.wikipedia.org/wiki/Industrial_internet_of_things

Key Performance Indicator. (2024, December 29). In *Wikipedia.* https://en.wikipedia.org/wiki/Performance_indicator

Network Effect. (2025, January 22). In *Wikipedia.* https://en.wikipedia.org/wiki/Network_effect

Role-Based Access Control. (2025, January 16). In *Wikipedia.* https://en.wikipedia.org/wiki/Role-based_access_control

# CHAPTER 3

# Operationalizing Data as the Fourth Pillar

## *The Data Operating Model*

The DOM aims to enable efficient, effective, and governed production and consumption of data assets required by the use cases. Operationalizing the DOM is essential for realizing data as the fourth pillar of the operating model (see Figure 3.1).

An enterprise may choose a centralized, federated, or decentralized setup for its DOM, depending on factors such as its size, organization structure, and data landscape. This chapter shares high-level perspectives on the setup of each layer.

> ***Food for Thought:*** *Which DOM setup would work well for your enterprise? Would you consider having different setups for each layer?*

Keeping these questions in mind, let us explore how to operationalize each layer by combining the required people, processes, and technologies.

We first cover the supporting layer, which enables the primary layers to function. After that, we will cover the primary layers: Data products, data intelligence, and raw data.

DOI: 10.1201/9781003512776-4

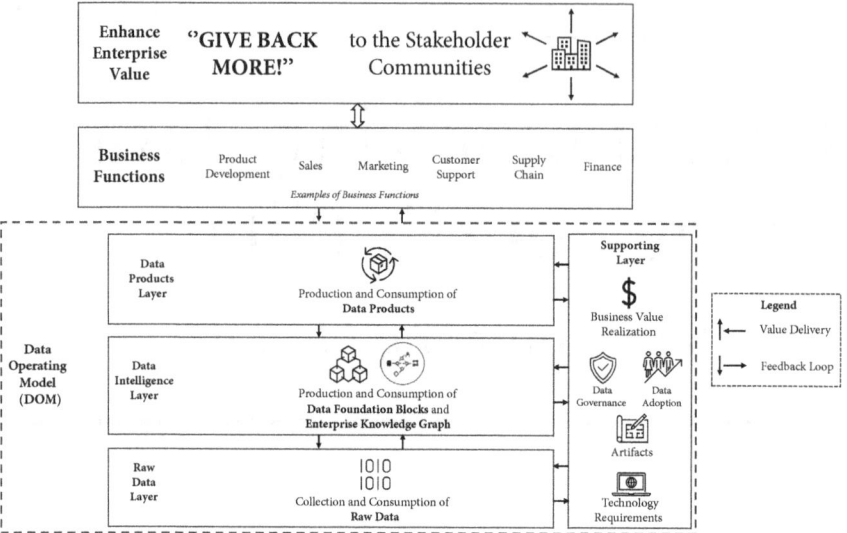

FIGURE 3.1   Operationalizing the DOM.

## 3.1 SUPPORTING LAYER

*The supporting layer enables the standardization of the primary layers. Additionally, it promotes the adoption of data assets and enables governed and secured use of data.*

The supporting layer performs the following functions based on the requirements of the Level 1 business capabilities and prioritization of the Level 2 data capabilities (see Figure 3.2):

1. **Develop the data strategy and architecture:** The data strategy and architecture capabilities are explained in Chapter 2. The supporting layer creates and regularly updates the data strategy and architecture based on established processes.

2. **Develop the reusable artifacts:** Reusable artifacts such as frameworks, templates, rules, and guidelines are leveraged by the stakeholders, including the business functions, the data office, and the IT office, to standardize their activities and improve time-to-value. A few examples of such artifacts would be a data quality rule, a data engineering template, or a GDPR policy guideline. It is important

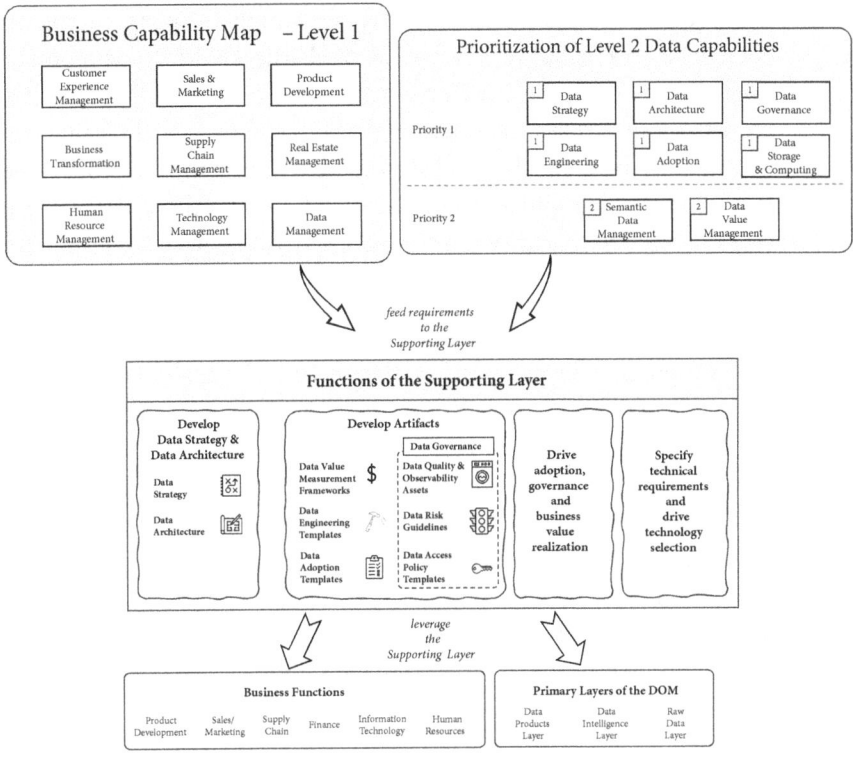

FIGURE 3.2    Functions of the Supporting Layer.

to note that all the artifacts are not developed simultaneously in the supporting layer – their development would be staggered. The sequence of their development would depend on the prioritization of the data capabilities and the data pillar's maturity journey. Chapter 4 delves into the maturity journey.

*With an increasing number of artifacts, stakeholders can accelerate the fulfillment of their data needs and improve their time-to-value.*

3. **Drive adoption, governance, and value realization through the DOM:** The data adoption, governance, and value management capabilities are explained in Chapter 2. The supporting layer executes enablement programs in collaboration with the CHRO and the HR office to enable data adoption and governance. They develop the data culture in the enterprise, i.e., treating data as a strategic asset and developing

the required data skills and competencies among the people across the enterprise. For value realization through the DOM, the supporting layer defines, measures, and shares the KPIs for the DOM. The CDO reports these KPIs to the Board and CEO to showcase the value contribution of the data pillar and secure the required funding for further maturing the data pillar. The CDO also leverages these KPIs to plan and execute the maturity journey of the data pillar. Chapter 4 delves into the maturity journey.

4. **Specify technology requirements and drive technology selection:** The supporting layer specifies the technical capabilities required to enable the prioritized data capabilities. It collaborates with the IT office to select or develop the necessary technology solutions. Consideration must be given to the composability[1] and interoperability of the technology solutions across the data capabilities and how the supporting layer teams can provide the required artifacts used in the technology solutions. The supporting layer coordinates with the IT office to deploy and maintain the technology solutions, such as accelerating the underlying technology landscape by leveraging "Infrastructure as Code (IaC)."[2]

Next, let us delve into how the capabilities of people, processes, and technologies enable the supporting layer.

### 3.1.1 People Capabilities Enabling the Supporting Layer

In collaboration with the CHRO and the HR office, the CDO creates teams within the data office to execute the functions of the supporting layer. The teams' roles and responsibilities are aligned with the data capabilities explained in Chapter 2.

The following teams are set up within the data office (see Figure 3.3):

- **Data Strategy Team:** This team creates and regularly updates the data strategy, as per the process illustrated in Figure 3.4. It also tracks its execution, engages with the stakeholders to resolve hurdles, and identifies and reports deviations to the CDO.

- **Data Architecture Team:** This team creates and regularly updates the data architecture, as per the process illustrated in Figure 3.5. This team also guides and clarifies the other DOM stakeholders who need to refer to the data architecture to perform their activities.

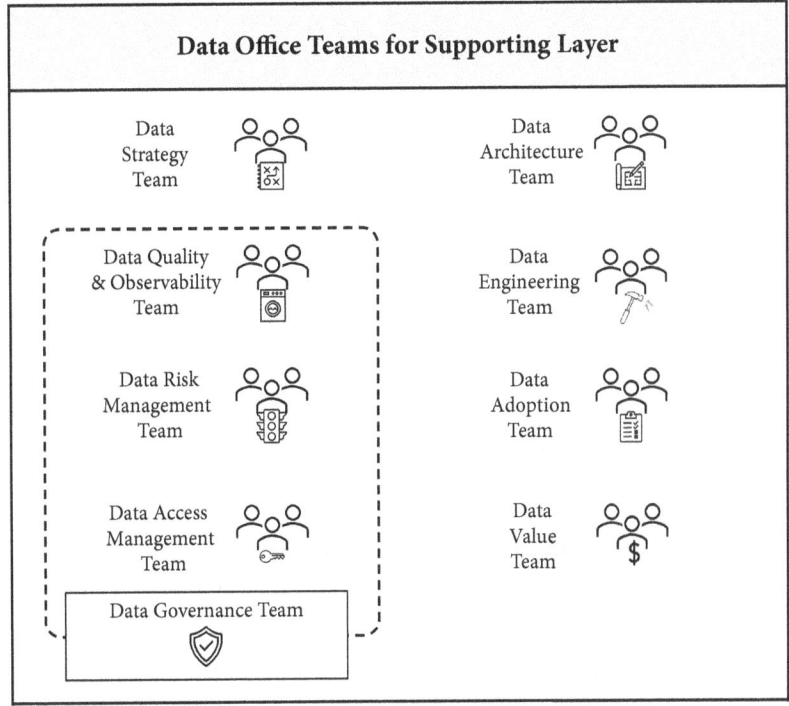

FIGURE 3.3　Data Office Teams for the Supporting Layer.

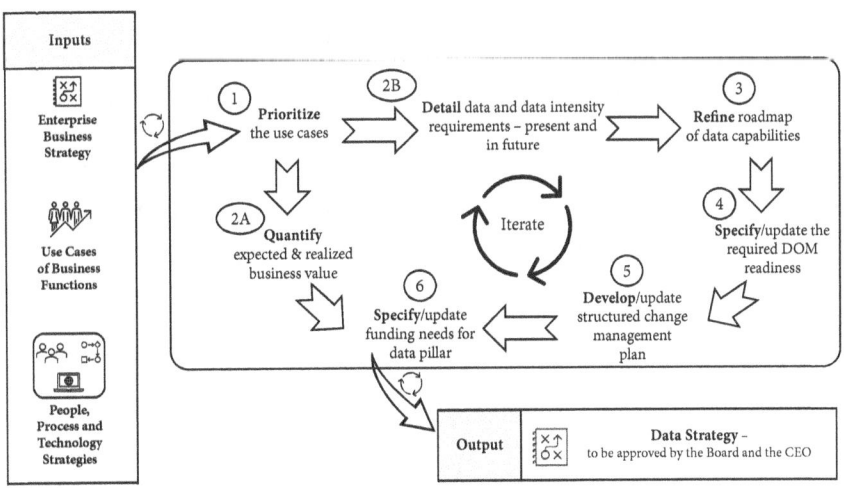

FIGURE 3.4　High-Level Process to Create a Data Strategy.

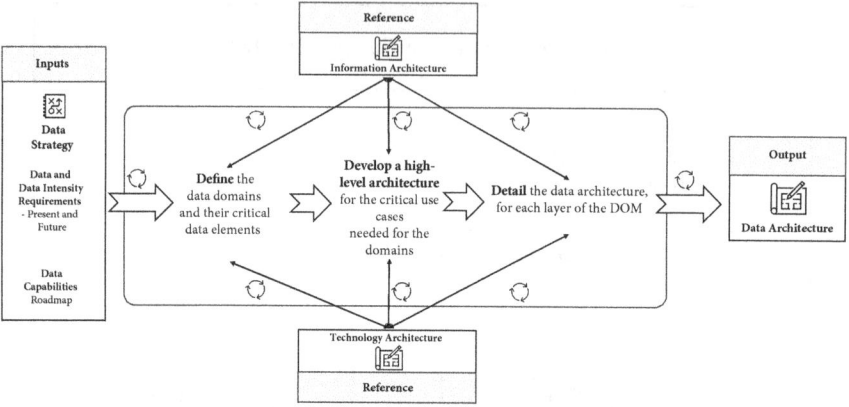

FIGURE 3.5    High-Level Process to Create and Extend a Data Architecture.

- **Data Engineering Team:** This team has two roles. One is to develop the data engineering templates, and the other is to provide data engineering services to the primary layers of the DOM.

- **Data Adoption Team:** This team continuously engages with data producers and consumers and enables them to fulfill their needs through the data assets provided by the DOM. During this process, the team learns about gaps in the expectations of the data consumers and shares those with other DOM stakeholders to take steps to fill them. Examples of such gaps could be the unavailability of required data products, DFBs, or data products not adhering to the specific terms in the data contract (see Section 3.2.1).

- **Data Value Team:** This team is responsible for defining, measuring, and sharing the KPIs for the DOM (see Sections 3.1.4, 3.2.5, 3.3.4, and 3.4.4). They engage with the data adoption team for the data intensity requirements. They also engage with data consumers and producers of the data assets provided by the DOM to measure the KPIs. To ensure consistency of measurement, this team also creates the frameworks to calculate the KPIs.

- **Data Governance Team:** Typically, under a data governance lead, this team can have sub-teams:

1. *Data Risk Management Team:* This team has two roles. The first is to publish the data risk management guidelines, and the second is to identify and mitigate risks with the required stakeholders.

2. *Data Access Management Team:* This team has two roles. The first is to prepare the data access policy templates. The second is to support the primary layers governing authorized access of the data assets.

3. *Data Quality and Observability Team:* This team has two roles. The first is to develop data quality and observability assets, and the second is to provide data quality and observability services to the primary layers.

### 3.1.1.1 Setup of the Supporting Layer Teams

It is important to note that not all the teams in Figure 3.3 may be required simultaneously. This would depend on the prioritization of the data capabilities and the maturity journey of the data pillar.

A critical consideration for setting up the supporting layer teams is whether they operate in a centralized, federated, or decentralized setup. Table 3.1 shares the high-level perspectives on the differences between these setups.

TABLE 3.1   Supporting Layer Teams in a Centralized, Federated, or Distributed Setup

|  | Centralized Setup | Federated Setup | Decentralized Setup |
|---|---|---|---|
| Meaning | The supporting layer team operates as a central team | The supporting layer team has a central hub and multiple spokes in business functions/operating units | The supporting layer team is distributed across business functions/operating units |
| Example of enterprise | An SMB enterprise with centralized business functions | A large enterprise that promotes the reuse of core business capabilities yet provides independence to its business functions/operating units | A large enterprise that has grown through acquisitions with decentralized business functions/operating units |
| Supporting layer functions | All supporting layer functions are performed centrally | Data strategy, architecture, and artifacts, such as data governance policies, are developed in the central hub. The execution of data adoption, governance, engineering, and value realization happen in each spoke | All supporting layer functions are performed in each business function/operating unit |

> *Food for Thought: Would your enterprise consider varying the setup of different teams – for example, a centralized data strategy team with a federated data governance and engineering team?*

### 3.1.1.2 Potential Pitfalls While Setting Up the Supporting Layer Teams

While establishing the teams for the supporting layer, the CDO must be aware of the multiple potential pitfalls and address them in collaboration with other stakeholders. Table 3.2 shares the potential pitfalls and suggested approach to address those.

### 3.1.2 Process Capabilities Enabling the Supporting Layer

Guided by the scope of the data capabilities, processes in the supporting layer enable the involved teams to perform their functions in a standardized manner that can be scaled and automated, aligned to the data pillar's maturity journey. This chapter presents high-level processes, which must be detailed and adjusted for every enterprise. The processes may vary based on the size of the enterprise, the dynamic nature of its business operations, the demand for data, and the organization setup, such as a centralized versus federated or decentralized setup. The CDO must collaborate with the COO to develop the required processes, which may require changes to the existing working methods.

TABLE 3.2    Potential Pitfalls While Setting Up the Supporting Layer Teams

1. *Finding people with the required skills and competencies is a challenge.* The CDO and CHRO should upskill the existing people performing data roles and/or recruit people from outside or other parts of the enterprise

2. *Lack of balance between artifact development and value generation roles.* The CDO and the data office teams should be agile and actively prioritize activities based on the demand for data and the maturity level of the data pillar

3. *Deviating from standardized artifacts and developing custom ones to meet delivery priorities.* Custom artifacts to fulfill specific requirements from use cases would sometimes be developed. The CDO and the data office teams must try to minimize that through proactive alignment with the users of the artifacts. Also, the teams must merge or convert the custom artifacts into the standard ones in the next version of the artifact

4. *Lack of collaboration between each team and the business and IT stakeholders.* The roles, responsibilities, and expectations of all stakeholders must be aligned. The supporting layer teams must collaborate to ensure that their capabilities are aligned and their artifacts are interoperable. The CDO should clarify roles and remove ambiguity in each team's roles. The expectations and responsibilities of the business and IT stakeholders must also be clearly stated

### 3.1.2.1 Process of Developing Data Strategy, Data Architecture, and Artifacts

*3.1.2.1.1 Data Strategy*  Developing a data strategy must be one of the CDO's prioritized tasks. Chapter 2 covers the five principles of the data pillar, which includes the data strategy. When the CDO decides to develop the data strategy at an enterprise level or within a large enterprise's business function or operating unit, the data strategy team can follow the high-level process as presented in Figure 3.4.

A data strategy must be developed iteratively due to the dynamic nature of the inputs.

The process can be broken down into the following steps at a high level:

- **Step 1 – Prioritize the use cases:** The process inputs are the enterprise business strategy; the use cases of the business functions; and the strategies of the people, processes, and technology pillars. In this step, the data strategy team analyses the use cases from the process inputs to understand their data needs at a high level. These use cases are then prioritized, in discussion with the stakeholders providing the inputs, into in-scope use cases for the DOM. The CDO is critical in finalizing the in-scope use cases and setting appropriate expectations with the stakeholders.

  After this step, the process is split into two tracks.

- **Step 2A – Quantify expected and realized business value:** Collaborating with the stakeholders, the data strategy team details and quantifies the EAV through data from in-scope use cases. This step also captures the RV for in-flight use cases.

- **Step 2B – Detail data and data intensity requirements:** The data strategy team details the data and intensity requirements (refer to the QCS framework in Figure 1.4) for in-scope use cases. It is important to note that in-scope use cases may also include expected future data needs. The CDO and the data office must improve the DOM readiness to fulfill such expected future needs.

- **Step 3 – Refine the roadmap of data capabilities:** The data strategy team refines the roadmap of the data capabilities needed to meet the defined data and data intensity requirements. This also provides feedback on prioritizing the data capabilities (see Figure 2.13).

- **Step 4 – Specify or update the required DOM readiness:** With an understanding of the roadmap of the data capabilities, the data strategy team specifies or updates the required DOM readiness to meet the defined data and data intensity requirements. Chapter 4 delves into improving the DOM readiness throughout the maturity journey of the data pillar.

- **Step 5 – Develop or update the structured change management plan:** The data strategy team develops or updates the structured change management plan required to develop or enhance the data capabilities, operationalize the DOM, improve its readiness, and realize business value through the DOM.

- **Step 6 – Specify or update the funding needs for the data pillar:** Based on the inputs of RV, EAV, the required DOM readiness, and expected ROI, the CDO and the data strategy team specify or update the funding required for the data pillar to execute the data strategy.

> *Food for Thought: Do you have a data strategy, and is it being executed to achieve the EAV defined in the strategy?*

To secure their continued sponsorship and involvement, the CDO must get every version of the data strategy approved by the Board and the CEO. To enable them, the CDO must provide them with an executive summary along with a detailed data strategy. Figure 3.6 provides an example of the executive summary "on a page" for a retail consumer brand enterprise.

| Business Imperatives | Foster Direct Customer Relationships | Improve Net Promoter Score (NPS) | Achieve Revenue Growth Targets | Achieve Sustainability Targets | **Expected Addressable Value through Data (EAV)** |
|---|---|---|---|---|---|
| **Business Use Cases** | Pivot towards a D2C retail model | Deliver new customer experiences | Expand into new territories (APAC, Middle East) | Build more sustainable products | 10M D2C Customers |
| | | | | | Improve NPS from 61 to 75 |
| **Data Requirements** | Data partnerships with wholesalers | Build a 360-degree view of customers | Support local data compliance & regulations | Collecting and reporting sustainability related data | Increase Revenues by 35% |
| | | | | | 100% Accurate Reporting of Sustainability Metrics |
| **Prioritized Data Capabilities** | Data Adoption & Governance | Semantic Data Management | Data Access Management | Data Risk Management | |
| | | | | | **Budget Ask** |
| **DOM Readiness** | External & internal facing Data Products | Customer, Product, Supplier Data Foundation Blocks | Enterprise Knowledge Graph w/ D2C & local compliance and regulations | Collection and parsing of unstructured raw data | USD 15M for 2026; USD 20M for 2027 |
| | | | | | **Expected ROI** |
| **Structured Change Management Plan** | Data Literacy Program | Data Intelligence Layer – Process and organization setup | Improving Technology Capabilities | Improving Adoption of DOM by Business Stakeholders | 120% for 2026; 150% for 2027 |

FIGURE 3.6 Example: Executive Summary of Data Strategy "on a Page" for a Retail Consumer Brand Enterprise.

The CDO leverages the approved data strategy to secure the budget allocated for the data pillar and execute the data strategy.

*Potential Pitfalls with Data Strategy*
The CDO must also watch out for multiple potential pitfalls with a data strategy and address those in collaboration with other stakeholders (see Table 3.3).

*3.1.2.1.2 Data Architecture*   This is a broad topic; here, we cover it at a summary level.

Data architecture supports operational, transactional, and analytical use cases and considers immediate and future requirements. The data strategy acts as a prerequisite for the data architecture. If the data strategy does not exist, enterprises must consider the data and data intensity requirements of the use cases and the roadmap of the data capabilities as inputs for the data architecture.

The data architecture must also align with the information and technology architectures. Section 2.5 of Chapter 2 clarifies the differences and interdependency among information, data, and technology architectures.

TABLE 3.3   Potential Pitfalls with Data Strategy

---

1. *Developing a data strategy as a one-time exercise.* The inputs to the data strategy would be dynamic. The CDO must develop a new version of the data strategy biannually or annually to update the in-scope use cases and the downstream impact based on that, including the funding required.
2. *The data strategy stays on paper and is not executed.* Once developed and approved, the data strategy must be executed to establish and mature the data pillar. The CDO must periodically, like biannually, share the status of the execution of the data strategy with the Board and the CEO and secure their continued involvement to remove any hurdle they face
3. *The data strategy lacks quantified business value.* Without it, the data strategy cannot be leveraged to secure the required funding for the data pillar. Chapter 4 provides the approaches to determine the EAV
4. *Lack of buy-in into the data strategy by the Board, CEO, and other CxOs.* The CDO must involve them in prioritizing the use cases in the data strategy and highlight the EAV and ROI to secure their buy-in. An executive summary of the data strategy on a page would be helpful
5. *Procrastinating the development of the data strategy.* Some CDOs might become busy executing important activities like modernizing the technology capabilities or helping business functions with their data requirements. Procrastinating the development of the data strategy may lead to multiple challenges, such as a lack of clarity on the EAV, a lack of rationale for requesting the required budget for the data pillar, and an inability to secure a continued involvement from stakeholders in executing the data strategy

Let us examine each step of the data architecture development process outlined in Figure 3.6, assuming that the data strategy exists.

- **Define the data domains and CDEs:** The first step is to identify and define the data domains and their CDEs[3] based on the inputs from the data strategy. Based on those, the key entities and attributes are interrelated using data model(s).

- **Develop a high-level data architecture:** The next step is developing a high-level data architecture for critical use cases in each data domain across the DOM layers (Figure 3.7). This step specifies the interrelation between the layers and the assets that will be leveraged from each layer.

- **Detailed data architecture:** This step includes detailing the data architecture for each layer of the DOM based on the high-level data architecture. The data model is accordingly adjusted and/or expanded. The architecture detailing for each layer can occur in parallel, with frequent cross-collaboration, to ensure that the detailed data architectures for each layer are aligned. The data architecture becomes a reference for developing the data capabilities.

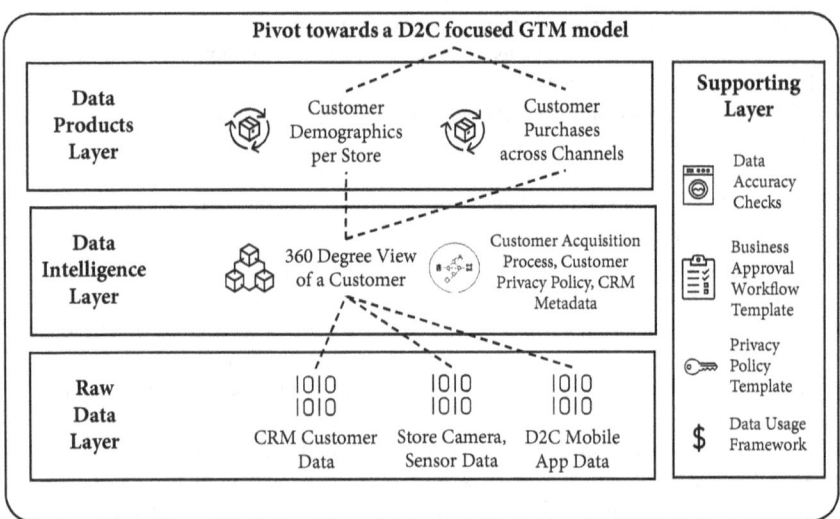

FIGURE 3.7 High-Level Data Architecture for a Retail Consumer Brand Enterprise Transforming Its GTM to D2C Model.

TABLE 3.4    Potential Pitfalls with Data Architecture

1. *Data architecture is used interchangeably with information architecture.* Information architecture provides a blueprint for critical information in the business functions' processes. The data office must clarify the differences and interlinkages with the stakeholders involved

2. *The DOM's operationalization is not aligned with the data architecture.* The data architecture must be referred to while operationalizing the DOM, and the data office must monitor it and provide feedback.

3. *Data architecture is incompatible with technology architecture.* – Data architecture cannot be realized without enabling technologies, and the existing legacy technologies may restrict its implementation. The CDO and the data office must collaborate with the CIO/CTO and the IT office to resolve incompatibilities.

4. *Data architecture is not future-looking.* This likely happens when a data strategy is not implemented before developing the data architecture. As a data strategy would include future business requirements, the CDO should prioritize the development of the data strategy

5. *Data architecture is developed as a one-time exercise.* The CDO and the data office should update the data architecture biannually or annually, based on the changes to inputs mentioned in Figure 3.6

Feedback received during the data architecture development or implementation process, such as changes in the data strategy, information, and technology architectures, would trigger another iteration of the data architecture.

To elaborate on the high-level data architecture, let us examine it in the context of a specific example – the retail consumer brand enterprise transforming its GTM to a D2C model.

The high-level data architecture can be called the data architecture "on a page" version. The detailed data architecture further drills each component and links interdependencies across the DOM.

### Potential Pitfalls with Data Architecture

The CDO and the data office must monitor multiple potential pitfalls in data architecture and address them in collaboration with other stakeholders (see Table 3.4).

*3.1.2.1.3 Artifacts Provided by the Supporting Layer*  For the artifacts provided by the supporting layer, we propose a process that could be repeated and reused across the DOM layers. We call it the "Demand-to-Deploy (5D)" process (see Figure 3.8).

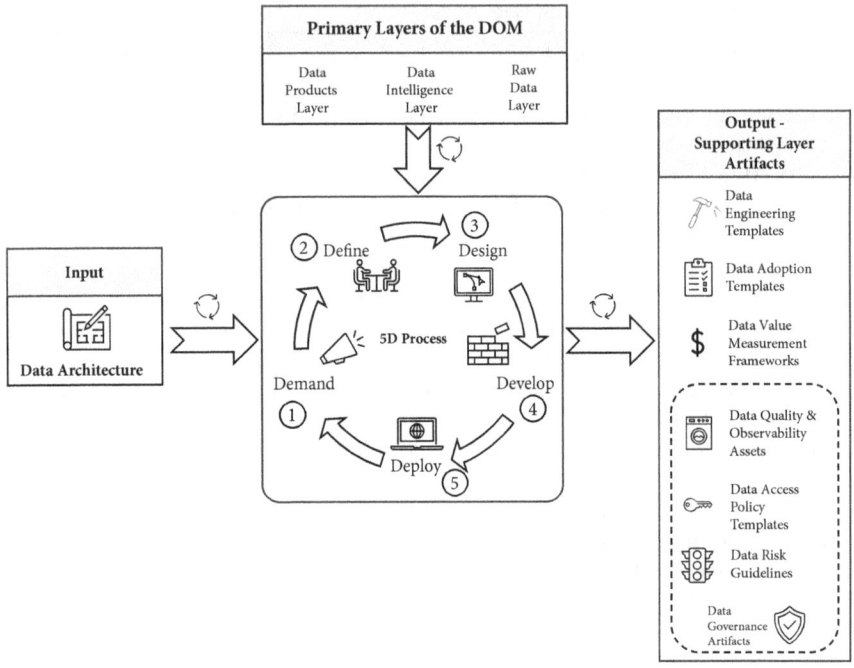

FIGURE 3.8    5D Process for the Artifacts Provided by the Supporting Layer.

Let us delve into each step in the 5D process (see Figure 3.8):

- **Demand capture:** This step identifies the demand for artifacts based on the data architecture. Additional demand might also come from the primary layers of the DOM. Based on the aggregate demand, this step prioritizes the artifacts to be developed and/or updated.

- **Define:** The detailed requirements for the prioritized artifacts are defined on the basis of the demand captured for them. The expected value from the artifacts is also defined.

- **Design:** In this step, artifacts are designed on the basis of the defined requirements. For example, the design specification for a data engineering pipeline template incorporates the elements in the template, such as the inputs, outputs, and transformation logic, as well as the process of building the template, including the documentation, testing, and deployment process.

- **Develop:** The artifacts are developed on the basis of the design speci-fication. Note that an artifact is a reusable template, rule, guideline, or framework, and not the final deliverable applied to the physical data. For example, a data quality rule would be leveraged to develop a data quality rule to remove inconsistencies in raw data.

- **Deploy:** This step makes the artifacts ready to use. They are deployed into a shared repository, and their availability and usage information are broadcast to the required stakeholders. Feedback is collected on the artifacts, which may trigger a new iteration of the 5D process. This process step should also track the artifacts' usage.

### 3.1.2.2 Processes for Driving Adoption, Governance, and Value Realization Through the DOM

These get embedded into the processes in DOM layers explained in Sections 3.2.3, 3.3.2, and 3.4.2.

### 3.1.2.3 Process for Specifying the Technical Requirements and Driving the Technologies Required for Enabling the In-Scope Data Capabilities

- The supporting layer teams engage with the stakeholders involved in the primary layers of the DOM, gather their technical requirements, aggregate, and work with the IT office to onboard the required tech-nologies or improve the existing technologies.

- The supporting layer teams also provide feedback to the IT office on technology requirements and technology enhancements based on usage.

With an understanding of the supporting layer's people and processes, let us now look at the technology capabilities required to automate the processes, improve people's productivity, and enhance the supporting layer's maturity.

### 3.1.3 Technology Capabilities Enabling the Supporting Layer

This section covers the key technology components needed. It does not cover specific technology providers or decisions such as "build versus buy" or "open-source versus proprietary software."

Let us delve into the key technology components needed for the supporting layer.

### 3.1.3.1 Technology Components for Data Strategy, Data Architecture, and Artifacts

- **Data Strategy:** The technology component must enable collaboration to create and amend the data strategy, which should be traced back to previous versions. It must also enable the interfacing of the data strategy with other technology components such as the one for data architecture.

- **Data Architecture:** The technology component must be capable of interfacing with the data strategy, information and technology architectures, and data modeling. It must also provide a mechanism to export a data model depicting the CDEs and DOM relationships.

- **Artifacts:** The technology component must automate the execution of the 5D process for all artifacts. A single or multiple technology solutions provide the required technology components for all artifacts. In addition, an artifact portal would be required where all deployed artifacts can be listed.

### 3.1.3.2 Technology Components for Driving Data Adoption, Data Governance, and Value Realization through the DOM

- **Data Adoption:** The technology component should enable the promotion and marketing of data assets to data producers and consumers across the DOM, aligned to the data adoption capability covered in Chapter 2.

- **Data Governance:** The technology for data governance would include subcomponents for data quality and observability, data risk management, and data access management. These components should enable the realization of the respective capabilities covered in Chapter 2.

- **Data Value Realization:** The technology component should support defining, measuring, and reporting the KPIs. Sections 3.1.4, 3.2.5, 3.3.4, and 3.4.4 provide examples of KPIs.

### 3.1.3.3 Technology Components for Specifying the Technical Requirements and Driving the Selection of Technologies for Enabling In-Scope Data Capabilities

The technology component should enable listing the functional and non-functional technical requirements, prioritizing them, and assigning them to stakeholders in the IT office.

### 3.1.3.4 Potential Pitfalls with Technologies in the Supporting Layer

The CDO and the data office must monitor technologies in the supporting layer for potential pitfalls and address them in collaboration with the CIO/CTO and the IT office (see Table 3.5).

## 3.1.4 KPIs for the Supporting Layer

Let us delve into examples of KPIs for the supporting layer. See Table 3.6 for example KPIs.

Next, let us delve into the primary layers of the DOM. We start with the data products layer, which enables data consumers to enhance their business outcomes by accessing ready-to-use data with the required data intensity.

TABLE 3.5    Potential Pitfalls with Technologies in the Supporting Layer

---

1. *Creation of technology silos.* The technology components must be composable, sharing relevant information seamlessly and optimizing the total cost of ownership (TCO). This also enables a seamless user experience
2. *Data architecture is not aligned with technology architecture.* Data architecture cannot be realized without enabling the technology components. On the other hand, the existing legacy technology components may restrict its implementation. The CDO and the CIO must collaborate to resolve the gaps
3. *Adopt a "big bang" approach.* The technology components should be prioritized on the basis of the prioritization of data capabilities and the current technology landscape. Deployment should be gradual and accompanied by a structured change management program
4. *Focus on deploying technology components and not their adoption.* Intended users must adopt the deployed technology components to derive value from them. The data adoption team must execute enablement initiatives to improve adoption
5. *Not future-proof.* The technology components must be able to support the maturation of the data pillar and not become bottlenecks. Chapter 4 elaborates on the data pillar's maturity journey

---

TABLE 3.6   Example KPIs for the Supporting Layer

| KPI Name | Calculation | Description |
|---|---|---|
| These KPIs apply to the data strategy. | | |
| EAV through data | Sum of the EAV from all in-scope use cases | Tracks the business value expected from the use cases leveraging the data pillar |
| RV | Sum of the RV from all in-scope use cases | Tracks the business value realized from the use cases leveraging the data pillar |
| Funds allocation %age | (Released funds divided by approved budget) × 100 | Tracks the funds released for the data pillar compared to the approved value in the data strategy |
| These KPIs apply to the adoption of the DOM. | | |
| DOM penetration | %age of data consumers leveraging the data assets provided by the DOM | Tracks the penetration of the DOM among data consumers |
| Artifact reuse rate | Number of artifacts used more than once every month is divided by the total number of artifacts | Tracks the effectiveness of artifacts and enables optimizing the number of required artifacts |
| These KPIs enable the evaluation of the *effectiveness of the technology requirements* specified by the supporting layer and the selection of *technology components* by the IT office | | |
| TCO for technology | Sum of the TCO for each technology component used in the DOM | Tracks the TCO and enables the alignment of the TCO with the funding and the business value from the data pillar |
| Technology change cost | Costs incurred to change technology components | Tracks the effectiveness of the specification and selection of technology components, also considering potential future requirements |

## 3.2  DATA PRODUCTS LAYER

The production and consumption of data products are executed in the data products layer (see Figure 3.9).

> *A critical aspect of success with data products is "partnerships." These are internal partnerships with stakeholders across business functions or external partnerships with customers, suppliers, business partners, etc.*

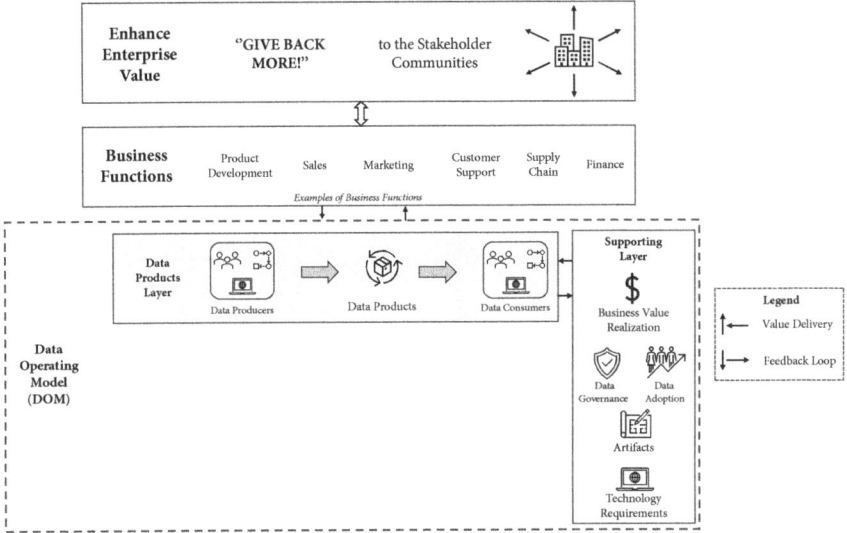

FIGURE 3.9  Data Products Layer Enabling the Production and Consumption of Data Products.

A corollary to partnerships is "trust." This is where a "data contract"[4] comes in.

### 3.2.1  Data Contract

> *A "data contract" helps build "trust" between partners in adopting data products by setting a structured mechanism to define, measure, and confirm the delivery of the required data intensity for data consumers and producers.*

A data contract (see Figure 3.10) is a formal agreement between the data producers and consumers for a specific data product. The data producers specify the data, the data intensity fulfilled by the data product, and the authorized purposes for using the data product. The data consumers accept the terms in the data contract or request changes to align with the requirements of their use cases. The underlying processes for producing and consuming data products are executed by referring to the data contract. Establishing an upfront data contract fosters trust through transparency, improves the adoption of data products, and eliminates the negative downstream impacts when a data product does not meet the required data intensity or is used in

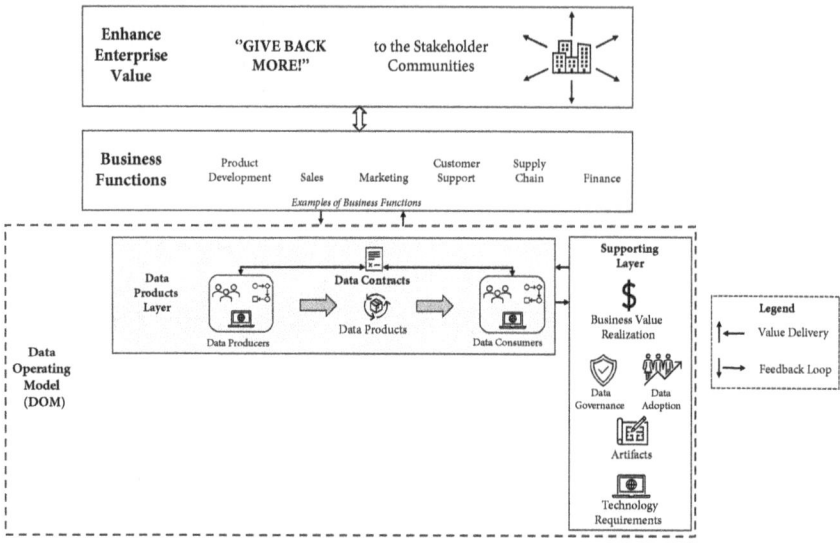

FIGURE 3.10   Data Contracts between Data Producers and Data Consumers.

an unauthorized manner. The data office plays a crucial role in the process – it considers the interests of both data producers and consumers. It facilitates the execution of the data contract between the involved stakeholders.

### 3.2.1.1 Example of a Data Contract

Let us take the example of the marketing team in a retail consumer brand enterprise. The marketing team needs to access the "regional customer segmentation" data product to execute a promotional program for a particular region. The data contract for this data product may include the following terms.

#### 3.2.1.1.1 Quality Requirements in a Data Contract   Example quality requirements in a data contract are outlined in Table 3.7.

TABLE 3.7   Example Quality Requirements in a Data Contract

| Example Requirement | Description |
| --- | --- |
| Validation checks | The "customer email" should always have a valid verified email. Any other values are a violation |
| Missing data | The "customer segment by age" cannot be missing or blank. That would mean no segment has been established for the customer. Such missing or blank values are a violation |
| Time-sensitive refresh | All data in the "regional customer segmentation" data product must be refreshed daily. Any data older than 1 day is a contract violation |

TABLE 3.8   Example Compliance Requirements in a Data Contract

| Example Requirement | Description |
|---|---|
| Data confidentiality | The data product should include only "year of birth" information. Having the "date of birth" data is a contract violation as this is determined as a privacy identification attribute |
| Consent check | The data product must include only customers who have consented to be approached for promotional programs |
| Risk assessment | The data product is classified as medium risk. This means related requirements, such as validation checks and data confidentiality, are linked. Not performing a risk assessment every 6 months is a violation |
| Comply with regulations | This varies based on the type of compliance and the underlying requirement. For example, in the case of the "right to be forgotten" (RTBF)[5] in GDPR, conditions can be placed on customer-specific fields to ensure they are removed upon request |

*3.2.1.1.2 Compliance Requirements in a Data Contract*   Examples of compliance requirements in a data contract are outlined in Table 3.8.

*3.2.1.1.3 Speed Requirements in a Data Contract*   Examples of speed requirements in a data contract are outlined in Table 3.9.

*3.2.1.1.4 Authorized Usage Scenario in a Data Contract*   In addition to specifying and agreeing on the terms of a data contract, the data producer should put checks and measures in place to verify if any term is violated

TABLE 3.9   Example Speed Requirements in a Data Contract

| Example Requirement | Description |
|---|---|
| Data pipeline performance | This is related to the performance of the data pipelines that feed data downstream. The performance required would be linked to the "time-sensitive refresh" requirement under data quality |
| Data access speed | This is related to the time between the request and grant of access to a data product. Here, the data access speed is 2 hours, for instance |
| Data infrastructure performance | This is related to the performance of the underlying technology infrastructure for data storage and computing, either when writing new data to a data product or when reading data as a consumer from a data product. For instance, reading should occur within 30 milliseconds and writing within 60 milliseconds |

or at risk of violation, and notifications should be provided to the relevant stakeholders. See Table 3.10 for an example usage scenario that is authorized in a data contract.

Data contracts increase trust through transparency and enable communities of data consumers and producers to adopt data products. The extent of use of data contracts also depends on the maturity of the data pillar (see Chapter 4).

> **Food for Thought:** *Are you already using data contracts or considering? What hindrances are you facing or expecting when adopting them?*

Table 3.11 provides some good practices to follow to succeed with data contracts.

With the understanding of data contracts, let us explore how people, processes, and technologies should be set up to enable the data products layer.

TABLE 3.10   Example Authorized Usage Scenario in a Data Contract

| Usage Scenario | Description |
| --- | --- |
| Not for use by external parties | External parties, including business partners, cannot access and use the data product |

TABLE 3.11   Good Practices to Follow to Succeed with Data Contracts

1. *Positioning of data contracts.* Data contracts must be positioned as an "aid" for business stakeholders to help them get data that meets their data intensity requirements. The focus must be on empowering rather than creating another guardrail
2. *Buy-in from business stakeholders.* Business stakeholders might perceive data contracts as an additional overhead. Showcasing the benefits of adopting data contracts would enable achieving their buy-in
3. *Extensive communication.* The data office must act like an internal marketing organization, promoting the benefits of data contracts to business stakeholders, celebrating early wins, and sharing adoption stories internally
4. *Ease of use.* Make data contracts easy for business stakeholders to adopt. Technologies that enable ease of use and self-service would be critical for success
5. *Automating data contracts.* The development and execution of data contracts must be automated to scale their usage

## 3.2.2 People Capabilities Enabling the Data Products Layer

Data consumers and producers are the primary people personas for the data products layer, and the data and IT offices enable them. Figure 3.11 summarizes the people personas for the data products layer.

### 3.2.2.1 Data Consumers

Data consumers need to consume data with the required data intensity to enhance business outcomes from their use cases. While data consumers are primarily based inside the enterprise, they may also be based in stakeholder communities external to the enterprise, e.g., business partners, customers, suppliers, and regulatory agencies. With the increasing automation in enterprises, business processes and enabling technologies will increasingly become data consumers. Table 3.12 provides the key responsibilities of data consumers.

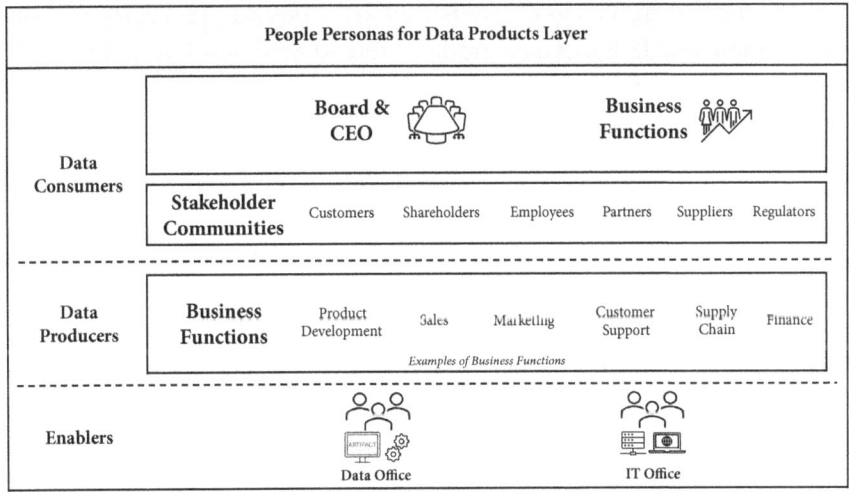

FIGURE 3.11   People Personas for the Data Products Layer.

TABLE 3.12   Key Responsibilities of Data Consumers

1. Creating demand for data products and collaborating with the stakeholders involved during the data product production process. Providing information on the expected addressable value, purpose of use, etc.
2. Adhering to the data contract terms while consuming the data products. They may need to seek changes in the terms to align with the requirements of their use cases
3. Providing feedback on the data products. Positive feedback would help promote the products and improve their adoption, while critical feedback would help improve them

### 3.2.2.2 Data Producers

As the name suggests, data producers produce data products in an enterprise. Some data producers might be "pseudo-producers" – they take in data from external data providers and leverage it to produce data products. Data producers must be equipped and empowered to produce data products.

We recommend that stakeholders within the business functions, accountable for their data, should be the data producers. This approach provides multiple benefits:

- First, the business functions responsible for establishing and maintaining their business capabilities, mentioned in Chapter 2, are the best positioned to determine the data intensity required (i.e., QCS requirements) for the business use cases and thus produce the data products that meet the consumption requirements.

- Second, as data is closely connected to the business processes, the definition and design of data products should be closely interlinked to the in-scope business processes. Stakeholders in the business functions who understand the business processes are best positioned to do that.

- Last but not least, adopting the philosophy "for the business functions, by the business functions," the production of data products by the business functions enables faster adoption of the data products by themselves, compared to that by the data or IT office.

The data office may initially support the data producers in the business functions in producing data products. Later, as data maturity increases, they will become self-competent, or the production process will be automated.

> **Food for Thought:** *Are you considering or already have data producers in the business functions? If not, how do you plan to scale the production and adoption of data products?*

Enterprises may face multiple challenges in getting the data producers in business functions to execute their responsibilities. Table 3.13 lists such challenges. Knowing the challenges, they should plan to mitigate those.

The production and consumption of data products must be scaled to enhance the realization of business value through data, i.e., the RV and EAV. To enable that, data consumers in the business functions should also produce data products and become data producers, thus creating a "network effect" (see Figure 3.12) from data products.

TABLE 3.13   Challenges in Getting the Data Producers to Execute Their Responsibilities

1. *Cultural or mindset issue.* Business stakeholders may feel that managing data is the responsibility of the IT or the data office. To change this mindset, the CDO must collaborate with the COO and leaders of the business functions. Business stakeholders should be reminded that they are accountable for their data. The Board and the CEO may also be required to help with the culture change. The CDO should leverage the approved data strategy to seek their active involvement

2. *Lack of bandwidth.* Pressure from business execution may limit the bandwidth business stakeholders could spend on producing data products. The CDO must leverage the approved data strategy and seek collaboration from the COO and leaders of the business functions to allocate bandwidth to the identified data producers

3. *Lack of data skills and competencies.* Business stakeholders may lack the skills and competencies in data engineering or data quality improvement to produce data products. To this end, they can initially seek the data office's help. In parallel, the data office should execute enablement programs to train the business stakeholders

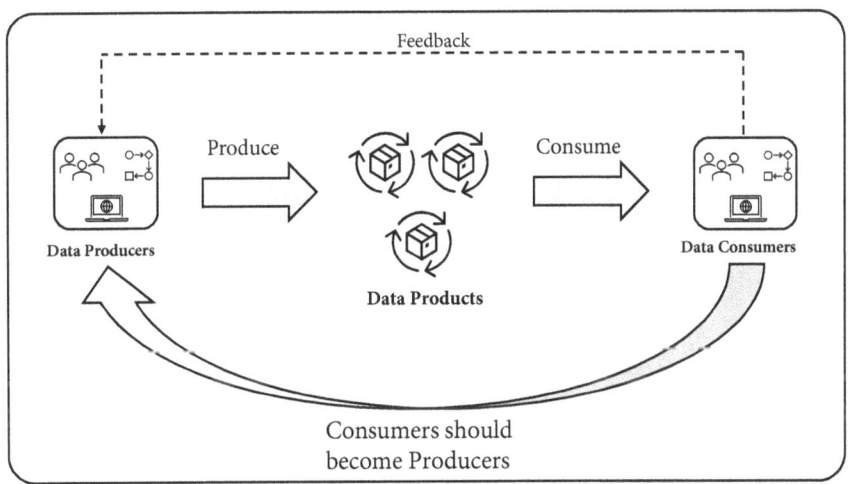

FIGURE 3.12   Data Consumers Should Become Data Producers and Create the "Network Effect."

> *Scaling the adoption of data products requires creating a "network effect," wherein data consumers also become data producers.*

### 3.2.2.3 Data Products Enabler – Data Office

The data office supports data producers in delivering and deriving business value through the data products. The data office may initially help produce the data products for business functions. It would also interface with the HR office to execute enablement programs for the data producers and consumers, enabling them to adopt data products. It also enables the governance of data products.

### 3.2.2.4 Data Products Enabler – IT Office

The IT office deploys and maintains the technology components for the data products layer. Data consumers and producers need them to execute and automate their processes. To meet the required data intensity and improve data maturity, the IT office must deploy technologies, including AI, that provide tailored and seamless user experiences for data consumers and producers and drive self-service and automation. These technology components must be aligned with the data and the technology architecture; the technology architect and the data architect play vital roles in aligning the technology architecture with the data architecture.

### 3.2.2.5 Setup of the Data Products Layer Teams

Depending on factors mentioned earlier in this chapter, enterprises can have a centralized, federated, or decentralized setup for producing data products. Table 3.1 shares high-level perspectives on the differences between these setups. We extend this reasoning to the data products layer, as presented in Table 3.14.

TABLE 3.14   Setup of the Data Products Layer Teams

| Theme | Centralized | Federated | Decentralized |
|---|---|---|---|
| Meaning | Data products are produced centrally by the central data office | This is a hybrid setup, wherein some business functions produce their data products, while the data office produces for others | All data products are produced in business functions. The data office provides the artifacts and drives adoption, governance, and business value realization |
| Enterprise example | An enterprise in the early stages of data maturity with low demand for data products | A large enterprise with varied data maturity across business functions and high demand for data products | A large enterprise with high data maturity and high business demand for data products |
| DOM readiness | The data intelligence layer is not set up, requiring the data office to produce data products by leveraging the raw data layer | The data intelligence layer is partially set up, enabling some business functions to leverage it to produce data products | The data intelligence layer is ready to use, enabling all business functions to leverage it to produce data products |

### 3.2.3 Process Capabilities Enabling the Data Products Layer

Processes in the data products layer enable enterprises to standardize, automate, and scale the production and consumption of data products.

To produce data products, we reuse the "5D" process mentioned in the supporting layer, although the activity in each step differs. For the consumption of data products, we introduce a process called the "FRAAU (find, request, approve, access, and use)."

Let us now delve into these processes.

#### 3.2.3.1 Production of Data Products through the 5D Process

The core objective of the 5D process would be to produce standardized data products that are reusable and interoperable while optimizing the productivity of data producers and improving the time-to-value for data consumers.

To illustrate the 5D process presented in Figure 3.13, let us again consider the example of the "regional customer segmentation" data product in a retail consumer brand enterprise.

*3.2.3.1.1 Demand Capture* This process step captures the demand for data products. The data producer evaluates requests for a data product from data consumers. Other data consumers are notified of the request for a potential

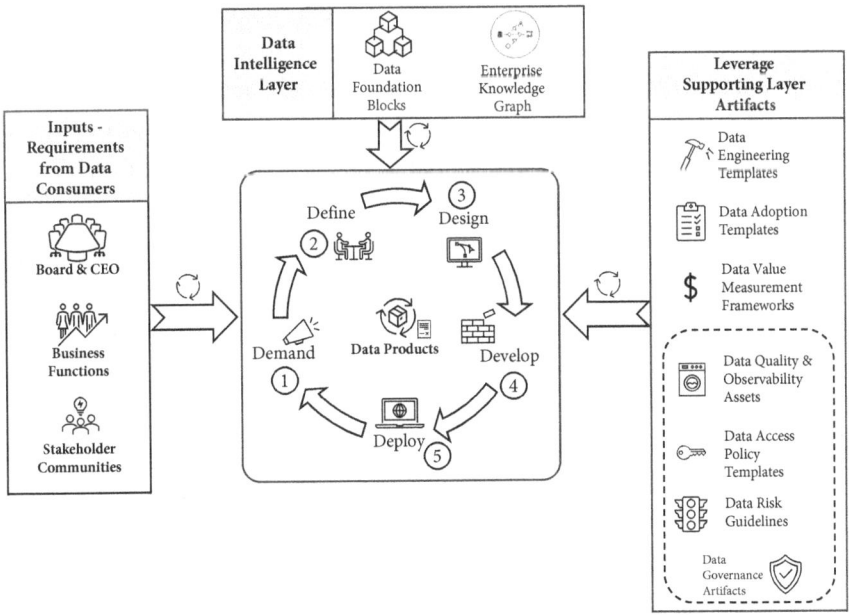

FIGURE 3.13   5D Process for Producing Data Products.

data product, to identify additional demand for it. Once all the demand for a potential data product is captured, the data producer collaborates with the data office to align options to fulfill the demand. The expected outcome of this demand capture process step is a confirmation that either a new data product is needed or the demand could be fulfilled by the existing data product(s) or DFBs. If the conclusion is to produce a new data product or make changes to the existing data product(s), the process moves to the "Define" step. Otherwise, the data consumers are guided by the data office to the data intelligence layer to fulfill their needs through the existing DFBs.

In the example, the brand manager, i.e., a data consumer, has a use case to improve the effectiveness of the promotional program. For this, the brand manager must better understand customers' buying behavior at a regional level. In the demand capture process step, the brand manager requests information on regional customer segmentation. The request for this information is channeled to the appropriate data producer, in this case, to the stakeholder responsible for the customer information data domain. Next, other data consumer communities are notified of the request for regional customer segmentation data to determine if there would be additional demand for the potential data product. Another data consumer, the supply chain operations team, must use regional customer segmentation data to track returned products by customer segments at a regional level. This will enable them to improve regional supply chain planning and reduce inventory carrying costs. Thus, the demands from the brand manager and the supply chain operations team are aggregated for the "regional customer segmentation" data product.

Let us now consider the potential pitfalls to watch out for during the demand capture process step. These have been provided in Table 3.15.

TABLE 3.15   Potential Pitfalls during the Demand Capture Process Step

---

1. *Missing out on broadcasting the initial demand* across different data domains and business functions. Broadcasting ensures that additional demand across the enterprise is captured for the potential data product. This helps with a more holistic design of the data product that could cater to multiple use cases and higher adoption. The additional demand must be carefully assessed and accepted on the basis of the readiness of the DOM so that the right expectations are set for fulfilling the demand
2. *Not involving the data office might result in missing quick-win opportunities* such as extending an existing data product or leveraging a DFB to fulfill the demand. The data office should be involved early in and throughout the process
3. *Bypassing the technology* setup provided by the data and IT offices to capture demand for data products across the enterprise. This would create silos of demand across the enterprise and hinder the creation of appropriate data products that could be adopted across the enterprise. Structured change management is, therefore, essential to prevent this. The data office should lead it in collaboration with the business leaders

---

*3.2.3.1.2 Define the Data Product*   In this step, the data producer defines how the data product will be used to fulfill the requirements in scope. The required data intensity, i.e., QCS requirements for the data product, is also defined. The data producer, the data consumers, and the data office collaborate to define the data contract required for the data product. Based on the EAV of the use cases the data product would fulfill, the overall EAV for the data product is also assessed at this stage.

Continuing with the example, the data producer, i.e., the customer information data domain for the "regional customer segmentation" data product, collaborates with the data office and the data consumers, such as the brand manager and the supply chain operations team, to describe the in-scope business use cases. These may be improving the promotional program's effectiveness, supply chain planning, and product design and packaging. The EAV for this data product would be an aggregate of the EAV of each use case, such as a 10% additional revenue impact from the promotional program, a 5% reduction in inventory carrying cost, and 5% additional revenues from the improved product design and packaging. Finally, the data contract terms are discussed between the stakeholders and defined by the data producer.

Let us now consider the potential pitfalls to watch out for during this process step. These have been provided in Table 3.16.

*3.2.3.1.3 Design the Data Product*   The design specification for the data product is developed in this step. The design specification should be developed iteratively. It involves determining the composition of the data product, such as the attributes of the data product, based on the

TABLE 3.16   Potential Pitfalls during the Define Process Step

1. *Lack of participation from data consumers.* This might result in defining a data product that does not align with the needs of data consumers, resulting in poor adoption when the data product is available for use. It might also result in a data contract getting defined in such a way that the data consumers are not able to accept. The data product will not be used in such a situation
2. *Not collaborating with the data office.* This may result in a narrow definition of a new data product and data contract, limiting the possibility of its reuse for other data products
3. *Not using a framework for business value determination.* This might result in different data consumers giving values of expected business benefits based on gut feelings or vague assumptions. The data value team from the supporting layer should be leveraged for this exercise

definition of the data product. This step also involves determining the DFBs that can be used to produce the data product. In exceptional situations, if DFBs are unavailable, raw data might need to be used due to the unavailability of the required foundation blocks or the time to build those. If raw data is also unavailable, feedback must be provided to the raw data layer so that the required raw data can be urgently sourced. The EKG should be leveraged to gather information about the availability of DFBs or raw data and to gather contextual information on the data product to be designed. The design specification also details the terms in the data contract that would apply to the data product. Based on the details of the data contract, the design specification also specifies the workflow to be followed when exceptions happen, such as when a specific term in the data contract is violated. The design specification defines the role and responsibilities of stakeholders involved in developing and deploying the data product in the next steps of the 5D process. The design specification also mentions the usage metrics that need to be captured in the consumption process of the data product. With guidance from the data office, the data product must be designed to promote interoperability and reusability of the data product (refer to the five principles for the data pillar presented in Figure 2.3). At this stage, the design also includes a potential data modeling exercise to detail the specifications. The design should include implementation details to guide the "develop" process step. Based on this, the required technology components are leveraged. Finally, the KPIs for the data product are also captured in the design specifications.

The design specification will form the basis for developing the data product in the next step of the 5D process.

Continuing with the example, the design includes data product attributes such as customers' demographic details, geographic information, and buying behavior based on the data product's definition. The "regional customer segmentation" data product can leverage the "customer 360" DFB, which contains all information about individual customers. KPIs such as unique daily access by the data consumers are identified for the data consumption process.

Before proceeding to the next process step, let us examine the potential pitfalls during the design process step. These have been provided in Table 3.17.

TABLE 3.17   Potential Pitfalls during the Design Process Step

---

1. *Delegating the responsibility of creating the design specification to the data office.* Even though the data producer needs to collaborate with the data office to create the design specification, the responsibility must remain with the data producer. Based on the business function, the data producer would have the best understanding of the use of the data product in the business processes, the data intensity (i.e., QCS requirements) to be fulfilled, and the business context of the data. The data office may guide the data producer to the relevant data intelligence layer assets to be used and/or the data architecture knowledge

2. *Delegating the responsibility of creating the design specification to the IT office.* Although collaboration with the IT office is needed for the data producer to create the design specification, the responsibility must remain with the data producer. For instance, the IT office can guide the choice of virtualizing or physically persisting a data product based on the underlying performance capabilities of the technology landscape. The data office should also be consulted to guide the data product's consistency, reusability, and interoperability

3. *Not taking an iterative approach to developing the design specification.* An iterative approach enables the data producer and the data office to initially cater to the demand of some data consumers, thereby providing fast value to the business. Subsequently, the demand from other data consumers could be met iteratively

---

*3.2.3.1.4 Develop the Data Product*   Data product development is done in this step based on the design specification. Data products are to be produced from DFBs. In exceptional situations, raw data might need to be processed and transformed due to the unavailability of required DFBs or time to build those. This step also involves performing activities to meet the terms of the data contract, e.g., checking and improving data quality, and protecting sensitive data. Enabling activities such as auditing and logging metrics and data observability notifications are also performed. For performing these activities, artifacts developed in the supporting layer must be leveraged to enable standardization and scaling of the data product development process. Enterprises that are low in data maturity may need to involve the data and IT offices to develop the data products. In higher-maturity enterprises with self-service capabilities, data producers execute this step. Chapter 4 delves into the data maturity journey.

Continuing the example, the "regional customer segmentation" data product is developed on the basis of transforming the relevant attributes from the "customer 360" DFB. The data contract contains relevant terms such as the accuracy of the customer segments, hiding specific customer

TABLE 3.18    Potential Pitfalls during the Develop Process Step

| |
|---|
| 1. *Delegating the responsibility of developing the data product to the data and IT offices.* The data producer has the best view of the design of the data product. Development of the data product must adhere to the design. The data producer must treat the data and IT offices as resources that could help them during the development of the data product. The responsibility of developing data products must remain with the data producer |
| 2. *Not leveraging artifacts from the supporting layer*, such as the data quality libraries, data engineering templates, data contract APIs, and usage logging frameworks, might result in nonstandardized data products that are not reusable or interoperable. Also, when the artifacts are unused, more time and effort are consumed in developing data products |
| 3. *Not involving the data consumers while testing the data product* as per the design specification. The data consumers understand the data in the data product, the use cases that need it, and the data contract in scope for the data product. They must be involved in testing the data product during the development process |

names and addresses and checking that the data is not older than a day. Data engineering and governance activities are performed to meet and test the terms of the data contract.

Let us now consider the potential pitfalls to watch out for during this process step. These have been provided in Table 3.18.

*3.2.3.1.5 Deploy the Data Product*    This step makes the data product available for consumption and gathers feedback from the data consumers.

After executing the prerequisite activities, the data producer publishes the data product along with the metadata information and contract terms of the data product. The data producer should leverage a checklist provided by the data office to confirm that all the prerequisites are completed before publishing the data products. Before the data product is published, the data producer should perform the lifecycle management activities such as data product versioning. Data consumers may still be using older versions of data products. After the data product is published, the data office and the data producer promote it and monitor its usage metrics. Feedback on the data product from the data consumers is also gathered. The improvement feedback is provided as input for the next iteration of the 5D process.

Continuing with the example, the "regional customer segmentation" data product is checked against criteria such as description, scope, usage purpose, and data delivered through the product. All terms of the data product are also verified. The data product is then published and marketed for consumption. Feedback is captured, such as the data product missing data for some specific regions, which can be part of the next iteration.

TABLE 3.19    Potential Pitfalls during the Deploy Process Step

1. *A data producer's work is considered done when a data product is deployed.* A data product is successful only when the data consumers adopt it, and it delivers business value after deployment. The data products should be promoted and marketed to the communities of data consumers. This promotion could be done through videos, newsletters, success stories, or other marketing content. The data producer and the data office must collaborate to continue promoting the data product after deployment

2. *Not actioning on feedback received from data consumers.* Feedback must be gathered and provided as input for the next iteration of the 5D process. Missing the feedback would lead to dissatisfaction among the data consumers, and adoption would decline over time

Let us examine the potential pitfalls during the "deploy" process step. These have been provided in Table 3.19.

After a data product is deployed, it delivers business value only when consumed.

> **Food for Thought:** *Will your enterprise wait to produce "perfect" data products or improve them iteratively?*

Let us now delve into the process of consuming data products.

### 3.2.3.2 Consumption of Data Products through the FRAAU Process
Consuming data products involves the following FRAAU process steps as depicted in Figure 3.14: Find, request, approve, access, and use data products. The core objective is to enable self-service and the ease of use for data consumers while providing them with governed access to the data products.

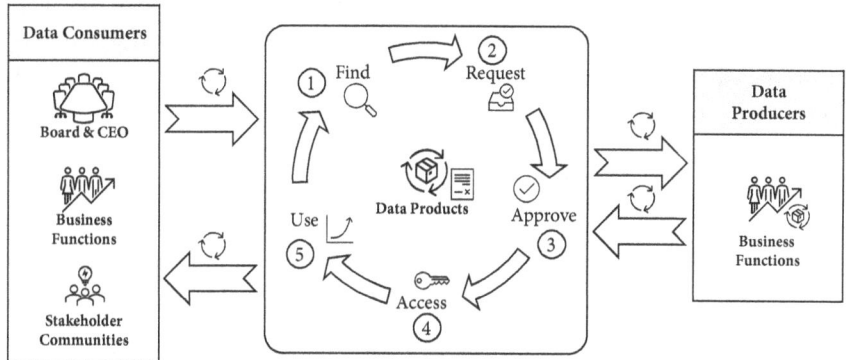

FIGURE 3.14    The FRAAU Process for Consuming Data Products.

To illustrate the FRAAU process, let us continue with the example of the "regional customer segmentation" data product in the retail consumer brand enterprise.

*3.2.3.2.1 Find a Data Product*   In this step, data consumers search for data products required for their use cases. Then, they confirm that the terms in the associated data contract fulfill their required data intensity and purpose of use. If changes are needed, they create change requests to the relevant data producer. If the data consumers do not find any data product that could serve their use case, they submit their demand for new data products, which goes as inputs to the demand capture step of the 5D process.

In the example, a brand manager looking for regional customer segmentation data can search and find the relevant data product. Once they find the "regional customer segmentation" data product, they review the associated data contract. Therein, it is mentioned that the regional data is refreshed daily. However, the brand manager needs this information updated every hour to analyze the performance of the regional social media campaign. The brand manager creates a change request for the customer information data domain data producer to update the refresh frequency in the data contract and update the data product accordingly.

*3.2.3.2.2 Request the Data Product*   In this step, data consumers request the identified data products. While placing the request, the data consumer provides information on the purpose of use and the EAV from using the data product. They also confirm that they will adhere to the data contract.

Continuing with the example, the brand manager creates a request to access the "regional customer segmentation" data product. The purpose of use is provided as a regional social media campaign analysis. The EAV from using the data product is provided as a 10% additional revenue impact from the campaign. The data consumer also confirms that they will adhere to the data contract. The request is then raised.

*3.2.3.2.3 Approve the Request*   In this step, the requests from the data consumer are either approved or denied. The approval request may be directed to the data producers or data product owners appointed by the data producers. Based on the information provided through the request, the approvers must determine if the data consumers' requests can be approved. The primary checks in this step would be from authentication and authorization perspectives, i.e., whether the data consumers are verified as valid users and are authorized to access the data contained in the data products, as per the policies linked to the data contract. Enterprises may require multiple approvals for specific data products based on the criticality or sensitivity of data. A balance should be considered between the approval levels versus the lead time for approval, as delays in approval would negatively impact the RV and time-to-value from the data products.

Continuing with the example, the brand manager who placed the request to access the "regional customer segmentation" data product is authenticated as a verified and valid user. It is also confirmed that the brand manager has the authorization to access the data for its specific region. The customer information data domain data producer then approves, noting that data for other regions must not be shared with the brand manager.

*3.2.3.2.4 Access the Data Product*   In this process step, the data consumers access the data products after receiving approval. They gain access to only the authorized data as per the access policies linked to the data contract. In enterprises with automated policy-based fine-grained access management technology, data consumers would automatically get access only to the authorized data based on their roles and policies; unauthorized data would be automatically masked, anonymized, or hidden. Otherwise, the approval would need to be routed to the IT office to mask, anonymize, or remove unauthorized data and then provide access to the requested data products to the data consumers.

Continuing the example, the brand manager gets access to the required data in the "regional customer segmentation" data product. Leveraging an automated policy-based fine-grained access management technology, customers' "date of birth" field gets anonymized, but the age segments are retained.

*3.2.3.2.5 Use the Data Product*   In this step, after receiving access to the data products, the data consumers use them to perform their tasks/execute their use cases while adhering to the data contracts. Also, in this step, after using the data products, the data consumers confirm or update the earlier communicated RV and EAV for the data products. The data office also captures the usage KPIs for the data products. Such KPIs would be critical for the data office to track the business value delivered by the data pillar, report to the Board and the CEO, and secure further funding for the data pillar.

TABLE 3.20   Potential Pitfalls during the Consumption Process

---

1. *Finding a data product is complicated.* It is the first step in the consumption process. A critical pitfall will be if findability is not universal across the enterprise, such as when different business units create their data marketplaces for publishing their data products. This would likely create confusion and bottlenecks that hinder the rest of the consumption process and significantly affect the realization of business value from data products
2. *The long time it takes to approve.* If there are multilevel approvals and they are time-consuming, this may negatively impact their use case and frustrate the data consumers. This might result in them finding alternate ways to access the data
3. *Not capturing usage metrics.* It can result in missed opportunities to increase business value from the data product. It also results in feedback from usages not being tracked or acted upon

---

While using the data products, the data consumers might need changes to the data products and the terms in the data contracts. They might discover gaps like data quality issues in the data products. The data consumers would provide such feedback to the data producers and the data office, which would be considered as inputs for the next iteration of the 5D process for updating the existing data product.

Continuing with the example, after using the "regional customer segmentation" data product, the brand manager confirms an 8% revenue increase due to the social media campaign – this would be the updated RV from the data product. The data office also captures the usage metrics, which show that brand managers in multiple regions use the data product an average of three times a day.

*Potential Pitfalls during Consumption of Data Products*
Let us now consider the potential pitfalls to watch out for during the consumption process. These have been provided in Table 3.20.

> **Food for Thought:** *How can you remove any hurdles for data consumers during the consumption process and maximize the usage of data products?*

### 3.2.4 Technology Capabilities Enabling the Data Products Layer

Technology components serve the needs of data producers and consumers to enable business value delivery through the data products layer.

Technology components, including AI, would help automate the 5D and FRAAU processes, scale the adoption of data products, and improve productivity and time-to-value for the data producers and consumers. Technology components must be agile, composable, and scalable to cater to data producers' and consumers' varied, changing, and growing data needs based on business dynamics.

Let us delve into the key technology components for the data products layer.

- **Enterprise Data Marketplace:** It is a digital gateway for data consumers to execute their FRAAU process. Think of it as your favorite e-commerce store, wherein the producers or suppliers publish their products, and you find and shop for your required products. Similarly, in the enterprise data marketplace, data producers publish their data products that are ready to be consumed, and data consumers find and request access to the data products in a self-service manner to fulfill their needs.

   Data producers can also leverage the enterprise data marketplace to collaborate and track the execution of the 5D process. The marketplace also enables data producers to manage the lifecycle of data products and facilitates collaboration and feedback sharing between the communities of data producers and data consumers.

   Enterprises may open the data marketplace, in a governed manner, to external data consumers and providers to enhance collaboration with them.

- **Data Contract Management:** It enables the execution and automation of data contract lifecycle management and the leverage of data contracts during the 5D and FRAAU processes.

- **Data Engineering:** It enables data transformation of the DFBs to produce or update data products during the 5D process. In exceptional situations, raw data might need to be processed and transformed due to the unavailability of required DFBs or the time required to build those. Optionally, enterprises may choose a *Data Virtualization* technology component to leverage the DFBs.

- **Data Governance:** This would be the same technology component leveraged for the supporting layer, including sub-components for data quality and observability, risk management, and access management. These components would be leveraged across the 5D and FRAAU processes.

- **Data Storage and Computing:** These technology components consist of the data storage component, where the data contained in the data product are stored, and the computing engine component, which processes and combines data to produce the data product. These components must be capable of storing and computing structured, semi-structured, and unstructured data. These components must also provide the required performance by scaling horizontally and vertically independently to meet the "speed" dimension of the data intensity requirements from the data products.

*Potential Pitfalls with Technologies in the Data Products Layer*

Let us now consider the potential pitfalls in the technologies for the data products layer. These have been provided in Table 3.21.

## 3.2.5 KPIs for the Data Products Layer

Let us look at example KPIs for the data products layer. These have been provided in Table 3.22.

Next, let us delve into the data intelligence layer of the DOM.

TABLE 3.21    Potential Pitfalls with Technologies in the Data Products Layer

---

1. *Not leveraging the enterprise data marketplace.* A critical pitfall would be if some communities of data consumers leverage other modes of data consumption instead of the deployed enterprise data marketplace. The CDO must collaborate with the COO and leaders of the business functions to identify the root causes and resolve them
2. *User experience unsuitable for business users.* The overall user experience from the technology components should be suitable for business users, as data producers and consumers primarily come from business functions
3. *Establishing technology without the required people and processes.* Although technologies will significantly aid in automating and scaling the usage of data products, required people and processes must also be set up along with these technologies

---

TABLE 3.22   Example KPIs to Measure in the Data Products Layer

| KPI | KPI Calculation | Description |
|---|---|---|
| These KPIs help understand the *relevance* of a data product | | |
| EAV for a data product | Sum of the EAV from all use cases a data product serves | Tracks the business value to be expected from a data product |
| RV for a data product | Sum of the RV from all use cases a data product serves | Tracks the realized business value from a data product |
| Daily users for a data product | Total number of users who access a data product daily | Tracks the usage of a data product |
| These KPIs help understand the *adoption* of the data products layer | | |
| Number of data products | Total number of published data products | Tracks the growth in data products |
| Daily users for all data products | Total number of users who access all data products daily | Tracks the growth in usage of data products |
| Average user rating | Average overall user rating for a data product | Tracks whether the data products are delivering the expectations of the users |
| These KPIs help understand the *efficiency* of processes in the data products layer | | |
| Average time to produce data products | Time duration between the start of the "demand capture" step and the end of the "deploy" step in the 5D process for all data products | Tracks the lead time to complete the 5D process |
| Data contract violations | Total number of reported data contract violations over a period | Tracks adherence to the data contracts |
| Time to get access to data products | Time duration between requesting access to a data product and getting access | Tracks the time-to-value for data consumers |

## 3.3  DATA INTELLIGENCE LAYER

The data intelligence layer (see Figure 3.15) builds and delivers the DFBs and the EKG. Raw data is processed and transformed to create the DFBs, and information on business and technical metadata and their relationships is used to create the EKG.

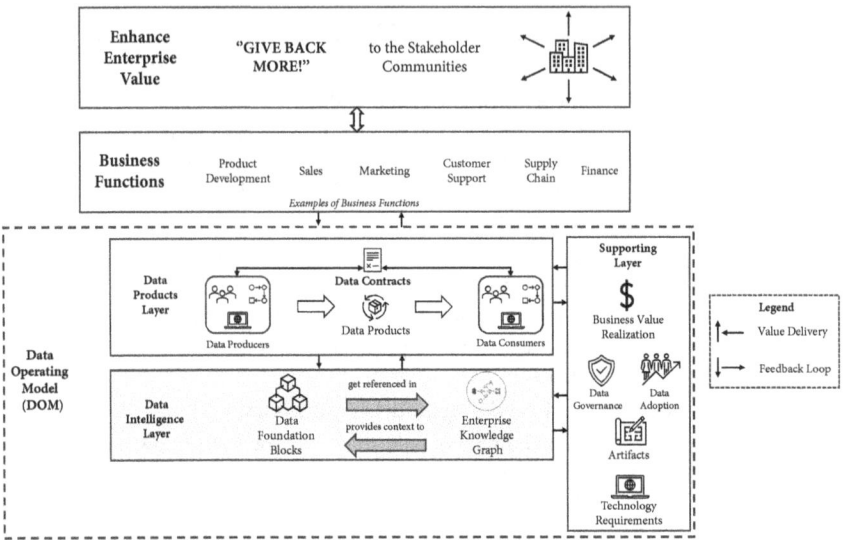

FIGURE 3.15   Data Intelligence Layer with the DFBs and the EKG.

*The data intelligence layer serves as the "brain" of the DOM. It provides the "context of data" by interconnecting metadata across the people, process, technology, and data landscape and accelerates data maturity.*

The data intelligence layer, performing the critical functions of providing the building blocks of data and its context, must stay steps ahead of immediate data needs. It must anticipate potential future requirements and be ready to support them. For example, expecting the enterprise to leverage AI at scale for various business use cases, the data intelligence layer must include relevant unstructured data in the DFBs and their context in the EKG.

Let us understand how to establish the data intelligence layer with the required people, processes, and technologies.

### 3.3.1  People Capabilities Enabling the Data Intelligence Layer

The following execution teams are set up in the data office for the data intelligence layer (See Figure 3.16).

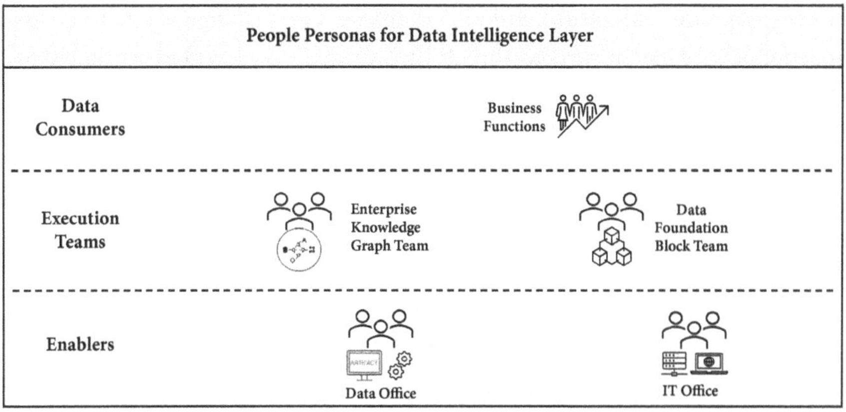

FIGURE 3.16   People Personas for the Data Intelligence Layer.

### 3.3.1.1 EKG Team

The EKG team is responsible for building, enhancing, and delivering the EKG. This involves documenting and maintaining all metadata reflected in the EKG. This team collaborates with different stakeholders in the business functions and IT to detail each metadata module in the EKG. The business stakeholders help define the key business terms, metrics, processes, and policies. For instance, a domain owner in a business function would help coordinate with the EKG team to define and manage these metadata modules. The IT stakeholders help harvest and maintain the technical metadata from the technology landscape. They also help develop and maintain the technical metadata lineage.

### 3.3.1.2 DFB Team

The DFB team builds new DFBs and manages the lifecycle of the existing ones. This team leverages the data engineering team in the data office to perform the required data engineering activities.

### 3.3.1.3 Data Intelligence Layer Enabler – Data Office

The data office teams in the supporting layer play critical roles in the adoption and governance of the EKG and the DFBs, as well as in value realization from them. Adopting the EKG is critical for the stakeholders to understand the context of data and make accurate data-enabled operational and strategic decisions. Adopting the DFBs is key to improving the time-to-value for the data producers and consumers. When adoption increases, value realization will also increase. Governance is key to ensuring that authorized access to the DFBs and EKG is provided while ensuring that the growth in the DFBs and enhancement of the EKG happen systematically and in a controlled manner.

### 3.3.1.4 Data Intelligence Layer Enabler – IT Office

The IT office deploys and maintains the technology components required for the data intelligence layer. The IT office also helps the EKG team extract the technical metadata and technical lineage from the data sources. To meet the required data intensity and improve data maturity, the IT office must deploy technologies, including AI, that enable tailored user experiences for data producers and drive self-service and automation. These technology components must be aligned with the technology and data architectures; technology and data architects play vital roles in aligning the technology architecture with the data architecture.

Figure 3.17 explains the collaboration between different teams for the data intelligence layer. We have reused the domains in the EKG (see Figure 2.11). Linked to the product domain, the DFB team builds the product foundation block. This team collaborates with various business functions that provide parts of the required data. For instance, the R&D business function provides

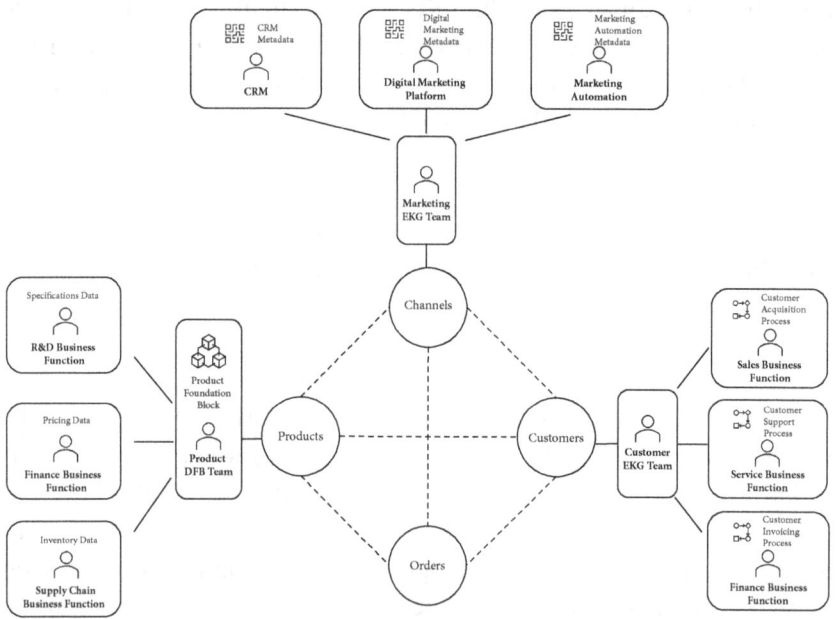

FIGURE 3.17   Roles and Collaborations in the Data Intelligence Layer.

the product specification data, the finance business function provides the pricing data, the supply chain business function provides the inventory data, and so on. All information is combined into the unified product foundation block. Linked to the customer domain, the EKG team collects the business metadata, such as process metadata from different business functions like sales, service, and finance. Linked to the marketing domain, the EKG team collects the technical metadata, such as those from CRM, digital marketing, and marketing automation applications.

> *Effective collaboration is key to succeeding with the data intelligence layer, enabling the "brain" to develop, and its power can be harnessed.*

### 3.3.1.5 Setup of the Data Intelligence Layer Teams

Like other DOM layers, an enterprise's critical decision is whether the data intelligence layer will be executed in a centralized, federated, or decentralized setup. Table 3.23 shares high-level perspectives on the differences between these setups.

TABLE 3.23  Setup Options for Producing Data Products

| Theme | Centralized | Federated | Decentralized |
|---|---|---|---|
| Meaning | The EKG and DFB teams, as part of the central data office, build and maintain the data intelligence layer assets while consulting the business functions when needed | The EKG and DFB teams in the data office build and maintain core domain elements, and the business functions manage some metadata modules | EKG: Business functions create and maintain their respective EKG metadata modules, while the data office is responsible for the enterprise-level EKG DFB: Business functions create and maintain their DFBs, with the data office as a facilitator |
| Enterprise example | An SMB enterprise that runs in a lean setup or a large enterprise in the early stage of maturity of the data intelligence layer | An enterprise with varied data maturity across business functions requires a strong core data office team to guide it | A large enterprise with several business function/operating units that function independently |
| DOM readiness | The initial phase of the data intelligence layer is operational with a handful of domains represented in the EKG | A high volume of data products is created in multiple domains and is represented in the EKG | A high volume of data products across business functions leveraging their DFBs and a mature EKG |

*Potential Pitfalls while Setting Up the Data Intelligence Layer Teams*
While establishing the data intelligence layer teams, the CDO may experience multiple pitfalls and needs to be prepared to address those. Table 3.24 provides potential pitfalls and suggestions to address those.

### 3.3.2 Process Capabilities Enabling the Data Intelligence Layer

Figure 3.18 depicts the processes for developing the EKG and DFBs in the data intelligence layer.

TABLE 3.24   Potential Pitfalls while Setting Up the Data Intelligence Layer Teams

1. *Lack of skilled resources required for the DFB and EKG teams.* People in these teams need to understand business well across multiple domains while understanding technology applications. Finding such skilled resources may be challenging, or it may take time to develop such skills. The CDO should consider onboarding stakeholders from the business functions who will likely understand the technology application used in their business functions

2. *Lack of business involvement.* The EKG cannot be enhanced without the active involvement of the business functions. To continuously build and enhance the EKG, it is necessary to secure the continued participation of the stakeholders in the business functions

3. *Siloed way of working.* The people in the data intelligence layer have a risk of working in siloes across multiple data domains, resulting in a fragmented data intelligence layer. The CDO must actively work with the DFB and EKG teams in the data office to mitigate this from happening

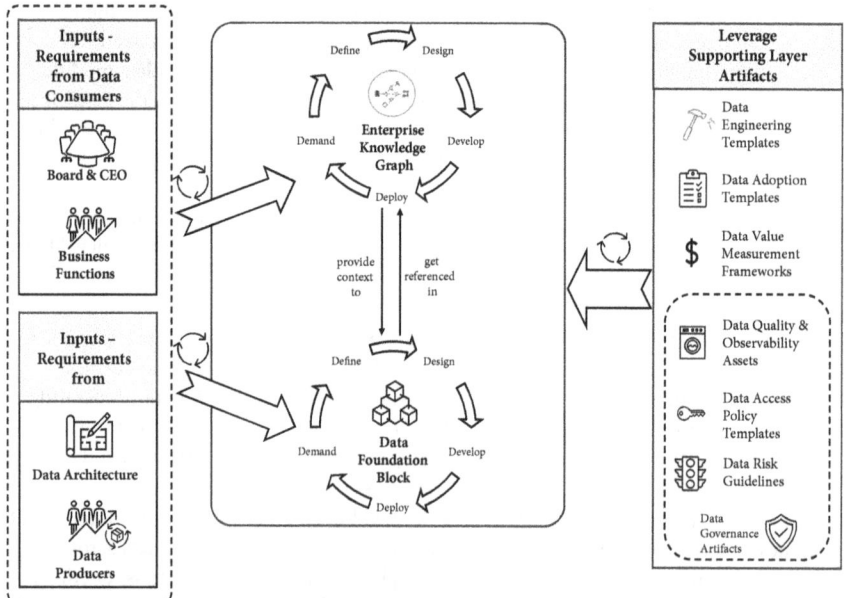

FIGURE 3.18   Processes for Developing the EKG and DFBs in the Data Intelligence Layer.

The inputs to the processes include the requirements of the use cases from the producers of data products and data consumers and the data architecture, which provides the guidelines and interaction flows to deploy the data intelligence layer. Given the dynamic nature of the inputs and the need for accelerated time-to-value, an iterative approach to building the DFBs and EKG is recommended.

### 3.3.2.1 Process for Developing the EKG

The EKG consists of two key sub-elements:

- The first sub-element is metadata modules. These include glossaries, policies, processes, people, technical metadata, and lineage. Each metadata module's development will follow its "5D" process, similar to the supporting layer's artifacts and the data products layer's data product production process.

- The second sub-element is the interrelationships between those metadata modules and the DFBs for each domain, such as customers, products, suppliers, and partners.

The orchestration of the development of the EKG mimics a "microservices[6] architecture." It requires defining the EKG's core elements, i.e., the metadata modules. This can then be designed and developed in parallel. Similarly, the interrelationships between the metadata modules can also be designed and developed in parallel to the metadata modules. The execution of all sub-processes is standardized and accelerated using the supporting layer's artifacts.

### 3.3.2.2 Process for Developing DFBs

Each DFB will independently follow its "5D" process. The DFB team executes the "demand capture," "define," and "design" steps. Producers of data products provide input to the "demand capture" step for their immediate and future needs. In the "define" step, the stakeholder responsible for the domain linked to the DFB aligns with the respective business functions to ensure that all requirements are captured for the DFB. Interfacing the DFB with the EKG is critical during the "design" step. The data architecture team and the data modeling exercise aid this process, such as by creating and/or extending enterprise identifiers to connect the DFBs. The "develop" step requires the data engineering team to transform the raw data to the DFB as designed. In the "deploy" step, the DFBs are deployed in the technology component for storage and published in the data marketplace. After the "deploy" step, the DFBs are physically linked to the EKG. Figure 2.18 depicts this. The EKG thus provides a rich context to the DFBs. During the 5D process, appropriate artifacts from the supporting layer, such as the data quality and observability rules, and data engineering templates are leveraged. While reusing such templates, feedback is provided to the supporting layer for the required improvements in the artifacts.

### 3.3.2.3 Process for Consuming the EKG and the DFBs

A robust and secure consumption process (see Figure 3.19) for the data intelligence layer is key for the users to derive value. The EKG and the DFBs can be consumed through the FRAAU or FAU (find, access, and use) process. The FRAAU process is similar to the consumption process for the data products layer (see Figure 3.14). The FAU process eliminates the "request" and "approve" process steps. Whether the FRAAU or FAU process is chosen depends primarily on data sensitivity and whether any policies need to be adhered to. The "request" and "approve" process steps can also be automated to provide faster access while governing access

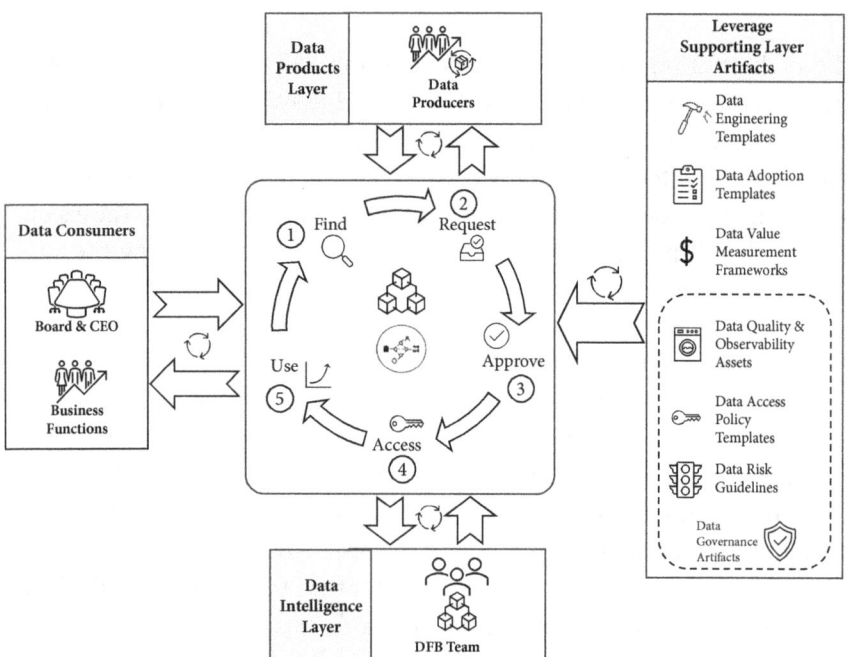

FIGURE 3.19 Processes for Consuming the EKG and DFBs from the Data Intelligence Layer.

to the EKG and DFBs. Management of required access restrictions or anonymization of specific data or metadata in the DFBs and EKG will be done during the "access" process step by leveraging the data access management technology component. The EKG also enables data access automation with fine-grained access management leveraging the data access management technology component. The users of the data intelligence layer can be broad, including the Board and CEO, CxOs, business functions, data office, and IT office.

Finally, based on the consumption, the data value team measures the KPIs and provides feedback to the data office on the value of the EKG and DFBs, which acts as input for subsequent iterations to build or enhance them.

> **Food for Thought:** *How will you scale the data intelligence layer in a controlled manner?*

*Potential Pitfalls in the Data Intelligence Layer Processes*
Let us now delve into the potential pitfalls and mitigations to watch out for in the processes for the data intelligence layer. These have been provided in Table 3.25.

## 3.3.3 Technology Capabilities Enabling the Data Intelligence Layer
Let us delve into the technology components required for the EKG and DFBs.

TABLE 3.25    Potential Pitfalls in the Processes for the Data Intelligence Layer

1. *Bottlenecks in the development of the EKG.* The EKG has multiple interdependent metadata modules, like the technical and business metadata. Each metadata module will follow its 5D process. These individual processes must be executed in parallel and in sync with each other. The EKG team must have a skillful program manager to eliminate the bottlenecks and continuously update the EKG. The CDO and their relationship with the CxOs and leaders of the business functions should be leveraged to resolve bottlenecks

2. *No business and/or IT involvement.* The business functions and the IT office may consider the data intelligence layer outside their scope of responsibility. This requires a structured change management program, and their involvement in each process step is critical

3. *Not considering potential future demand.* The data intelligence layer thrives on reuse and a broader set of use cases than data products. It is, therefore, essential to understand potential future demand and design it for the future

- **Enterprise Knowledge Graph:** The EKG is set up on a graph database. The metadata modules in the EKG, which contain business metadata, technical metadata, and data lineage, can be interfaced with a data catalog technology component. Leveraging AI technology components can automate metadata harvesting and interfacing with those in the EKG.

- **Data Foundation Blocks:** The DFBs leverage the core underlying storage technology components like a database, data warehouse, data lake, data lakehouse, document database, and NoSQL database extending to unstructured data storage. This is because DFBs can contain structured, semi-structured, and unstructured data. Enterprise IDs are used to link across these underlying storage components. The DFBs can also contain data management technology components such as master data management (MDM) or reference data management (RDM), which interact with the raw data layer and applications. The ready-to-consume DFBs are published in the data marketplace for the data producers in the data products layer to find, access, and use them for building data products. Leveraging AI technology components can automate steps involved in building and consuming DFBs.

*A "data catalog" is critical to understanding the data context provided by the EKG, and a "data marketplace" is critical to leverage DFBs.*

- **Reused Technology Components from the Supporting Layer:** The EKG and DFBs are augmented with technology components reused from the supporting layer. It includes the data engineering technology component that helps convert raw data into DFBs. It can also transform and parse unstructured and semi-structured data into a structured form. The data quality and observability technology component helps clean data and proactively monitor data discrepancies. The data access management component enables governed access to the EKG and DFBs and provides information on users' access. The data value technology component provides information to the data office and business stakeholders on the KPIs for the data intelligence layer.

*Potential Pitfalls with Technologies in the Data Intelligence Layer*
Let us now delve into the potential pitfalls to watch out for in the technology components of the data intelligence layer. These have been provided in Table 3.26.

TABLE 3.26   Potential Pitfalls with Technologies in the Data Intelligence Layer

1. *Lack of support for semi-structured and unstructured data.* As use cases increasingly demand semi-structured and unstructured data and metadata, the technology components must support them
2. *Lack of metadata lineage capability.* The data intelligence layer is the glue to the rest of the DOM layers. It is, therefore, essential for the EKG to track end-to-end lineage
3. *Technology components are not composable.* To provide a seamless user experience for data producers and consumers, the technology components deployed in the data intelligence layer must be composable, i.e., interface well and enable each other
4. *User experience unsuitable for business users.* The overall user experience from the technology components should enable the business users, as data producers primarily come from the business functions

TABLE 3.27   Example KPIs for the Data Intelligence Layer

| KPI | KPI Calculation | Description |
|---|---|---|
| These KPIs help understand the *adoption* of the data intelligence layer | | |
| Daily active users (DAU) | Total daily users for EKG and DFBs | Tracks the usage of the EKG and DFBs |
| Reusability of a DFB | *Average number of times a DFB is reused to create data products* | *Tracks the reuse of DFBs* |
| These KPIs help understand the *efficiency* of the data intelligence layer | | |
| EKG freshness | Current date minus the last updated date | Tracks the freshness of the EKG |
| EKG richness | Number of domains or number of metadata modules | Tracks the richness of the EKG and its growth |
| DFBs – average time to produce | The time duration between the start of the "demand capture" step and the end of the "deploy" step in the 5D process | Tracks the average lead time to develop DFBs |

## 3.3.4  KPIs for the Data Intelligence Layer

Let us look at examples of KPIs for the data intelligence layer. These have been provided in Table 3.27.

The data intelligence layer, with its rich data and context of data, will be a strategic differentiator for enterprises when it is leveraged extensively by technical and business users. Conversational AI interfaces enable business users to interact with and benefit from this layer. Scaling the usage of this layer would be key for attaining the highest level of data maturity. Chapter 4 delves into the maturity journey.

*Conversational AI interfaces are like the smart assistants on your phone, enabling an easy interface to derive value from the data intelligence layer. This interface allows users to provide information to enrich the layer further.*

Now that we have discussed the data intelligence layer; its value; and what it should comprise regarding people, processes, and technologies, let us look at the layer providing data to the data products layer and the data intelligence – the raw data layer.

## 3.4 RAW DATA LAYER

The raw data layer (see Figure 3.20) collects raw data and metadata from operational, transactional, and analytical data sources, both internal and external, for enterprises. External data from Bloomberg,[7] Dun & Bradstreet,[8] or other third-party providers is also considered raw data. Enterprises already collect raw data; however, the raw data might be scattered across the enterprises' data stores. Enterprises struggle to provide governed access to the raw data for use cases that need data with the required data intensity. The silos of raw data and the struggles with providing governed access with the required data intensity result in the underutilization of the raw data.

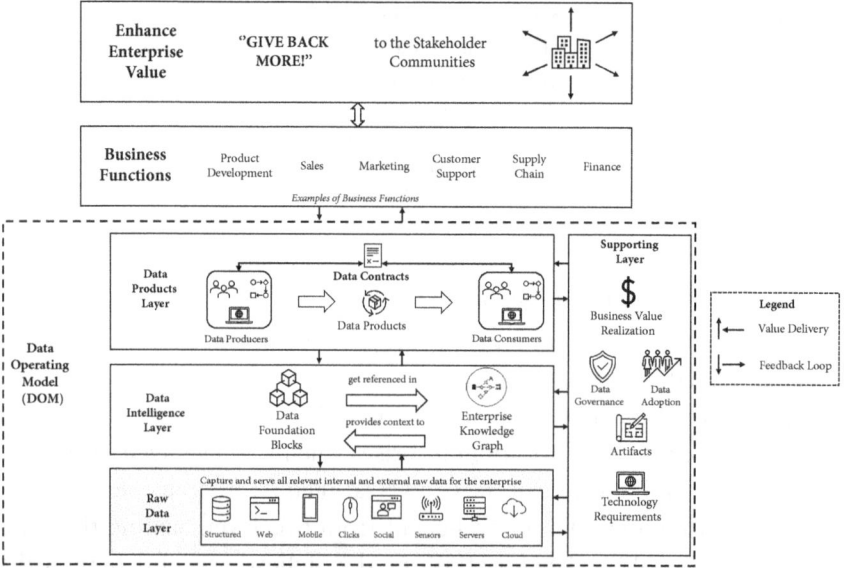

FIGURE 3.20  Raw Data Layer Capturing All Data for the Enterprise.

*The raw data layer is the foundation for the rest of the DOM. Its critical success factor is the "speed" of providing data required by the other DOM layers.*

The raw data layer plays the vital role of unifying the data silos by collecting all raw data, structured, semi-structured, and unstructured, from all data sources, internal and external to the enterprise. The technical metadata from the raw data layer is linked to the EKG from the data intelligence layer, enabling it to provide the context of data.

The raw data layer has two primary functions:

- Collect and provide raw data and metadata based on the requirements of producing DFBs. This would be a reactive approach to fulfill demand.

- Proactively collect and provide raw data and metadata to meet potential future requirements. The EKG guides toward that.

Let us now delve into how people, processes, and technologies should be set up for standardizing and scaling the usage of the raw data layer.

### 3.4.1 People Capabilities Enabling the Raw Data Layer

Figure 3.21 presents the people personas for the raw data layer.

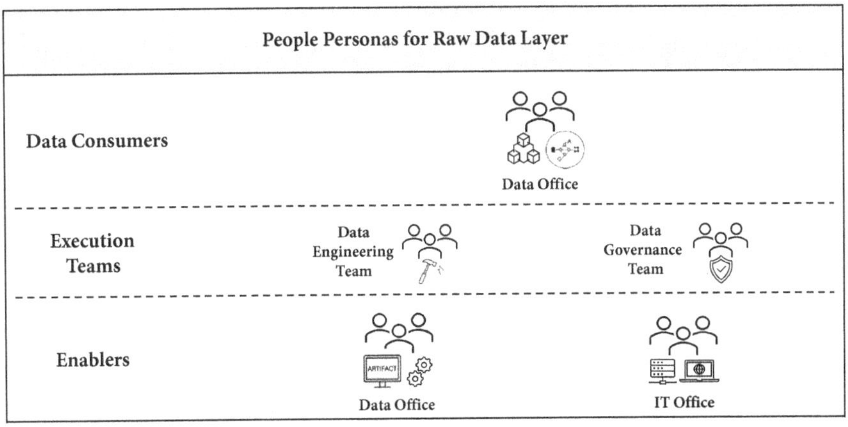

FIGURE 3.21 People Personas for the Raw Data Layer.

### 3.4.1.1 Data Consumers

The DFB team in the data office builds DFBs using raw data, and the EKG team links technical metadata from the raw data layer.

### 3.4.1.2 Execution Teams

The following execution teams are involved in the raw data layer:

- **Data Engineering Team:** This team in the data office collects and ingests, replicates, and/or virtualizes raw data based on an enterprise's data architecture decisions. This team leverages the artifacts provided by the supporting layer to improve its productivity and standardize its activities.

- **Data Governance Team:** This team in the data office enables governed access to raw data while fulfilling the required data intensity. This team relates to the data architecture to perform its activities. It also leverages the artifacts provided by the supporting layer to improve its productivity and standardize its activities.

### 3.4.1.3 Raw Data Layer Enabler – Data Office

- **Data Adoption Team:** This team in the data office collects the demand for raw data from the DFB team responsible for building the DFBs.

### 3.4.1.4 Raw Data Layer Enabler – IT Office

The IT office is critical in providing the technologies powering the raw data layer and ensuring their performance, stability, and scalability. The execution teams of the raw data layer interface with the IT architecture and operations teams of the IT office, which are responsible for the underlying technology applications and infrastructure.

### 3.4.1.5 Setup of the Raw Data Layer Teams

The raw data layer can be executed in a centralized, federated, or decentralized setup. Table 3.28 shows some high-level considerations for the same.

*Potential Pitfalls while Setting Up the Raw Data Layer Teams*
While setting up the raw data layer teams, the CDO may experience the multiple pitfalls and must be prepared to address those. Table 3.29 provides potential pitfalls and suggestions to address those.

TABLE 3.28  Setup of the Raw Data Layer Teams

| Theme | Centralized | Federated | Decentralized |
|---|---|---|---|
| Meaning | The execution teams in the central data office collect and govern raw data | The data office collects and governs the raw data required across the business functions, and the respective business functions collect and govern the raw data of specific business functions | Business functions collect and govern their respective raw data |
| Enterprise example | SMB enterprise or a large enterprise that manages raw data sources centrally | Large enterprise with varied data maturity across business functions and a central data office to guide them to leverage raw data | Large enterprise with business functions and/or operating entities functioning independently |
| Operationalization of DOM | Centrally managed supporting layer and data intelligence layer | Federated supporting layer and data intelligence layer | Decentralized supporting layer and data intelligence layer |

TABLE 3.29  Potential Pitfalls while Setting Up the Raw Data Layer Teams

1. *Lack of active involvement of the data consumers.* Without their participation, the raw data layer risks becoming a "data swamp"
2. *Lack of collaboration with the supporting layer teams.* Supporting layer artifacts enable the execution teams to scale the build-up and use of the raw data layer in a factory-like approach. Collaboration is critical for that
3. *Lack of collaboration with the IT office.* The execution teams should collaborate to ensure the required performance, stability, and scalability of the technology applications and infrastructure powering the raw data layer

## 3.4.2  Process Pillar Enabling the Raw Data Layer

Processes in the raw data layer enable enterprises to standardize, automate, and scale their activities for raw data.

We propose to reuse the "5D" process to make raw data available for consumption (see Figure 3.22). However, the raw data layer steps should be more straightforward in execution.

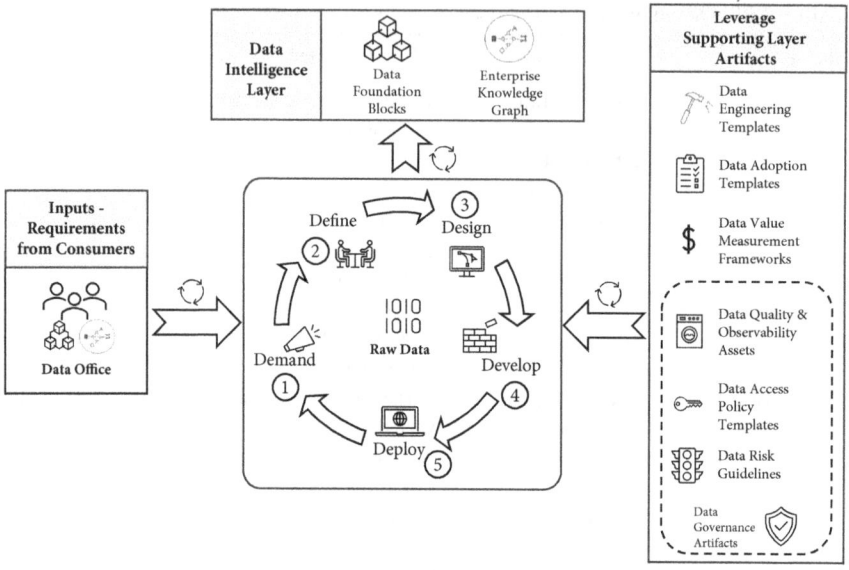

FIGURE 3.22    Process for Raw Data Layer and Making It Available for Consumption.

The following would be the scope of the process steps in this layer:

- **Demand Capture:** In this step, the demand for raw data is collected from the DFB team of the data intelligence layer. The demand should capture immediate and potential future needs based on the data strategy and architecture. The data adoption team in the data office drives this demand capture and collaboration.

- **Define:** In this step, the demand captured for the raw data is detailed, including information on the structured, semi-structured, and unstructured data needed and the required data intensity. The operational, transactional, and analytical data sources for the raw data in scope are defined. Leveraging the EKG, assessments are also performed to identify the additional raw data that needs to be sourced into the raw data layer.

- **Design:** In this step, the data engineering team designs the data flow, including the required data ingestion, transformation, and/or virtualization activities. Relevant data quality and data observability rules are specified. The technical metadata requirements are also designed. The design should be standardized on the basis of the type of data, data intensity requirements, and data volume.

- **Develop:** This step involves data engineering, computing, and storage activities. Technical metadata collection is also performed. The data governance team executes the required data quality and observability checks.

- **Deploy:** In this step, the IT office deploys the raw data to be consumed. The data office team promotes the availability of raw data for consumption and tracks usage and access patterns. Any relevant feedback and additional requirements are collected and fed back to the "demand capture" process step of the 5D process.

A critical process that may be overlooked in many enterprises is the consumption process for the raw data layer. Traditionally, the raw data layer contains varied data, and it is left to the downstream consumers to figure out how to access their required data. However, with the operationalization of the DOM and the criticality of the raw data for creating DFBs, a defined and structured consumption process for the raw data becomes essential.

We recommend reusing the FAU process for consumption. This is because the DFB and EKG teams in the data office consume raw data, which avoids the need to request and approve it. However, in the "access" step, the data governance team ensures that the DFB and EKG teams do not consume unauthorized data and metadata from the raw data layer.

*Potential Pitfalls in the Raw Data Layer Processes*
Let us now delve into the potential pitfalls and mitigations to watch out for in the raw data layer processes. These has been provided in Table 3.30.

TABLE 3.30   Potential Pitfalls in the Raw Data Layer Processes

1. *Reacting to current demand.* Speed of delivery is critical for the raw data layer to provide data to use cases and value across its consumers. The demand process should proactively consider future data needs by referencing the data strategy and architecture
2. *Not reusing design templates.* Another critical factor toward the speed of provisioning raw data is reusing the artifacts to design raw data processing
3. *Not incorporating feedback from consumers.* Consumers of raw data are critical in providing feedback regarding data intensity, performance, etc. These should be incorporated in subsequent process iterations

### 3.4.3 Technology Capabilities Enabling the Raw Data Layer

The technology components in the raw data layer depend on the enterprise's choices of technology and data architectures.

#### 3.4.3.1 Primary Technology Components

- *Data virtualization* component enables data to be captured from source applications without physically copying the data, enabling a dynamic view of the underlying source landscape.

- *Data ingestion* component allows data to be ingested into a data storage layer.

- *Data replication* component also serves the same purpose by replicating the data typically in near real time, with a latency usually in seconds.

- *Data storage* component may include a data lake, warehouse, lakehouse, etc.

- *Data computing* component can either be part of the data storage or a different component that helps ensure that data can be processed and/or consumed in a performant and scalable fashion.

- *Data catalog* component collects technology metadata from the raw data and links it to the EKG in the data intelligence layer.

> **Food for Thought:** *How can your enterprise balance the trade-offs between data virtualization and physical persistence, and between cost and performance?*

The technology components should be composable using standard interfaces like APIs. They should also facilitate a federated and/or decentralized setup. For instance, multiple data catalogs in different business functions/operating units may integrate with an enterprise-level data catalog for federation. Similarly, different data storage technologies might be present and be connected with a data virtualization component. These technology components should also embed AI functionalities such as automatic parsing for unstructured data.

The technology components should support the delicate balance of not impacting the operational performance of the source landscape while collecting the data in an optimized fashion to fulfill the data intensity requirements.

### 3.4.3.2 Supporting Layer's Technology Components

The technology components in the supporting layer can augment and add value to the raw data layer. For instance, the data engineering technology component may have out-of-the-box connectivity to the source applications, whose data must be ingested into the raw data layer. These tools, along with their artifacts, are reused in the raw data layer.

### Potential Pitfalls with Technologies in the Raw Data Layer

Let us now delve into the potential pitfalls to watch out for in the technology components of the raw data layer. These have been presented in Table 3.31.

### 3.4.4 KPIs for the Raw Data Layer

Let us look at examples of KPIs for the raw data layer. These have been provided in Table 3.32.

This chapter has covered how enterprises can establish data as a pillar of their operating model and how people, processes, and technology

TABLE 3.31    Potential Pitfalls with Technologies in the Raw Data Layer

1. *Lack of search capability.* An easy search interface should facilitate the raw data layer, enabling consumers to easily find and understand the existing raw data. Using a data catalog enables this with the required business and technology context
2. *Limited unstructured data support.* The technology components must support unstructured data formats to meet the requirements of use cases like leveraging AI at scale
3. *Lack of proactive cost optimization controls in place.* As the volume of data increases, resulting in rapidly increased storage and compute costs with a high number of consumers, the technology components should facilitate proactive cost optimization controls

TABLE 3.32    Example KPIs for the Raw Data Layer

| KPI | KPI Calculation | Description |
| --- | --- | --- |
| Average time to ingest | The time duration between the start of the "demand capture" step and the end of the "deploy" step in the 5D process | Tracks the time from demand capture till the actual deployment of raw data |
| Retrieval performance | Average time to retrieve the required raw data | Tracks the speed of processing raw data assets |
| Unavailability of raw data | Number of times a DFB producer is missing required raw data | Tracks proactive collection and processing of raw data based on potential future demand |

are critical in operationalizing the DOM. The layers of the DOM are also interdependent – the operationalization activities in one layer might necessitate activities in another. Audi's approach to operationalizing their DOM provides practical insights.

With the scope of activities required for the DOM, neither can it be operationalized in a short timeframe, such as a quarter, nor can it ever be considered a completed task. The DOM needs to evolve continuously to meet changing business needs. The CDO must plan to mature the DOM consistently to fulfill the dynamic demand for data from the use cases. Each enterprise is unique and so would be its maturity journey. The next chapter covers the maturity journey with multiple scenarios and approaches to measure the maturity level. It also covers Audi's case study to guide enterprises in understanding their maturity level and planning their maturity journey.

---

### 3.5 CASE STUDY: HOW DOES AUDI MAKE DATA A NEW PILLAR?

Since Audi's digital journey has progressed to the "data-centric" phase (see Figure 1.10 in Chapter 1), data has become a fundamental pillar of its new DOM. To enable this transformation, Audi has followed an internal path of continuous adaptation, including upskilling staff, reallocating internal funding, and iterating methodically to establish best practices. As a result, the adoption and maturity of the data pillar continue to evolve.

Today, Audi Production benefits from solid supporting structures that provide frameworks, policies, and KPIs to guide its business transformation toward efficient data utilization. This includes breaking down the organization into a limited number of data domains, each managed by data domain managers and information architects. Together with representatives from business domains, they form a "hub-and-spoke" data organization responsible for managing change and setting data strategies. On an operational level, shared data domain service teams execute initiatives such as data harmonization[9] projects.

Unlikely as it may seem, Audi did not establish new data roles at the outset. As a technology-focused company, it initially prioritized implementing data analytics solutions – such as "semi-semantic"[10] data warehouses and data engineering platforms – before addressing organizational changes. These solutions were aimed at consolidating disparate application-centric data stores and have since been reinforced by robust layers of data governance principles and processes.

Given Audi Production's legacy of locally distributed data silos across its manufacturing sites, early efforts focused on setting up data connectivity and abstraction layers, with a priority on data quality over quantity or speed of implementation. However, organizing business functions around cohesive data flows proved challenging due to a lack of jointly agreed process hierarchies and documented workflows. These issues were mitigated by establishing cross-site business working groups tasked with harmonizing process clusters and assigning data ownership roles.

One of the first successful projects implemented under this approach was the provisioning of cross-site rework data as a "data product." This data product captures the root causes of mechanical or electrical manufacturing errors and the faults identified during quality control. While relevant for day-to-day shopfloor management, its true value lies in enabling medium-term fault correction cycles by linking manufacturing process findings to inherent design issues.

The initial phase of establishing Audi Production's DOM involved centralizing previously distributed data experts into joint data product teams, working alongside IT specialists. This collaborative structure laid the foundation for Audi Production's formal recognition of its DOM as the "Data Factory." The term "factory" underscores the analogy that data products should follow standardized "production processes," ensuring consistent quality and efficiency, like physical manufacturing.

While the initial setup of the DOM had delivered notable business outcomes, the next challenge lay in scaling it to achieve broader, strategic leverage of data products (the underlying goal of the data transformation). This scaling effort aimed to elevate data products beyond operational utility to provide true informational insights, linking them to their source/consuming business processes. Achieving this required extensive cross-business collaboration and is still the focus of ongoing activities. These activities pursue two interdependent yet distinct goals:

- Making critical business data universally accessible across the organization: This is the primary responsibility of the data lead role, supported by the data factory.
- Optimizing the creation and flow of data: This is led by the data architecture team, which works to make information flows more data-centric by influencing technology architecture decisions during the scoping of new IT applications.

The maturity of Audi's data capabilities varies significantly across its business units. While some units are more advanced, overall maturity levels – scaling the DOM and meeting business demands for high-data intensity – still require substantial effort. Audi Production, as the internal lead in this transformation, continues to spearhead efforts within the Audi Group to develop a fully scaled data factory and pursues this journey as follows on the four layers of the DOM, as presented by the authors in this book.

## Raw Data Layer

This layer focuses on managing and integrating raw data from various sources, including manufacturing, logistics, and planning systems. While significant progress has been made with manufacturing data, a considerable portion of logistics and planning data is managed through centralized Volkswagen Group IT services, shared across multiple brands. This setup requires extensive group-wide coordination to restructure systems effectively. To address this, Audi Production is working to establish cross-brand business and IT working groups while organizing appropriate funding models.

Audi's data integration and warehousing solutions have already been accepted as group standards, with existing systems being refactored to reduce IT complexity and costs. However, harmonizing OT communication and integration, which involves data exchange between machines and cloud applications, poses greater challenges. This effort requires the following:

- Addressing thousands of legacy machinery across all production sites.
- Engaging traditionally independent machine builders and automation teams to support broader use cases beyond their immediate responsibilities.

Additionally, the growing importance of infrastructure data collection (e.g., building and energy data) necessitates the development of strategies and the creation of technical working groups focused on this often-overlooked area.

## Supporting Layer

The supporting layer provides architectural frameworks, governance templates, and policies, such as platform principles or a data-sharing code of conduct. However, a key challenge lies in ensuring that these guidelines are effectively implemented in real-world IT projects. Historically, well-defined policies often lost relevance during the lengthy demand-to-solution process.

To address this issue, Audi Production is focusing on the following:

- Iteratively defining clear, measurable framework deliverables.
- Embedding these deliverables throughout the demand-to-solution lifecycle.

Shifting IT's role from being viewed as a cost center to a strategic enabler is critical for success in this layer. This requires introducing new methods that are not only innovative but also adaptable from other industries or business areas.

## Data Products Layer

The data products layer focuses on creating actionable insights by developing reusable, high-quality data products. The next steps involve initiating cross-business data products in areas where data management has already been harmonized across Audi Production sites to ensure a strong foundation for data quality. Key priorities here include the following:

- Defining the required "level" of a data product based on measurable, value-driven use cases.
- Conducting value definition workshops with business units to identify needs and derive consumable ("shoppable") datasets.
- Extending these efforts from production-focused use cases to cross-business contexts.

The ultimate goal is to create well-documented data products that are easily accessible through a data marketplace, supported by automated processes for seamless utilization across the organization.

### DATA INTELLIGENCE LAYER

The authors have introduced the data intelligence layer in Section 3.3. Audi Production is aligned with the value this layer would provide. This layer focuses on leveraging data for advanced insights and decision-making. The data factory leads it in collaboration with Audi's data domain structure. Immediate efforts include the following:

- Establishing a joint understanding of tools and business artifact metamodels between IT and production.
- Finalizing methodical discussions around architecture tools, roles, and responsibilities.
- Launching organization-wide activities to fill informational knowledge gaps.

As this layer matures, it will play a pivotal role in integrating additional insights into architectural decision-making processes and the development of data products. Over time, it will enable more business use cases to leverage data intelligence for improved outcomes, thereby driving the demand for high-quality data solution.

## KEY TAKEAWAYS FROM THIS CHAPTER

*"Without a well-architected DOM, enterprises risk data silos, operational inefficiencies, and AI initiatives that fail beyond experimentation."*

*– Rainer Deutschmann, Senior Executive in Telecom and Technology Industries. Board Director, Advisor, and Investor*

- The DOM must evolve to meet changing business needs continuously. Changes in one layer of the DOM impact the rest of the DOM.

- The supporting layer is pivotal, from building the data strategy and architecture to providing reusable artifacts and frameworks for the rest of the DOM. It also drives data adoption, governance, and business value realization through the DOM.
- The data products layer enables data consumers to effectively consume data products packaged by the producers and ready to be consumed. Data contracts establish trust through transparency between data consumers and producers by setting up the proper mechanism to define, measure, and fulfill the required data intensity.
- The data intelligence layer is the brain of the DOM, providing the context of data across the enterprise through the EKG. It also enables scaling the production of data products through the DFBs.
- The raw data layer provides internal and external transactional, operational, and analytical data to the rest of the DOM. To fulfill business needs, it must proactively provision data to produce DFBs.
- Each layer of the DOM should be established with clear roles and responsibilities across its people, with standardized and repeatable processes and modern technologies that enable its usage to scale for the enterprise's current and future data needs.
- The DOM can be centralized, federated, or decentralized. Each enterprise must determine the setup that suits it best.

## NOTES

1 Composability. (2024, November 23). In *Wikipedia*.
2 Infrastructure as Code. (2024, November 23). In *Wikipedia*.
3 They are attributes essential for the strategy, key business processes, and analytics of the enterprise.
4 Data contract. (n.d.). *Data Contract*.
5 Right to be forgotten. (2025, February 12). In *Wikipedia*.
6 Microservices. (2025, February 8). In *Wikipedia*.
7 Bloomberg. (n.d.). *Bloomberg Data*.
8 Dun & Bradstreet. (n.d.). *D&B Data*.
9 "Data harmonization" – We understand that the informational context of identical data fields is different between different partners using the same data points but describing different information, e.g., rework. Two partners use the data field "repair time": One partner is including the time to order material (much longer), whereas the other partner would only include the actual time of the repair. Without harmonization, this data field cannot be used in any data-driven application.
10 Some metadata was attributed to ingested data; however, the source of this metadata was not necessarily from a single point of truth.

## REFERENCE LIST

Analytics Vivid. (2024, June 29). *What Is Data Harmonization.* https://analyt-icsvivid.com/data-harmonization-explained-what-is-data-harmonization/

Bloomberg. (n.d.). *Bloomberg Data.* https://data.bloomberg.com/

Composability. (2024, November 23). In *Wikipedia.* https://en.wikipedia.org/wiki/Composability

Data Contract. (n.d.). *Data Contract.* https://datacontract.com/

Dun and Bradstreet. (n.d.). *D&B Data.* https://www.dnb.com/en-us/marketplace/data.html

Infrastructure as Code. (2024, November 23). In *Wikipedia.* https://en.wikipedia.org/wiki/Infrastructure_as_code

Microservices. (2025, February 8). In *Wikipedia.* https://en.wikipedia.org/wiki/Microservices

Right to Be Forgotten. (2025, February 12). In *Wikipedia.* https://en.wikipedia.org/wiki/Right_to_be_forgotten

# CHAPTER 4

# Maturity Journey for the Data Pillar

In Chapter 3, we covered the people, processes, and technologies required to be put in place for the DOM to function. However, that cannot be achieved quickly. Enterprises must go through a journey to mature their data pillar gradually. Each enterprise is unique, as is its present maturity level and journey.

To enable enterprises to assess their present maturity level, create their maturity goal, develop the plan for that goal, and execute toward achieving it, we have developed a two-dimensional "maturity framework." This framework is simple to understand and follow throughout the journey. Each enterprise has its unique positioning in the maturity framework based on multiple factors like the size of the enterprise, number of use cases in scope for the data pillar, addressable business value in the use cases, data intensity required for those, and the resources available to improve the readiness of the DOM. Audi's case study provides insights into their maturity level and maturity journey.

In the maturity framework:

- **The Y-axis represents the "demand for data":** We propose to measure the demand for data by taking the percentage of EAV to the TAV. Enterprises that cannot measure their EAV and TAV can consider the required data intensity of their use cases as a proxy for the EAV and TAV. We will present examples for both approaches later in this chapter.

DOI: 10.1201/9781003512776-5

- **The X-axis represents the "supply of data":** We propose to measure the supply of data through the DOM's readiness level. We will present an example to measure that later in this chapter.

The Y- and X-axis values enable an enterprise to identify its positioning in the maturity framework.

We introduce three maturity stages to enable enterprises to structure their maturity journey: *Fundamental*, *scaled*, and *automated*. These stages can be plotted onto the maturity framework, as shown in Figure 4.1. As an enterprise increases the maturity of its data pillar, it will be able to increase the demand for data and match it with an increasing supply of data, thus moving toward the top-right corner of the maturity framework.

*Balancing growth in data demand and supply is key! Supply not fulfilling demand frustrates data consumers and impacts realized value, while the reverse results in wastage and untapped data potential.*

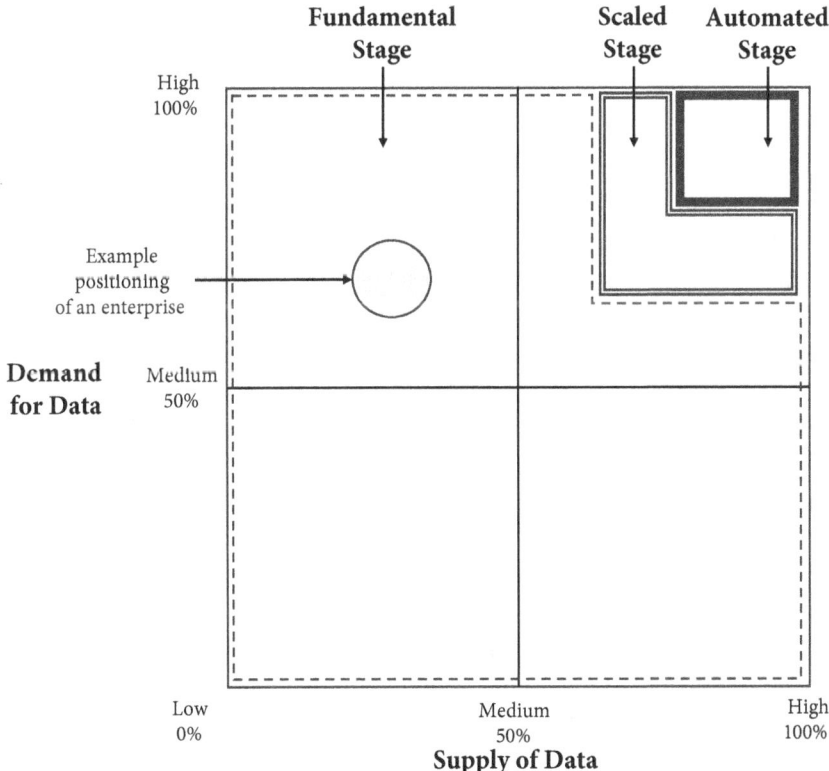

FIGURE 4.1   Maturity Framework and the Stages of Maturity for the Data Pillar.

Let us now delve into each stage of the maturity journey.

**Fundamental stage:** Enterprises build the essential foundation of the data pillar in this stage. The "dotted area" in Figure 4.1 represents the fundamental stage. The fundamental stage takes the largest area in the maturity framework. The CDO and the data office need to invest significant effort in increasing the RV, EAV, and TAV by aligning and highlighting the value of data with the relevant business stakeholders. The CDO and their collaboration with the Board and the CxOs play a critical role in driving stakeholders' adoption of the DOM in the use cases. The DOM's layers are prioritized on the basis of the required data intensity and Level 2 data management capabilities. In this stage, enterprises may leverage AI capabilities piecemeal for tasks like building data engineering pipelines, anomaly detection in raw data, and suggesting data quality and observability rules. As data demand and supply increase, enterprises come close to the fundamental stage's boundaries in the maturity framework's top-right quadrant. In such a position, the CDO's goal for the data pillar would be to move to the next stage, i.e., the "scaled stage."

> *In the fundamental stage, CDOs must continuously evaluate whether the DOM is ready to fulfill the data demand. Failing to do that would force data consumers to bypass the DOM, negatively impacting its adoption.*

**Scaled stage:** Enterprise-wise self-service of the data pillar's assets is achieved in this stage. As an enterprise reaches this stage, it generates data demand across its business functions. These stakeholders can leverage data across most use cases, achieving a medium-to-high level on the Y-axis. This is made possible through a DOM ready to enable "self-service" for the stakeholders across all layers of the DOM, i.e., achieving medium-to-high on the X-axis. The "double-lined L-shaped area" in the top-right quadrant in Figure 4.1 represents the scaled stage.

To accomplish the self-service goal, the data intelligence layer is critical, with its EKG providing the context of data across the enterprise and the DFBs enabling the data producers to fast-track the production of data products. In addition, data processes to produce and consume the data assets must be automated by leveraging technology capabilities, such as GenAI, data access management, and data marketplace.

Leveraging GenAI, enterprises provide a natural language-based "conversational AI" assistant, making self-service easy, time-saving, and fun. The AI assistant answers users' questions and guides them in real time. In the background, the AI assistant would interface with the EKG to become "context-aware" while providing answers and with the data access management to enable only authorized access to data. Few examples are as follows:

- Data consumers in business functions, typically lacking data engineering and querying skills, can ask questions in natural language such as "What is the latest revenue forecast for next quarter?" and get authorized answers immediately.

- Data consumers can ask for data to fulfill their use case. The AI assistant would refer to a specific data product in the data marketplace that provides more information and automates access.

- Data producers can ask how to fulfill a specific data engineering task. The AI assistant would refer to a specific data engineering template in the artifact portal that provides more information on the artifact and automates access.

*Vision for the scaled stage: "Conversational AI" assistant as the self-service gateway for all data consumers and producers!*

In addition, enablement programs must be executed so that data producers and consumers can adopt the self-service capabilities.

While the DOM is ready for self-service, the CDO and the data office must engage with the stakeholders of the use cases to increase the adoption of the DOM's assets. This increases the EAV and enables the enterprise to achieve a medium-to-high level on the Y-axis. The self-service maturity gained in the scaled stage frees up the bandwidth of the CDO and the data office and creates the required foundation for the data pillar to mature to the automated stage.

*The data pillar can achieve and sustain the scaled stage when people across the enterprise adopt the offered self-service capabilities.*

**Automated stage:** In this stage, enterprises achieve an AI-powered data pillar. The "bold square-shaped area" in the top-right quadrant in Figure 4.1 represents the automated stage. This is the highest stage of maturity, wherein enterprises accelerate the consumption of data assets by leveraging AI extensively, resulting in their EAV coming close to or becoming equal to their TAV. AI-powered automation is achieved within and across all DOM layers, accelerating the DOM's readiness level further and thus fulfilling the highest level of data demand.

With AI and especially AI agents[1] rapidly evolving, we believe that AI agents will be increasingly leveraged in the DOM and enable the data pillar to achieve and sustain the automated stage of maturity. In this stage, AI agents will power all the stakeholders in the DOM to accelerate their activities and outcomes.

Data consumers will leverage AI agents to use multimodal interfaces such as text, speech, images, videos, and APIs, for getting recommendations on data assets the DOM provides, accessing and consuming them, thereby accelerating the fulfillment of their data needs.

Data producers and the execution teams will leverage AI agents across the DOM to automate and, thus, accelerate the execution of their tasks. Examples of such tasks would be analyzing raw data continuously and creating notifications and/or taking actions; automating workflows and activities throughout the lifecycle of data products, DFBs, raw data, and the EKG; and recommending artifacts to be leveraged. People stakeholders are kept in the loop for accepting or rejecting predefined tasks performed by the AI agents, providing the business context, exception handling, and governance of the AI agents.

*AI agents are the future! They will enable accelerated data-driven decision-making across the enterprise in the automated stage!*

The teams responsible for the artifacts will leverage AI agents to automate and accelerate the lifecycle management of the artifacts. People stakeholders are kept in the loop to provide the business context and govern AI agents.

Additionally, AI agents will provide recommendations to the CDO and the data office on the "next best actions" for further maturing the data pillar; predictions on new use cases by tracking the enterprise business strategy and the strategies of other operating pillars; summarized insights on the EAV and TAV, or even suggestions for strengthening collaboration with the Board, the CEO, and other CxOs.

As AI technologies evolve, there may even be multiple AI agents interacting with each other with some human assistance to execute complex tasks across the DOM layers. For instance, AI agent #1 in the data intelligence layer will continuously evaluate the usage of the DFBs and the feedback received. Another AI agent, #2, will continuously evaluate the searches occurring on the EKG. A third AI agent, #3, will align with AI agents #1 and #2 and provide recommendations to the data office to further improve the data intelligence layer. Similarly, AI agent #4 will continuously observe real-time data discrepancies such as inaccurate, incompliant, or stale data and inform the relevant data product stakeholders of potential data contract violations. There may even be "super" agents, i.e., AI agents managing more AI agents who are trained to provide the business context and oversee other agents with appropriate governance by humans. A vision of AI agents across the DOM is presented in Figure 4.2.

Eventually, as AI technology evolves, these AI agents can become self-managing for recommending, developing, and maintaining new data assets and artifacts across the DOM layers.

It is essential to reiterate that humans are kept in the loop of tasks that AI agents perform for required governance, including quality checking, access management, and risk management. The level of leverage of AI agents and human governance would be a critical decision for enterprises.

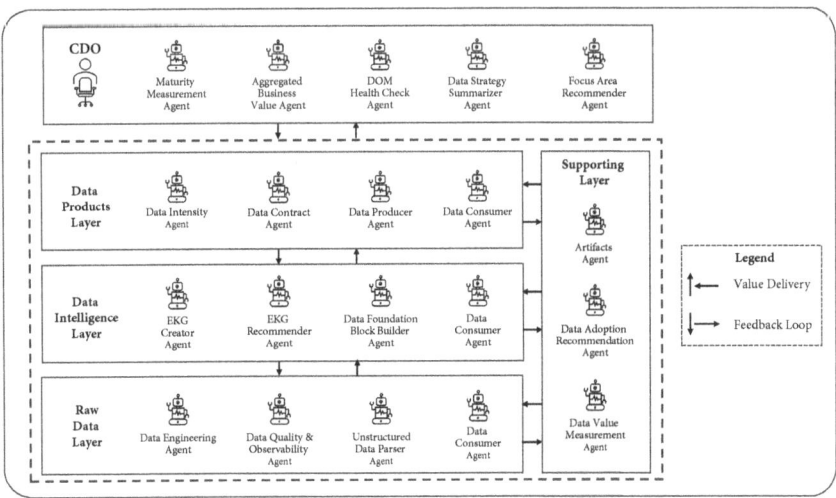

FIGURE 4.2   Example: AI Agents Interacting with Each Other in the Automated Stage.

As AI technology evolves and an enterprise matures further in the automated stage, each enterprise must evaluate the required levels periodically.

*AI agents must be governed by humans.*

With the understanding of the three stages of maturity, let us next delve into how enterprises determine their position in the maturity framework.

## 4.1 DETERMINING ENTERPRISE POSITIONING IN THE MATURITY FRAMEWORK

Let us continue with the example of the retail consumer brand enterprise pursuing a transformation of pivoting its GTM model from being wholesale-focused to D2C-focused.

### 4.1.1 Positioning on the Y-axis: Demand for Data

Enterprises may find it challenging to measure their demand for data for the first time. Enterprises should not be too concerned about the accuracy of the measurement when done for the first time. The accuracy of measurements would improve in subsequent iterations by incorporating learnings from previous measurements. In addition, we propose two approaches to provide flexibility to enterprises to measure their demand for data. If an enterprise can follow both approaches, we recommend taking the average value from both approaches to form a balanced view.

- **Approach 1 – Measuring the EAV and TAV:** This approach measures the demand for data as the "EAV to TAV percentage" KPI (see Chapter 2). That would require that enterprises quantify and measure the addressable business value from their use cases.

- **Approach 2 – Measuring the required data intensity:** This approach considers the data intensity required by the in-scope use cases as the proxy for data demand. This approach reuses the data intensity measurements obtained for the use cases the DOM would fulfill.

Let us next delve into examples of measuring the values in both approaches.

#### 4.1.1.1 Approach 1 – Measuring the EAV and TAV

The calculation of EAV and TAV in an enterprise is not straightforward. To calculate the values, we recommend enterprises reuse existing business plans for their capabilities, which should have the expected business outcomes from their use cases rather than starting from scratch. This would help achieve better alignment among stakeholders on the EAV and TAV and save time and effort.

*4.1.1.1.1 Measuring the TAV*   To measure the TAV, we have taken inspiration from a top-down approach typically taken to measure the widely used TAM metric.

In the top-down approach to measure TAV, we propose to consider the EV as a base, take the EV growth projection made by the Board and the CEO, and roughly estimate the percentage of the projected increase in EV that can be impacted by data.

To guide the estimation, enterprises can leverage the value driver tree[2] framework, develop the value driver tree for EV, and understand the impact areas.

> **Food for Thought:** *Do you want to "perfect" the value measurement or move ahead with rough estimates and adjust along the way?*

In our retail consumer brand enterprise example, for illustration purposes, let us assume that the current EV is estimated at $500 million. As the enterprise embarks on its D2C transformation initiative, the Board and the CEO have projected the EV to increase to $600 million in one year, i.e., a growth of $100 million in one year.

The next step is to estimate the percentage of this projected growth of $100 million, which can be achieved using data. The value driver tree for EV can provide guidance on the impact areas for making the estimation. Below are a few example impact areas to consider in this case:

- Direct impact on revenue through data, such as by upselling new products and reducing stockout situations based on the end customer data and storing transaction data, and data monetization by sharing aggregated customers' preferences with wholesalers in a compliant manner.

- Indirect impact on revenue through data such as reducing customer churn by improving customer satisfaction by leveraging end customer data.

- Impact on strategic programs, such as leveraging end customer data to improve Net Promoter Score (NPS).

- Impact on cost avoidance in existing business functions, such as enabling enterprise risk management function to avoid compliance fines by leveraging data.

- Impact on cost savings, such as leveraging data to improve the efficiency of people, processes, and technology pillars.

All these impact areas lead to deriving a "percentage" that should be applied to the projected $100 million growth in EV to determine the TAV.

For illustration, let us assume a 10% impact through data based on the aforementioned factors. Over time, based on the EAV and data maturity, this percentage can be better calibrated. We recommend that the CDO consult the Board, the CEO, and the CFO to form an aligned hypothesis on the impact percentage.

Based on the assumption in this example, the TAV is estimated as

TAV = (Impact on EV Growth through Data) × (Overall EV Growth)

= 10% of $100 million = **$10 million**

*4.1.1.1.2 Measuring the EAV* To measure the EAV, we propose a bottom-up approach by reusing the use cases of Level 1 business capabilities in the capability map. For performing the measurement, the use cases should be broken down to the lowest possible level of granularity to avoid overlap between them. At the lowest level of granularity, the use cases should have quantifiable business value. However, positive and/or negative correlation may exist between two use cases broken down to the lowest level of granularity, which would be unavoidable in a practical business situation.

For example, let us assume, for the sake of simplicity, that the Level 1 business capabilities (see Figure 2.6) have ten business use cases at the lowest level of granularity, such as

- "UC1" in supply chain management capability – reducing inventory carrying cost;

- "UC2" in sales and marketing capability – reducing lost sales due to stockout occurrences in stores, and so on.

To illustrate the possible correlation between the use cases, reducing the inventory carrying cost may increase lost sales due to increased stockout occurrences in stores – a negative correlation in this case. Such a correlation is unavoidable and must be accepted while calculating the EAV.

Let us further assume that the data strategy development process (see Figure 3.4) has prioritized six use cases in scope for the data pillar, including UC1 and UC2, to which data at the required intensity would be delivered through the DOM.

For UC1, the inventory carrying cost should be captured before leveraging the data assets through the DOM, and the target cost should be captured after leveraging the data assets through the DOM. The differential would provide the EAV for UC1. Let us assume the value to be $0.5 million.

Similarly, for UC2, the lost sales due to stockout in stores before leveraging the data assets through the DOM and the target after leveraging the data assets through the DOM should be captured. The differential would provide the EAV for UC2. Let us assume the value to be $0.6 million.

For illustration purposes, let us assume the EAV for other in-scope use cases, as presented in Table 4.1.

At an enterprise level, the EAV is calculated as the sum of EAV for all the use cases "in-scope" for data delivery through the DOM.

$$\text{EAV} = \Sigma \text{ EAV for In-Scope (UC1, UC2 ... UC10)}$$

$$= (0.5 + 0.6 + 0.6 + 0.7 + 0.8 + 0.8) = \textbf{\$4.0 million}$$

The scoring for the Y-axis (demand for data) as per Approach 1 would be equal to the "EAV to TAV percentage," i.e., (4.0 divided by 10) million = **40%**.

Let us assume that UC1 and UC2 have been delivered and that the RV is the same as the sum of the EAV of those use cases, which would be $1.1

TABLE 4.1   Example EAV of In-Scope Use Cases

| Use Case Number | EAV |
| --- | --- |
| UC1 | $0.5 million |
| UC2 | $0.6 million |
| UC3 | $0.6 million |
| UC4 | $0.7 million |
| UC5 | $0.8 million |
| UC6 | $0.8 million |

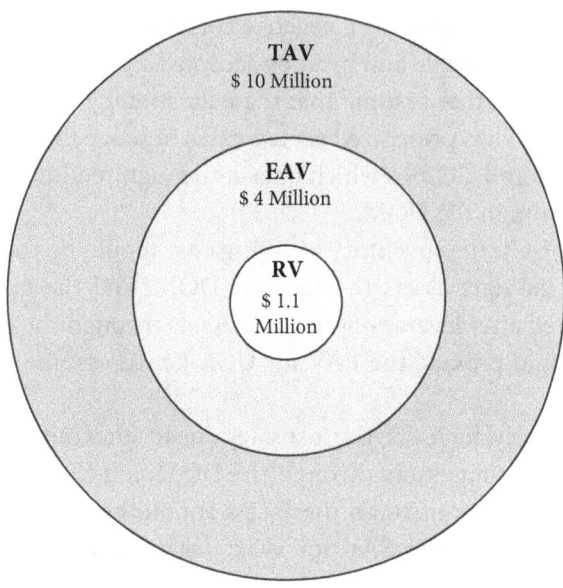

FIGURE 4.3   Example TAV, EAV, and RV KPIs.

million. Therefore, the TAV, EAV, and RV KPIs can be obtained as presented in Figure 4.3.

### 4.1.1.2 Approach 2 – Measuring the Required Data Intensity of the Use Cases

In this approach, we measure the demand for data through the required data intensity of the use cases.

Let us continue with the assumption that the Level 1 business capabilities (see Figure 2.6) have ten use cases in total, of which six use cases are prioritized in the data strategy to be delivered through the DOM.

As explained in Chapter 1, the data office, in collaboration with the stakeholders of the use cases, would assess the required data intensity (i.e., QCS requirements) for each use case. This assessment is required for the DOM to fulfill the demand for data. We reuse this assessment as a proxy for measuring the demand for data in this Approach 2.

To measure the Y-axis score, we measure each dimension of the QCS framework (see Figure 1.4) in three levels: Low, medium, and high and provide a score of 0 for use cases out-of-scope for DOM, 1 for low, 2 for medium, and 3 for high.

TABLE 4.2   Scoring for the Y-axis as per Approach 2: Demand for Data

| Use Case Number | Quality (Q) Dimension | Compliance (C) Dimension | Speed (S) Dimension | Score per Use Case/ Max. Score per Use Case |
|---|---|---|---|---|
| UC1 | Low (1) | Low (1) | Medium (2) | 4/9 |
| UC2 | Medium (2) | Low (1) | High (3) | 6/9 |
| UC3 | Low (1) | Medium (2) | Medium (2) | 5/9 |
| UC4 | High (3) | Medium (2) | Low (1) | 6/9 |
| UC5 | High (3) | High (3) | High (3) | 9/9 |
| UC6 | Low (1) | Medium (2) | Low (1) | 4/9 |
| UC7 | Out-of-scope for DOM (0) | Out-of-scope for DOM (0) | Out-of-scope for DOM (0) | 0/9 |
| UC8 | Out-of-scope for DOM (0) | Out-of-scope for DOM (0) | Out-of-scope for DOM (0) | 0/9 |
| UC9 | Out-of-scope for DOM (0) | Out-of-scope for DOM (0) | Out-of-scope for DOM (0) | 0/9 |
| UC10 | Out-of-scope for DOM (0) | Out-of-scope for DOM (0) | Out-of-scope for DOM (0) | 0/9 |
| **Required data intensity for all use cases** | | | | **34/90 = 38%** |

For illustration, let us assume the QCS levels for the use cases in this example and the scoring for the Y-axis, as shown in Table 4.2.

As per Table 4.2, four use cases (UC7, UC8, UC9, and UC10) are not in scope for leveraging data through the DOM. For instance, UC7 could be the new store staff onboarding use case, which is currently people- and process-driven and does not need any data assets provided by the DOM; this might change in the future.

Referring to Table 4.2, the maximum score of 90 can be considered a proxy for the TAV, and the score of 34 can be regarded as a proxy for the EAV.

The Y-axis (demand for data) scoring as per Approach 2 would be equal to 34 divided by 90, equal to **38%.**

- **Demand for Data – Positioning on the Y-axis:** The retail consumer brand enterprise in our example could take the average values through Approach 1 (= 40%) and Approach 2 (=38%), equal to **39%.**

### 4.1.2  Positioning on the X-axis: Supply of Data

We propose to measure the value for the X-axis representing the *"supply"* of data through the DOM's readiness level.

TABLE 4.3  Scoring for the X-axis: Supply of Data

| Layer of the DOM | People Readiness | Processes Readiness | Technology Readiness | Score per Layer/ Max. Score per Layer |
|---|---|---|---|---|
| Supporting layer | Low (1) | Low (1) | Low (1) | 3/9 |
| Data products layer | Not existing (0) | Not existing (0) | Not existing (0) | 0/9 |
| Data intelligence layer | Not existing (0) | Not existing (0) | Not existing (0) | 0/9 |
| Raw data layer | High (3) | High (3) | Medium (2) | 8/9 |
| **DOM readiness** | | | | **11/36 = 31%** |

To arrive at the scoring for the X-axis, we measure each layer of the DOM for its people, processes, and technology readiness. We measure readiness in three levels: "low," "medium," and "high." We provide a score of 0 for "not existing," 1 for "low," 2 for "medium," and 3 for "high" levels of readiness.

Let us assume that the retail consumer brand enterprise has set up parts of its supporting layer, such as developing a first iteration of the data strategy and architecture. It has also established the data governance process and technology to support it. However, they have not been able to put in the teams, processes, and technologies required to execute data adoption and data value management and develop the required artifacts. The enterprise has not yet set up the data products or data intelligence layer. However, the raw data layer has a high readiness level, i.e., people, processes, and technologies established for structured raw data. Still improvements in people and technology capabilities are needed to include unstructured raw data.

Given the DOM's readiness situation in the enterprise, let us assume the scoring for the X-axis, as shown in Table 4.3, for illustration purposes.

The scoring for the X-axis (supply of data) would be equal to 11 divided by 36, which is equal to **31%**.

It is essential to mention that the core objective of the exercise is for enterprises to identify their positioning in the maturity framework.

## 4.1.3 Positioning in the Maturity Framework

After plotting the Y-axis and X-axis values, the retail consumer brand enterprise finds its current position in the fundamental stage of the maturity journey, as depicted in Figure 4.4.

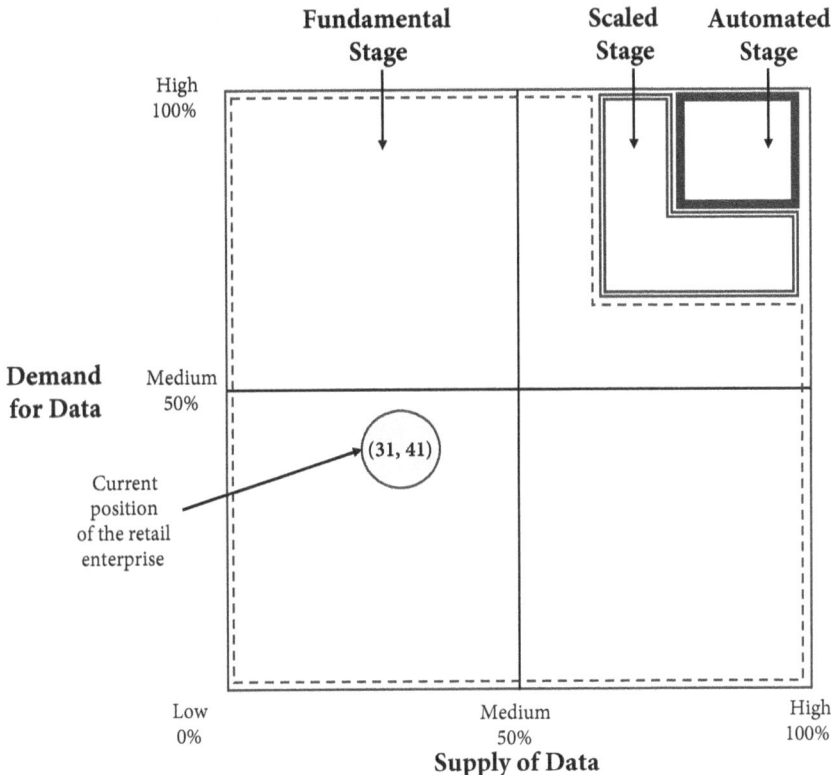

FIGURE 4.4   Current Position of the Retail Enterprise in the Maturity Framework.

The CDO must revisit the positioning in the maturity framework peri-odically. The frequency could be every 3 or 6 months, depending on the pace of the maturity journey.

## 4.2 SCENARIOS IN THE FUNDAMENTAL STAGE

The fundamental stage is a broad area in the maturity framework. To bet-ter understand it, let us consider a few scenarios of different enterprises in different positions in the fundamental stage (see Figure 4.5).

- **Enterprise Scenario 1:** In this scenario, the enterprise is "close to low" on both the Y- and X-axes. The smaller size of the circle signi-fies that it is a small enterprise. In this small enterprise, the demand for data from business use cases is low. This may be because data is

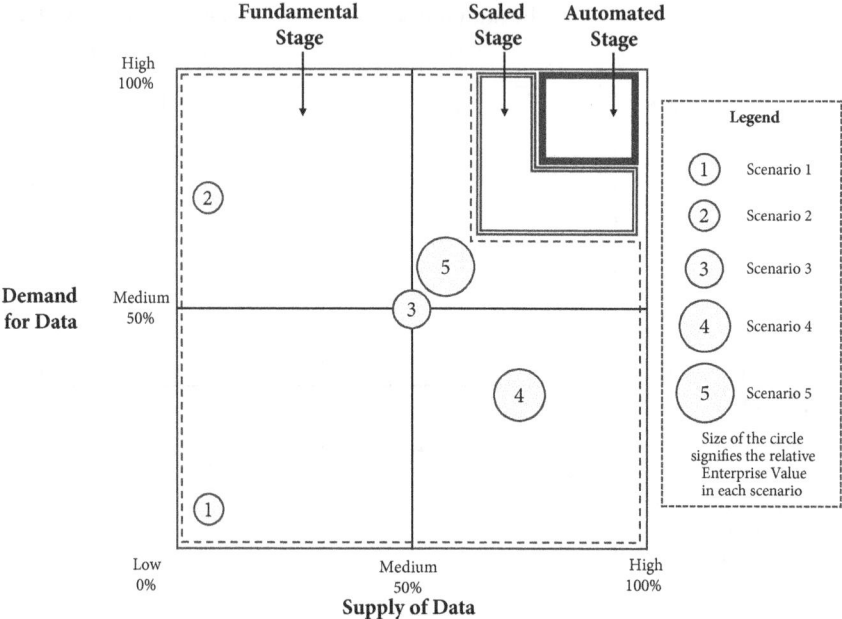

FIGURE 4.5 Scenarios of Different Enterprises Having Different Positioning in the Fundamental Stage.

treated as a by-product of executing its business processes. Without the business demand for data, there is no value in investing in establishing and scaling a DOM. The enterprise does not have a CDO as well. In that case, the CEO, playing the role of the CDO, should first focus on engaging with the business stakeholders and developing a shared understanding of the strategic value of data for the enterprise to enhance business outcomes. In other words, the demand for data must first be increased before investing in expanding the data supply.

- **Enterprise Scenario 2:** In this scenario, the enterprise is "between medium to high" on the Y-axis and "close to low" on the X-axis. This scenario represents a small enterprise. With a medium-to-high EAV to TAV percentage (the measure for the Y-axis), this small enterprise realizes the business potential from data, and its Board and CEO are pursuing data-driven decision-making across the enterprise. However, the data pillar's required people, processes, and technologies are not in place, leading to low DOM readiness. Due to its small size, the enterprise may still be able to fulfill the data needs of the business use cases. However, such an enterprise is expected to grow and have new business use cases. In this enterprise, the Board and the CEO must create the role of the CDO if it does not exist. With the sponsorship of the Board and the CEO's active involvement, the CDO's data office must rapidly deliver to increase the DOM readiness and prepare for future data demand. These efforts would enable the enterprise to move to the right on the X-axis. In other words, the data supply must be expanded rapidly to cater to the increasing demand for data.

- **Enterprise Scenario 3:** The enterprise is at a "medium" level on both the Y- and X-axes. This scenario may represent a medium or a large enterprise. In this enterprise, the CDO role exists. The CDO and the data office have set up the data products layer supported by the raw data layer, some DFBs in the data intelligence layer and some components in the supporting layer, such as data adoption and governance, data quality and observability, and some aspects of data value measurement. Data contracts are created for data products. EAV is also measured and reported. The CDO and the data office must focus on setting up the EKG and adding more DFBs and, in parallel, partner with additional business functions to obtain further use cases that need to leverage the DOM. The CDO would also need to reassess the required DOM readiness to deliver the demand for data from the additional use cases. For example, additional use cases may bring new requirements such as collecting and handling unstructured data for AI initiatives in the raw data layer and data risk management artifacts from the supporting layer. These efforts would enable the enterprise to move toward the top-right quadrant in the maturity framework.

- **Enterprise Scenario 4:** The enterprise is "between low to medium" level on the Y-axis and "between medium to high" level on the X-axis. This scenario may represent a large enterprise that has established a DOM with the raw data layer, data products layer, supporting layer, and the EKG in the data intelligence layer. Still, most business use cases across the enterprise do not leverage data through the DOM. At an initial glance, this might look like an impossible scenario. After all, why would an enterprise invest in its DOM without sufficient demand for data? This scenario may exist in a large enterprise wherein a specific business function, such as manufacturing or an operating entity, like a product area with its P&L, has its CDO and the data office focusing on the data pillar. The CDO of a business function has set up all layers of the DOM that deliver data and context of data to the specific use cases in that business function or operating entity. Still, the rest of the enterprise does not yet leverage the DOM. In this scenario, the CDO must secure sponsorship of the executive leadership of the enterprise, to partner with the other business functions and operating units. This can be achieved by sharing information on the achieved business value through leveraging data and showcasing the DOM's role in accelerating business outcomes. These efforts could enable the enterprise to increase the EAV to TAV percentage, thus moving up the Y-axis toward the scaled stage of maturity.

- **Enterprise Scenario 5:** The enterprise has crossed the "medium" level on the Y- and X-axes. This scenario may represent a large enterprise that has done well in creating demand for data from its business use cases and fulfilling those with a reasonably ready DOM, such as an established raw data layer, DFBs, data products, and an initial iteration of the EKG. The enterprise in this scenario must also plan to reach the "scaled stage" as its next step in the maturity journey. To move further toward the scaled stage, the CDO and the data office of this enterprise need to focus on further enhancing the data intelligence layer and providing artifacts across data management capabilities. These measures would enable the remaining business use cases to leverage data through the DOM to enhance their business outcomes, thus increasing the EAV to TAV percentage toward the required level for the scaled stage.

## 4.3 JOURNEY FROM THE FUNDAMENTAL STAGE TO THE SCALED STAGE

When an enterprise has identified its positioning in the fundamental stage and intends to mature toward the scaled stage, it needs to realize that it would need to undertake a journey with multiple steps from its current positioning in the fundamental stage to the scaled stage. Also, the enterprise's size, complexity of operations, and demand for data will change during the journey. The CDO and the data office must lead the enterprise; take the sponsorship of the Board; and involve the CEO and leaders of the people, processes, and technology pillars through the journey.

*The journey requires the CDO to develop a telescopic vision of multiple steps ahead while the data office team focuses on the immediate next step.*

To illustrate the journey, let us take the example of an enterprise beginning its journey from position "a" in the fundamental stage and targeting to reach position "h" in the scaled stage, while going through the positions of "b," "c," "d," "e," "f," and "g" over time, as shown in Figure 4.6. In that figure, the increasing size of the circles showcases the increasing EV of the enterprise throughout its journey.

In *position "a,"* the enterprise is small and has a low demand for data. Due to this, it has not yet established a DOM. This position matches Scenario 1 as mentioned in Figure 4.5.

As the journey progresses, the enterprise reaches *position "b."* In this position, the EV has grown and is getting demand for data from some business use cases. The CDO role has been recently created. The CDO and the data office establish the DOM and focus on delivering data to the business use cases through the raw data layer. The DOM also enables data adoption and governance through the supporting layer to drive the adoption of the raw data layer while enabling governed data consumption.

The enterprise continues increasing its value, expanding the demand for data from more business use cases. The supply of data also expands to meet

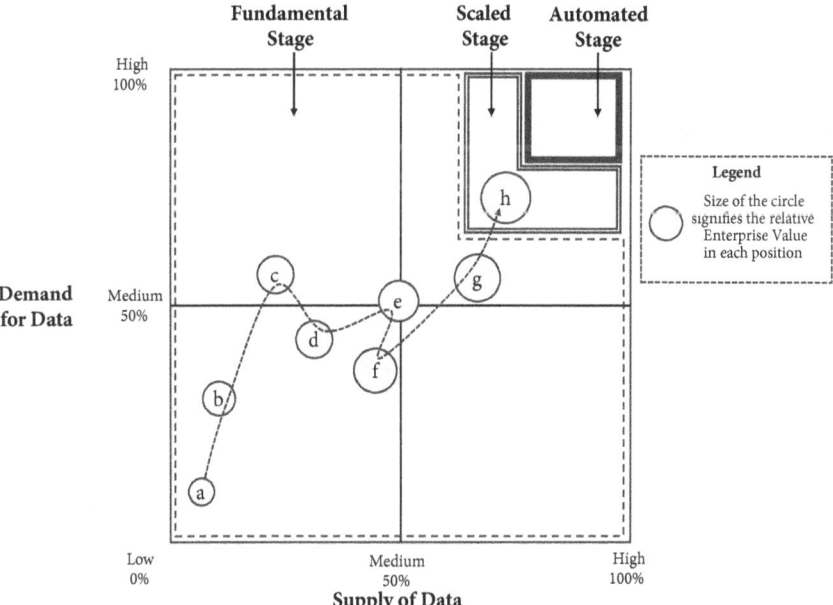

FIGURE 4.6  Example: Journey of an Enterprise from the Fundamental Stage to the Scaled Stage.

the demand. The enterprise reaches *position "c"* of its maturity journey. The CDO and the data office set up the data products layer in this position, create DFBs, and reuse those to build initial data products. However, the data office creates the data products in collaboration with the IT office. The other data requirements are fulfilled through the raw data layer. In addition, the data value measurement team has been set up in the supporting layer, and it has started measuring the EAV and TAV. At this position, the EAV to TAV percentage (the measure for the Y-axis) is more than 50%.

However, after reaching position "c," with the increased demand for data, some business use cases experience the DOM being unable to deliver data at their required intensity. Maybe the required speed is not provided, the quality/compliance requirements are not met, or combinations of those are not met. Also, with the growth of the enterprise, the TAV is expanding. These situations result in a drop in the score of the EAV to TAV percentage (the measure for the Y-axis) to below 50%. However, the CDO and the data office continue working toward improving the readiness of the DOM to match the data and data intensity requirements. They continue developing reusable artifacts like data engineering templates, quality rules, and risk guidelines. As a data strategy does not yet exist, the business capability map is leveraged to proactively build DFBs for future demand. The data adoption team also trains the data producers in the business functions to create their data products, leveraging the reusable artifacts. These actions result in increasing DOM readiness and, thus, an improvement on the X-axis. The enterprise, therefore, reaches *position "d"* of its maturity journey. Position "d" might be seen as disappointing from the heights of position "c"; however, the CDO and the data office must draw upon the positives the DOM has gained during the process.

> *Food for Thought: Does your company culture see setbacks as "opportunities" for growth?*

From there on, while taking steps to improve its DOM readiness, the data adoption team within the data office also communicates the increase in DOM readiness and its improved ability to meet the required data intensity of the business use cases. These efforts result in gaining the confidence of the business back and expanding the EAV. However, as the enterprise continues to grow, its TAV also continues to expand. Still, the expanding EAV results in a slight improvement in the EAV to TAV percentage (the measure for the Y-axis) to about 50%. The CDO and the data office continue their focus on increasing the DOM readiness. They develop a data strategy, get it approved by the Board, and get additional funding. With the funding, they develop the first iteration of the EKG, and further increase their DFBs across data domains. These actions further increase the DOM readiness and thus further improvement on the X-axis. The enterprise, therefore, reaches *position "e"* of its maturity journey.

However, after that position, the journey receives another setback. It falls back on both the Y- and X-axes and reaches *position "f."* This happened because the enterprise decided to leverage AI at scale, which brought in an influx of use cases that needed unstructured data. However, the data strategy has not included unstructured data in scope, and the DOM is not ready to collect, process, and deliver unstructured data.

> *A fall in the maturity level may not mean a decline in the enterprise's data capabilities. It may be due to a previous increase in maturity level resulting in higher data demand, for which the data supply is unavailable.*

After experiencing the setback, the CDO and the data office swiftly take corrective actions to enhance the DOM and manage unstructured data. The CDO creates the next iteration of the data strategy, gets it approved by the Board, and, based on that, receives additional funding for the data pillar. The CDO and the data office focus on the raw data layer to collect and process unstructured data. They also enhance the data intelligence layer with more DFBs for unstructured data and enrich the EKG with metadata and context for unstructured data. The data producers in the data products layer leverage the DFBs to build data products and do not need to reach out to the raw data layer. The supporting layer builds the entire range of required reusable artifacts. These actions enable the DOM to meet the requirements of AI use case data and data intensity. Business use cases across the enterprise now demand data to enhance their outcomes. The enterprise gathers momentum in leveraging data as the fourth pillar and reaches *position "g."* This position is close to the border of the fundamental and scaled stages, with the scaled stage as the next step for the enterprise in its maturity journey.

The position in the scaled stage is represented by *position "h"* in the maturity framework. In this position, the enterprise focuses on self-service for stakeholders in the business functions who participate in and interface with the DOM. The data consumers consume the data products, the DFBs, the EKG, and the raw data through the DOM in a self-service manner. The data producers in the business functions also produce data products from the DFBs by themselves, without the help of the data office or the IT office.

The execution teams in the primary layers of the DOM also leverage self-service capabilities to execute their tasks. New use cases that leverage the DOM reuse the existing artifacts from the supporting layer. In this position of the maturity journey, the CDO and the data office must closely watch the incoming business use cases and their data and data intensity requirements to confirm that the DOM can meet such requirements in a self-service manner. Any gaps identified must be swiftly filled to ensure that the maturity level does not fall back toward the zone of the fundamental stage. Sustaining itself in the scaled stage would not be easy for the enterprise.

While the enterprise takes multiple steps in the journey from positions "a"–"h," the key role of the CDO must be to zoom out and develop a long-term telescopic vision of the journey, proactively update the data strategy for the next steps ahead, and leverage it to secure sponsorship and commitment from the Board and the CEO to continue improving the maturity journey, even during possible situations of setback or disappointment.

Table 4.4 provides the key considerations for maturing from the fundamental stage to the scaled stage.

TABLE 4.4   Key Considerations for the Journey from the Fundamental Stage to the Scaled Stage

1. *People Capabilities and Change Management.* Enterprises would spend considerable time and resources to build the required people capabilities and foster a data culture. The CDO and the data office must develop a structured change management plan for each step and, under the Board and the CEO's sponsorship, secure collaboration from the CxOs to execute the plan

2. *Focus on Demand Generation.* The CDO must focus on increasing the demand for data. This would require continuous engagement with the stakeholders of use cases, promoting business impact from the data adoption success stories, and executing enablement initiatives to improve the leverage of data assets by the use cases

3. *Do not target Perfection.* Targeting perfection would mean planning and working to mitigate every potential adverse "what-if" scenario. With that approach, enterprises may find their progress painfully slow and stuck in the fundamental stage. Instead, adopt an agile approach, continuously improve along the journey, and progress toward the scaled stage

4. *Ups and Downs.* The maturity journey will not be linear. Enterprises may occasionally fall back due to "hype" or "disappointment." Enterprises' culture should promote considering the setbacks as natural characteristics of the journey and see them as opportunities for improvement. The CDO must stay resilient and continue driving the data pillar toward the scaled stage

5. *Disruption by external factors.* External factors like mergers and acquisition activities, macroeconomic conditions, or new regulations may force the CDO to alter the planned maturity journey. The CDO must adopt an agile approach to manage such disruptions

## 4.4 MATURING FROM THE SCALED STAGE
## TO THE AUTOMATED STAGE

Achieving the scaled stage of maturity is a significant milestone for enterprises. Many enterprises may continue to operate and sustain themselves in the scaled stage for long periods. However, enterprises growing their TAV and wanting to increase their DOM readiness to expand their EAV would decide to mature their data pillar to the automated stage (see Figure 4.7).

To increase DOM readiness, the focus should be to leverage AI capabilities, such as AI agents, in the processes (see Chapter 3) for each DOM layer. This would result in reducing manual efforts and improving the quality of outcomes, compliance, and speed of execution of the processes. Multiple AI agents across the DOM would interact with each other to synchronize between the layers of the DOM (see Figure 4.2). The role of people stakeholders in the DOM would be to participate in exception handling, make critical decisions, and govern the AI agents. The technology applications leveraged in each layer of the DOM must also be enhanced so that the AI agents can interact with them and get tasks executed through them.

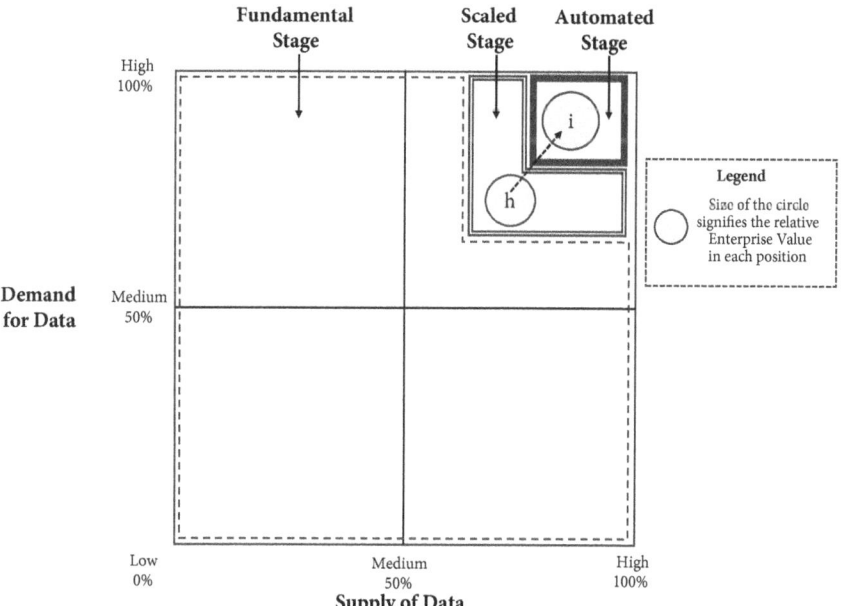

FIGURE 4.7    Example: Journey from the Scaled Stage to the Automated Stage.

Let us delve into some examples of leveraging AI agents in each layer of the DOM.

### 4.4.1 Supporting Layer

Table 4.5 provides examples of tasks performed by AI agents in the supporting layer.

TABLE 4.5    Examples of Tasks Performed by AI Agents in the Supporting Layer

| Agent Name | Examples of Tasks Performed by AI Agents in the Supporting Layer |
|---|---|
| Artifacts agent | *Creates and updates artifacts.* Executes the tasks of the supporting layer teams during the artifact creation and updation processes (see Figure 3.8) |
| Data adoption recommendation agent | *Recommends assets for data adoption.* Recommends data assets to data consumers. Confirms that the data consumers get data with their required data intensity, as captured in the data contract |
| Data value measurement agent | *Execution of business value realization.–* Continuously measures the KPIs defined for the data pillar. Also, provides recommendations to improve each KPI |

### 4.4.2 Data Products Layer

Table 4.6 provides examples of tasks performed by AI agents in the data products layer.

TABLE 4.6    Examples of Tasks Performed by AI Agents in the Data Products Layer

| Agent Name | Examples of Tasks Performed by AI Agents in the Data Products Layer |
|---|---|
| Data intensity agent | *Measures the data intensity required by the business use cases.* Measures and validates the required data intensity with the data consumers (see Figure 1.4) |
| Data contract agent | *Creates data contracts.* Creates data contracts as per the data intensity requirements of the use cases in scope for specific data products. Asks the data producers to confirm those or takes feedback for improvement |
| Data producer agent | *Creates data products.* Executes tasks for the data producers and seeks their go-ahead throughout the 5D process (see Figure 3.13). It also approves requests from data consumers. Thus, it frees up the bandwidth of data producers and speeds up the creation of data products while developing high-quality data products |
| Data consumer agent | *Recommends data products.* Recommends data products to individual data consumers based on their profile and their use cases |

### 4.4.3 Data Intelligence Layer

Table 4.7 provides examples of tasks performed by AI agents in the data intelligence layer.

TABLE 4.7   Examples of Tasks Performed by AI Agents in the Data Intelligence Layer

| Agent Name | Examples of Tasks Performed by AI Agents in the Data Intelligence Layer |
| --- | --- |
| EKG creator agent | *Creates nodes and adds metadata in EKG.* Creates, enriches, and extends the EKG based on new metadata, domains, or feedback |
| EKG recommender agent | *Recommends relevant information in EKG.* Over time, the EKG could become vast (in terms of breadth and depth of information). This agent provides the relevant information from the EKG to stakeholders based on their profiles and needs |
| DFB builder agent | *Creates DFBs.* Acts like the execution teams (see Figure 3.16) and executes their tasks during development (see Figure 3.18) |
| Data consumer agent | *Recommend DFBs.* Recommends them to individual data consumers and producers of data products based on their profiles and use cases |

### 4.4.4 Raw Data Layer

Table 4.8 provides examples of tasks performed by AI agents in the raw data layer.

TABLE 4.8   Examples of Tasks Performed by AI Agents in the Raw Data Layer

| Agent Name | Examples of Tasks Performed by AI Agents in the Raw Data Layer |
| --- | --- |
| Data engineering agent | *Collects and loads the raw data layer.* Collects data from various internal and external sources. Then, loads the data to the raw data layer and the technical metadata to the EKG |
| Data quality and observability agent | *Performs data quality and observability checks.* As new or changed data enters this layer, scans it and recommends data quality rules or flags any data observability violations |
| Unstructured data parser agent | *Parses unstructured data.* Recognizes and parses information from unstructured data. Then, loads the data to the raw data layer and the technical metadata to the EKG |
| Data consumer agent | *Consumption from the raw data layer.* Recommends raw data to the execution teams in the data intelligence layer based upon their use case. In addition, provisions access to the required raw data |

In addition to leveraging AI agents for each DOM layer, the CDO could also leverage AI agents. Table 4.9 provides some examples.

Table 4.10 presents the key considerations for maturing from the scaled stage to the automated stage.

Fast-paced innovations are happening in the AI domain. The CDO should apply the new AI innovations to the data pillar to extend its maturity journey further in the automated stage.

TABLE 4.9   Examples of Tasks Performed by AI Agents to Enable the CDO

| Agent Name | Examples of Tasks Performed by AI Agents to Enable the CDO |
|---|---|
| Maturity measurement agent | *Position in the maturity framework.* Measures the scores for the Y- and X-axes of the maturity framework to determine the positioning in the maturity framework |
| Aggregated business value agent | *Aggregate business value from the DOM.* Works with the data value measurement agent to aggregate key metrics for the CDO |
| DOM health check agent | *Health check of the DOM.* Performs regular health checks of each layer based on defined parameters to prevent the DOM from becoming ineffective and inefficient |
| Data strategy summarizer agent | *Summarizes the data strategy for the CDO.* Summarizes the data strategy, providing insights based on the CDO's focus areas. Interacts with the focus area recommender agent and the CDO for their feedback |
| Focus area recommender agent | *Recommends CDO attention areas.* Interfaces with other agents and recommends key areas requiring the attention of the CDO, with defined priority levels |

TABLE 4.10   Key Considerations for the Journey from the Scaled Stage to the Automated Stage

1. *Flywheel effect of Data and AI:* The criticality of AI for enterprises to achieve and continue being in the automated stage brings focus to the "flywheel effect" between data and AI in this stage of maturity. For the Boards and CEOs with a strategic goal of leveraging AI at scale, the data pillar operating in the automated stage must also become an associated strategic goal
2. *Falling back to the scaled or fundamental stage:* Once an enterprise is in the automated stage, it may fall back to the scaled or fundamental stage! This might happen because the DOM is not proactively prepared with AI and self-service capabilities to deliver data to new use cases, such as when unstructured data is needed for scaling AI
3. *Criticality of people involvement along with AI agents:* In the automated stage, while AI agents perform the execution tasks, skilled people govern and improve the AI agents

> **Food for Thought:** *Is your enterprise on the journey to leverage AI agents?*

Standing still would mean falling behind with the ever-increasing demand for data from use cases like leveraging AI at scale, data monetization, and more. Maturing the data pillar to become AI-powered after it has been established is critical for benefiting from data as a strategic asset for the enterprise in the long run. The Board, CEO, and CDO must prioritize identifying their maturity level, beginning their maturity journey, and continuously adapting and refining as their enterprise progresses.

> **Food for Thought:** *Are you already on the data maturity journey, or what is holding you back? How are you measuring your progress in the journey?*

## 4.5 CASE STUDY: MATURITY JOURNEY FOR THE DATA PILLAR AT AUDI

Audi Production's present maturity level, as per the maturity framework presented by the authors, would be in the "fundamental stage," as presented in Figure 4.8.

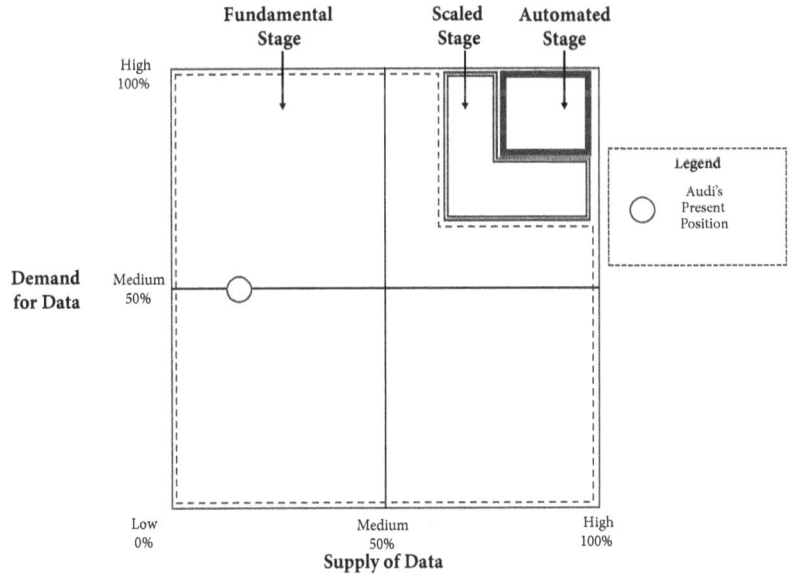

FIGURE 4.8   Audi's Present Position in the Maturity Framework.

Predicting the journey (see Figure 4.9), significant improvements are anticipated initially along the demand scale (Y-axis), given the current level of readiness in the data supply chain. However, as Audi progresses, there may come a point where business use cases perceive the DOM as lagging and unable to meet their increasing data intensity requirements. This phase could lead to a brief period of "disappointment," which is expected to act like a catalyst for the DOM to undergo another "leveling-up" in its readiness (X-axis).

This progression will gradually enable the DOM to meet the growing data demands, paving the way toward the "scaled stage." A key indicator of this advancement will be the proportion of data requests handled by the data domain teams. Once this ratio approaches 100%, it will signify that robust and effective data provisioning structures are in place. This milestone should mark the beginning of a new era of data productivity.

However, reaching the "automated stage" remains unpredictable at this point. Nevertheless, with ongoing advancements in AI, it is reasonable to expect this stage to be achievable within a 3- to 5-year timeframe.

With the maturation of Audi's data pillar well underway, numerous advanced data capabilities are expected to become accessible to Audi Production and other business functions. This progress is anticipated to

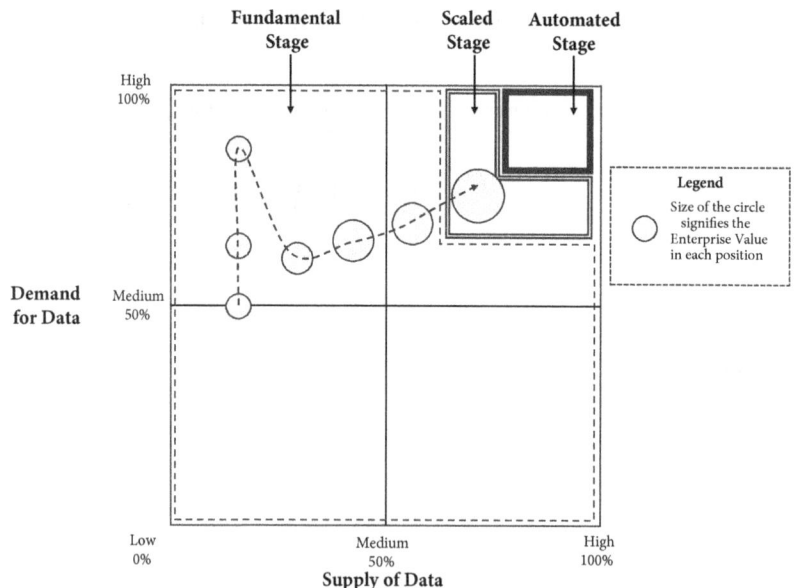

FIGURE 4.9   Audi's Predicted Maturity Journey.

unlock unprecedented business insights and improvements, such as significant reductions in equipment downtime and enhanced supply–demand quality. However, due to the transformational nature of these efforts, the journey is progressing more slowly than it could, as strategic directions are still under discussion. Achieving accountable (i.e., "real") financial business value requires excellence across all levels of the DOM, often making the journey feel like a continuous cycle through the "why," "what," and "how" phases of establishing the data pillar, as outlined in this book. Setbacks and disappointments may challenge the status quo, but it is in these moments that a company's culture and sponsorship from the Board become a decisive factor.

Since embarking on this transformation journey several years ago, Audi Production has grown increasingly resilient and efficient in driving change. Each success – whether in speed, collaboration, or data-enabled business value – reinforces the realization that data-centric solutions are becoming a new "superpower" for production. These solutions connect previously isolated process steps and extend optimization efforts beyond a small group of individuals. Informational metadata will further enhance insights by adding intelligence to data, giving overall transparency, and empowering the entire organization to identify solutions to existing or new business questions and thus foster further optimization. As more and more data are coherently available to the business, decision-making will change in a way that will aim to simulate cause-and-effect causalities as much as possible before proceeding. "Breaking out" from the digital twin[3] into the real, physical world will be as late as possible, and real-world business outcomes will be fed back to the data products wherever possible. This will increasingly make data "AI ready" and is likely to be a key requirement for any real-world business process. Once this AI readiness has been achieved, entirely new collaboration scenarios are likely to emerge. This evolution could lead to a fundamental shift in staff roles and skill allocation, transforming how the business operates and innovates.

While it is difficult to estimate long-term effects of this transformation, it seems clear that mastering this change is essential for any business to be relevant in the medium to long term. At Audi Production, this transformation was started several years back, and, today, surrounding business units and other brands regularly come forward, trying to understand how the current DOM was achieved, especially with regard to constraints on staff and financial resources. As all of this is the result of continuous internal restructuring and reallocation efforts (without increasing absolute staff numbers), the data factory has now become a stable, sustainable, and efficient business innovator. I am truly convinced that the concepts and practical advice, as portrayed in this book, are fundamentally correct and indispensable to successfully embark on this rewarding journey toward data proficiency.

## KEY TAKEAWAYS FROM THIS CHAPTER

*"By following the Maturity Framework, organizations can assess where they stand today, prioritize key enablers, and systematically progress toward AI-driven decision-making."*

*– Rainer Deutschmann, Senior Executive in Telecom and Technology Industries. Board Director, Advisor, and Investor*

- Enterprises must gradually mature their data pillar, aligning the data supply with their data demand. Each enterprise is unique, and so is its maturity level and maturity journey. The maturity framework, with demand for data on the Y-axis and supply of data on the X-axis, helps enterprises to assess their current maturity level and plan their maturity journey.
- The initial measurements of EAV and TAV may not be accurate but will become a basis for plotting the potential data demand. The measurements can be refined further as the enterprise monitors its maturity journey.
- **Fundamental stage:** Building the foundation
  - *Key actions*: Securing C-level sponsorship, creating success stories, promoting data adoption in use cases, establishing the DOM, and enhancing it along the journey.
  - *Key considerations*: Expect significant time and resources to be spent in this stage.
- **Scaled stage:** Achieving enterprise-wide self-service
  - *Key actions*: Adopting the data Intelligence layer and developing people's skills and technology capabilities required for self-service across the DOM.
  - *Key considerations*: Must mature through the fundamental stage to reach the scaled stage.
- **Automated stage:** AI-powered acceleration across the enterprise
  - *Key actions*: Rolling out the use of AI agents and developing people's skills to develop, train, and govern the AI agents.
  - *Key considerations*: Must mature through the scaled stage to reach the automated stage and keep humans in the loop of actions by AI agents.
- Throughout the maturity journey, while focusing on increasing the data supply, it is equally important that the CDO focuses on

increasing the data demand. The maturity of the data pillar increases when both data demand and supply increase in tandem.

- The maturity journey will not be linear. Enterprises may occasionally fall back due to "hype" or "disappointment." The CDO must stay resilient and continue driving the data pillar forward in the maturity journey.
- For the Boards and CEOs with a strategic goal of leveraging AI at scale, the data pillar operating in the automated stage must also become an associated strategic goal.

## NOTES

1 Agentic AI. (2025, February 27). In *Wikipedia*.
2 Obermatt. (n.d.). *Value Driver Tree Analysis*.
3 Digital Twin. (2025, February 16). In *Wikipedia*.

## REFERENCE LIST

Agentic AI. (2025, February 27). In *Wikipedia*. https://en.wikipedia.org/wiki/Agentic_AI

Digital Twin. (2025, February 16). In *Wikipedia*. https://en.wikipedia.org/wiki/Digital_twin

Obermatt. (n.d.). *Value Driver Tree Analysis*. https://obermatt.org/en/metrics/value-driver-tree-financial.html

# CHAPTER 5

# Visualizing the Future

## *An Autonomous Enterprise, with Data as the Lifeblood*

## 5.1 THE STATE OF ENTERPRISES IN 2035 – AUTONOMOUS ENTERPRISES

Imagine the year 2035. Enterprises have innovated and become "autonomous." In autonomous enterprises, business value with stakeholder communities is created with minimal human intervention. This would be made possible by autonomous processes powered by autonomous people, technology, and data operations. A few examples would be as follows:

- Business outcomes in processes are predicted through AI-powered digital twins. The supply chain management process predicts a disruption to a specific part of the supply chain, develops alternative options, and executes the most optimum option in real time when the disruption happens.

- Secure, compliant, and automated transactions are executed through smart contracts[1] built on blockchain.[2] In addition, AI constantly checks for fraudulent transactions.

- Personalized learning paths are automatically created for people based on their roles, performance, and career growth aspirations.

DOI: 10.1201/9781003512776-6

- New technology deployments and upgrades happen with zero human touch.

- Data requirements are fulfilled automatically.

- High-speed AI execution is powered by quantum computing.[3]

In autonomous enterprises, the technologies leveraged, such as AI, quantum computing, and blockchain, are standard. The Board and business leaders develop the enterprise business strategy that becomes a roadmap for autonomous operations: People, processes, technology, and data operations. They also receive real-time recommendations from their autonomous operations that enable them to adjust their strategy and its execution.

## 5.2 DATA AS A SOURCE OF DIFFERENTIATION FOR AUTONOMOUS ENTERPRISES

In autonomous enterprises, every action, predictive or reactive, performed by AI or humans, would need to be based on high-intensity data at scale, i.e., data high in quality, compliance, and speed simultaneously for all use cases across the enterprise (refer to the QCS framework in Figure 1.4). With the technologies common across enterprises, the ability to provision high-intensity data consistently and at scale would be the differentiator for enterprises. Attaining the automated stage of data maturity would be a prerequisite for enterprises (see Figure 4.1).

> High-intensity data will be the "lifeblood"[4] of autonomous enterprises!

With the automated stage of data maturity as a foundation, high-intensity data is woven intricately into the operations and is the "lifeblood" that flows through autonomous enterprises.

The boundaries between the people, processes, technologies, and data as discrete pillars diffuse. Referring to Figure 5.1, while data is the core strategic asset represented in the center circle, imagine the circles for people, processes, and technology pillars converging toward each other.

It is important to note that the journey to become an "autonomous enterprise" would be bumpy and challenging.

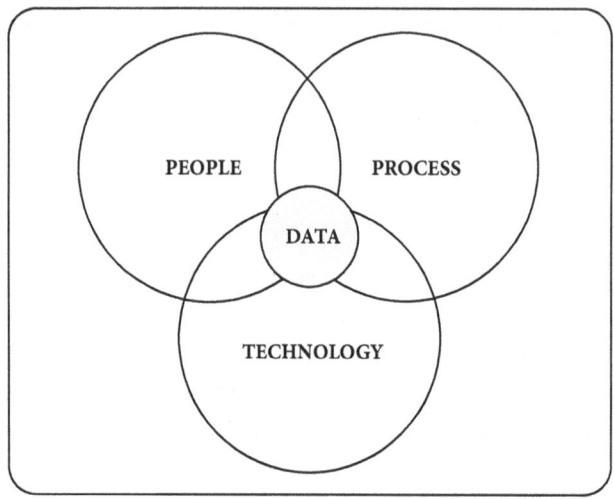

FIGURE 5.1    Data Woven into the Operating Model of Autonomous Enterprises.

## 5.3  THE COMPELLING REASON FOR ENTERPRISES TO ACT

Not all enterprises made it to 2035! They tried deploying AI, including AI agents, but could not scale their usage. AI or other required technologies were not the reason. They failed to consistently and at scale provide high-intensity data to the people, processes, and technology operations that were trying to be autonomous. This happened because they did not attain the automated stage of data maturity.

> **Food for Thought:** *Do you see your enterprise becoming "autonomous" by 2035? What actions should you take toward that?*

## 5.4  WHAT SHOULD ENTERPRISES DO NOW TO MAKE IT TO 2035?

> *Reflecting on Moore's law, we believe that enterprises must aim to double their EAV every 18 months. The supply of data must keep up with this exponentially increasing data demand.*

Enterprises must "urgently" treat data as their core strategic asset. Data must be leveraged in every enterprise's strategic and operational decision-making and action. The Boards, CxOs, and leaders of business functions must be accountable for their data. Together, they must accelerate their data maturity journey and attain the automated stage of maturity. Table 5.1 summarizes the key takeaways at an enterprise level.

*The urgency to act: Enterprises must prioritize to begin and then accelerate their journey to attain the automated stage of data maturity.*

TABLE 5.1    Key Takeaways at an Enterprise Level

1. Enterprises have varied data intensity requirements – not all use cases require high intensity. The *QCS framework* (see Figure 1.4) enables enterprises to understand their data intensity requirements

2. Enterprises face multiple challenges in meeting the data intensity requirements. They should *develop a scorecard* of their challenges leveraging the framework presented in Figure 1.8 and refer to the *scorecard shared by Audi* (see Figure 1.11). The scorecard would enable the Board, the CEO, and business leaders to align on the challenges in their enterprise that hinder them from meeting the data intensity requirements

3. To holistically and sustainably overcome the challenges identified in the scorecard and deliver on the data intensity requirements, enterprises must make *"data" the fourth pillar* of their operating model, alongside their people, processes, and technologies

4. When data is the fourth pillar, enterprises apply the *defined five principles* (see Figure 2.3) to the data pillar

5. The data pillar, together with the people, processes, and technology pillars, enables *enterprises' business capabilities* (see Figure 2.7)

6. Enterprises develop *data management capability* as an additional Level 1 business capability (see Figure 2.6). Multiple data capabilities, such as data strategy, data architecture, data adoption and governance, and semantic data management, are developed under the Level 1 data management capability

7. A *DOM* is established to deliver data to the use cases at the required data intensity by leveraging the developed data capabilities (see Figure 3.1). People, processes, and technologies (including AI) are required for each DOM layer to function effectively and efficiently

8. The DOM fulfills its purpose through data assets, i.e., *Data Products, DFBs, EKG,* and *raw data*, that are collected, created, and provisioned through the DOM

9. Establishing and maturing the data pillar cannot be done quickly. Time, resources, and commitment from the stakeholders are required. Enterprises must go through a journey of maturing the data pillar. Chapter 4 presents a *maturity framework* that acts as a guide throughout the journey

10. The maturity of the data pillar can be increased by increasing the *demand for data* from the use cases and matching the demand with the data supply through the DOM. The *starting position and the journey of maturing the data pillar would differ for each enterprise* based on their size, the enterprise strategy, the demand for data, the present status of the DOM, and the ability to invest in improving their DOM readiness. Business leaders have critical roles to play in accelerating to the *automated stage* of maturity

## 5.5 BOARDS AND CEOS MUST BE THE DATA CHAMPIONS

Boards and CEOs are accountable for ensuring that their enterprises exist and thrive in 2035. Their enterprises must continuously "give back more" to their stakeholder communities, but they have limited resources at their disposal. This situation makes it imperative for the Boards and CEOs to lead their enterprises to innovate and evolve, continuously delivering more business value with relatively fewer resources.

"Data" presents an opportunity for the Boards and CEOs to achieve their objectives while facing constraints. They can harness the power of data to create new business models, accelerate the execution of their strategic initiatives, and make timely and accurate strategic and operational decisions. They must become "data champions" and accelerate their enterprises' journey to the automated stage of data maturity. Table 5.2 summarizes the key takeaways for Boards and CEOs.

> *Food for Thought for the Board and CEOs: Have you developed a vision for leveraging data as a core strategic asset?*

TABLE 5.2　Key Takeaways for Boards and CEOs

1. The Board must provide its *sponsorship* and *commitment* to data as the enterprise's core strategic asset. They must also lead the way in fostering a *data culture* in their enterprise
2. The Board and the CEO are responsible for developing a *scorecard* of the enterprise's challenges that hinder the use of data as a strategic asset. Equipped with the scorecard, the Board must establish a *mandate* for the data pillar and the people, processes, and technology pillars to enable it. The mandate from the Board is crucial to work through and resolve the enterprise's challenges
3. The mandate from the Board must include the *creation of the role of the data pillar leader, i.e., the CDO*. We recommend that the *CDO reports to the CEO*
4. *Data strategy* is critical for leveraging data as a core strategic asset. The Board and the CEO must approve every iteration of the data strategy
5. The Board must *allocate the required budget* for the data pillar, which must be aligned with the *business value KPIs* defined for the data pillar
6. During the initial phase of developing the data capabilities and operationalizing the DOM, the Board and the CEO must focus on *helping the CDO resolve the challenges* identified in the scorecard and address any change management issues
7. As the CDO operationalizes the DOM, the Board and CEO must become its early data consumers, thus leading the way and *setting examples for the rest of the enterprise*
8. The Board and CEO have critical roles during the data pillar's maturity journey. They must actively support and enable the data pillar to *accelerate* to the automated stage of maturity

## 5.6 CXOS CREATE THE "FLYWHEEL" EFFECT – ENABLING THE DATA PILLAR AND BENEFITTING FROM IT

The CHRO, COO, and the CIO/CTO play critical roles in creating the "flywheel" effect with the data pillar – increasing the DOM readiness by enabling it with people, processes, and technology capabilities and increasing the demand for data from their use cases. Tables 5.3, 5.4, and 5.5 summarize the key takeaways for CHROs, COOs, and CIOs/CTOs respectively.

*Food for Thought for CHROs: Have you and the CDO developed a structured plan to build a data culture?*

*Food for Thought for COOs: Have you made your business process owners accountable for their data and leveraged it strategically to enhance their outcomes?*

TABLE 5.3   Key Takeaways for CHROs

1. Enterprises that treat data as a by-product of business cannot achieve the automated stage of data maturity. Enterprises must imbibe a *data culture*, considering data a core strategic asset. The CHRO plays a critical role in making this change happen, with the partnership of other CxOs and the sponsorship of the Board
2. The CHRO must support the CDO and the business functions in *developing or hiring people with the capabilities* required to mature and benefit from the DOM
3. The CHRO must be involved in the *CDO's hiring process,* help the CDO *build up the data office's teams,* and *partner with the data office* to execute upskilling or enablement programs required for maturing to the automated stage
4. In turn, the CHRO and the people operations team must increasingly *leverage data* delivered by the data pillar *to improve outcomes in their use cases,* such as making the right hiring decisions, identifying and fulfilling gaps in skills and competencies for the business functions' use cases, and initiatives like leveraging AI at scale

TABLE 5.4   Key Takeaways for COOs

1. The COO must partner with the CDO to *establish and automate the processes required in each layer of the DOM*
2. The COO and the stakeholders responsible for each business process must increasingly automate their processes and *leverage data to improve business outcomes*
3. Some business processes may need to be changed to enable leveraging data as a strategic asset and not as a by-product. To enable this, the stakeholders responsible for the business processes must imbibe the data culture. The COO is critical in resolving such challenges through a *structured change management program* executed with the CDO and the CHRO

TABLE 5.5   Key Takeaways for CIOs/CTOs

1. Imbibing the data culture would be an essential change within the IT office. The CIO/CTO is critical in executing the change through a *structured change management program* with the CDO and the CHRO
2. The CIO/CTO must partner with the CDO to establish the required *technology capabilities*, including AI, to *accelerate data maturity*
3. The CIO/CTO must also enable a *collaboration between the IT and data offices* to accelerate automation in each DOM layer
4. The CIO/CTO must update or change the existing technology applications to *unlock data* from them and enable the collection of such data in the raw data layer
5. The CIO/CTO must *enable the harvesting of technical metadata* from the technology applications required for building and continuously enriching the EKG
6. In turn, the CIO/CTO and the IT office must *increasingly leverage data* delivered by the data pillar *to improve outcomes in their use cases*

TABLE 5.6   Key Takeaways for CDOs

1. The North Star goal of a CDO is to *enhance business outcomes* for the business functions, the CEO, and the Board by enabling them to leverage data in their strategic and operational use cases
2. The CDO *addresses the enterprise's challenges* that hinder the use of data as a core strategic asset through a structured change management program in collaboration with the CEO and other CxOs and with the sponsorship of the Board
3. The CDO identifies, prioritizes, and develops the data capabilities required to *enhance the EV, EAV, and TAV*. Some data capabilities might already exist in an enterprise, albeit scattered across it or might need improvement, while others might need to be developed from scratch
4. The CDO and the data office *play a central role in the DOM*. The CDO secures the active involvement of the leaders of the business functions and the people, processes, and technology pillars in operationalizing the DOM
5. The CDO decides on the structure to adopt for the DOM: *Centralized, federated, or decentralized* – to make it effective and efficient
6. The CDO works to *increase the demand for data and the supply in tandem*, accelerating the enterprise to the automated stage of data maturity
7. When an enterprise leverages data as its core strategic asset, *a successful CDO will become a leading indicator of a successful enterprise*

> ***Food for Thought for CIOs/CTOs:*** *How can you speed up unlocking data from technology applications? Are you leveraging data strategically to improve outcomes from the IT office?*

## 5.7  CDO'S SUCCESS BECOMES THE LEADING INDICATOR OF THE ENTERPRISE'S SUCCESS

The CDO, leading the data pillar, addresses the enterprise's challenges that hinder the use of data as a core strategic asset in collaboration with the CEO and other CxOs and with the Board's sponsorship. Table 5.6 summarizes the key takeaways for CDOs.

*Food for Thought for CDOs: How will you continuously balance data demand and supply while accelerating toward the automated stage of data maturity?*

## 5.8 THE CALL TO ACTION FOR BUSINESS LEADERS: FUTURE-PROOF YOUR ENTERPRISE!

The future is fast unfolding.

As business leaders, you have an existential decision to make: Will you harness data as a core strategic asset to drive your enterprise toward becoming an autonomous enterprise or risk its existence in the future?

The time to act is now. Harness the power of data and thrive!

*Realize the Future – Become an Autonomous Enterprise with Data as the Lifeblood!*

## NOTES

1 Smart contract. (2025, January 3). In *Wikipedia*.
2 Smart blockchain. (2025, February 25). In *Wikipedia*.
3 Quantum computing. (2025, February 27). In *Wikipedia*.
4 An indispensable factor.

## REFERENCE LIST

Quantum Computing. (2025, February 27). In *Wikipedia*. https://en.wikipedia. org/wiki/Quantum_computing

Smart Blockchain. (2025, February 25). In *Wikipedia*. https://en.wikipedia.org/ wiki/Blockchain

Smart Contract. (2025, January 3). In *Wikipedia*. https://en.wikipedia.org/wiki/ Smart_contract

# Index

Note: Page numbers in *italics* indicate a figure and page numbers in **bold** indicate a table on the corresponding page.